Our Mothers

The Political Palate

A FEMINIST VEGETARIAN COOKBOOK

BY THE BLOODROOT COLLECTIVE
BETSEY BEAVEN
NOEL GIORDANO
SELMA MIRIAM
PAT SHEA

LAYOUT AND COVER DESIGN BY BUFFY PARKER
PHOTOGRAPHY BY NOEL GIORDANO

SANGUINARIA PUBLISHING
85 FERRIS STREET
BRIDGEPORT, CONNECTICUT 06605

Fourth Printing

© 1980 Sanguinaria Publishing
85 Ferris Street, Bridgeport, CT 06605

Library of Congress Catalog Card No. 80-53521

ISBN 0-9605210-0-3

DEDICATION

And yet the blackbird does not fly in us but is somewhere else free of our minds, and now even free of our sight, flying in the path of her own will . . . .

Susan Griffin, *Woman and Nature*

For one of our mothers
Fay Davidson
Fannie Gold
Faygele, little bird
1898–1979

As we do, she took cooking and reading seriously and believed in the necessity of a political consciousness. A suffragist, she had mixed feelings about the second wave, yet did much to make Bloodroot possible .

ACKNOWLEDGMENTS

Some women have been particularly helpful with this book: Adrianne Marks, Gloria Baldwin, Pat Mitchell, Sonja Bay and Donna Osborne. Buffy Parker's good taste in design made self-publishing a matter of pride.

Others have been part of Bloodroot's history and therefore, in some fashion, part of this book. Samn Stockwell helped begin. Denslow Brown, Sabrina Bunks, Sarah Ives, Jo Brooks, Jill Harker, Diane Remy, Beth Reasoner, Randi Parker, Charlene LaVoie, and Marcia Cameron have all expended significant effort here, as have others. Alicia Woodson and Sandy Anderson continue to do so. Bloodroot is something of all these women.

Some come to Bloodroot only once; some come weekly. Probably most women who make it clear how glad they are for our existence don't realize how much we need their appreciation. Many times visitors have canceled our tiredness or nullified the rudeness of some "customers" who require more service than we provide. To everyone who has encouraged us with their presence and understood or shared the struggle, thank you.

Spending time with Gwen Parker discussing legal options has been more fun than such events are supposed to be; that time has been most useful as well, and we are grateful.

And Barbara Beckelman has been and continues to be a constant reassuring part of our work and our lives. She has been integral from the beginning.

TABLE OF CONTENTS

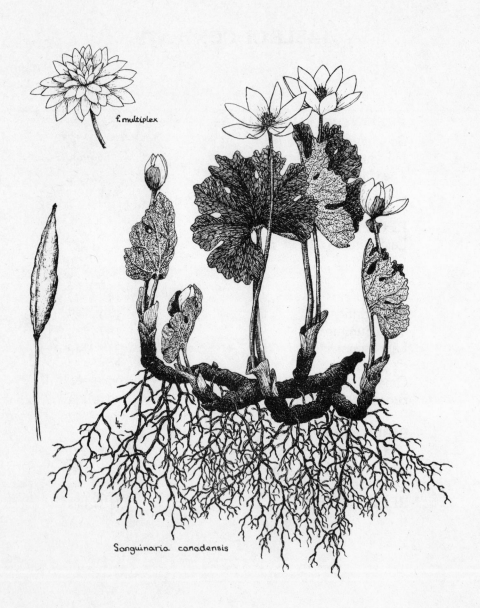

f. multiplex

Sanguinaria canadensis

SANGUINARIA CANADENSIS

We are named Bloodroot for an eastern woodland wildflower, *Sanguinaria canadensis*. One of us is a landscape designer who found something symbolic in its slow spreading rhizomatous root system and the way each piece of root throws up its own grey-green leaf furled protectively around the eight-petaled white flower. Any part of root, stem, or leaf "bleeds" a red juice. Though we have subsequently learned that Native Americans used Bloodroot as a dye plant and that some Hungarians have used it in cough medicines (it belongs to the poppy family), we chose it as a name for its habit of growth, which seemed appropriate to the way we work together. There seems a special beauty about a wildflower with a tough root system that is nevertheless so delicate. Many semi-double forms appear in the wild; we counted twelve and thirteen petaled flowers in our garden, and there is one very double form called "multiplex." All existing plants of this form are divisions of one Bloodroot plant found on an Ohio hillside.

The picture we use of the Bloodroot plant is a drawing by Laura Louise Foster, of Falls Village, Connecticut. A botanic artist, she is an expert in wildflowers and rock garden plants. She and the noted botanist H. Lincoln Foster maintain an exquisite collection of wild flowers from all over the world in an unparalleled garden. We are most grateful for her permission to use her fine work as a representation of our symbol.

INTRODUCTION

What is a feminist cookbook? What's a feminist restaurant? There's no such thing as feminist food! So people have said.

This is what we say: We are feminists, that is, we recognize that women are oppressed by patriarchy—the rule of the fathers—and we commit ourselves to rebellion against that oppression. Feminism is not a part-time attitude for us; it is how we live all day, everyday. Our choices in furniture, pictures, the music we play, the books we sell, and the food we cook all reflect and express our feminism. Our food is vegetarian because we are feminists. We are opposed to the exploitation, domination, and destruction which come from factory farming and the hunter with the gun. We oppose the keeping and killing of animals for the pleasure of the palate just as we oppose men controlling abortion or sterilization. We won't be part of the torture and killing of animals. [1] We know that humans, being omnivores, can live quite well

---

[1] *Woman's Creation* by Elizabeth Fisher examines in depth the connections between oppression of animals and of women. For example, ". . . the sexual subjugation of women, as it is practiced in all the known civilizations of the world, was modeled after the domestication of animals. The domestication of women followed long after the initiation of animal keeping, and it was then that men began to control women's reproductive capacity, enforcing chastity and sexual repression. . . . Animals, on the other hand, may well have been the earliest form of private property on any considerable scale, making animal domestication the pivot also in the development of class differences." p. 190 Fisher, Elizabeth, *Woman's Creation,* Anchor-Doubleday, Garden City, N.Y., and McGraw-Hill Paperback, 1980.

Also see Singer, Peter, *Animal Liberation: a New Ethics For a Treatment of Animals* (Avon Press New York, New York, 1975); and Mason, Jim, and Singer, Peter, *Animal Factories* (Crown Publishers, New York, New York, 1980). Both discuss vegetarianism from an ethical, that is, a political point of view.

without meat and that there is much evidence (the length of our intestines, the number of molars for grinding) to indicate that our bodies are best designed for the consumption of grains and vegetables. Meat eating can be justified in an environment that produces no other foods.[2] We are less exclusionary of fish and do sometimes serve it at our restaurant. Since, however, we wanted to prove how well people can eat on a vegetarian diet, we have included only eight recipes in this book which use fish.

Feminist food is seasonal. We use what's close at hand, what is most fresh and local and therefore least expensive and least "preserved". This seems obvious, but we know of no other serious attempt at a seasonal cookbook. Our lives are so disconnected from organic or natural timekeeping and the best efforts of the earth, that once we enter the sterile world of pre-packaged supermarkets it is hard to remember that strawberries and tomatoes are not worth eating in January and that onion soup and oranges don't make sense in August.

To us, being feminists or woman-oriented means celebrating holidays which predate Judaism and Christianity. The solstices and equinoxes are closer to the earth's rhythms, and celebrating the waning and growing light, seeds sprouting or the harvest brought in, makes more sense than the obscenity of noise and false jollity that is Christmas/New Years, or the celebration of masochism/

---

[2]"While humans are and always have been omnivorous, during the major part of our evolution, as in most parts of the earth even today, vegetables provided most of our sustenance, a fact which is reflected in our eight-yard-long gut, the shape and surface of our teeth, possibly in the fact that animal fats seem to contribute to hardening of the arteries and that most of the known long-lived peoples—the Hunzas, the Abkhasians, and the Ecuadorians—eat very little meat." p. 57–58, *Woman's Creation* by Elizabeth Fisher, op. cit.

martyrdom that is Easter. Despite the rationalization that these holidays derive from earlier pagan cultures, their continued observation in a Christian context is an endorsement of a theology and value system which continues opposition to abortion and the ERA, believes homosexuality to be a sin or disease, and confuses masochism and eroticism. We believe that carrying on "holiday" traditions of a system which is, per se, anti-woman, is concretely harmful to our minds and spirits. So we don't take note of these holidays. Instead this book is divided by solstices and equinoxes and by the cross-quarter days which would fall between, making eight break points in the year. While the Celtic calendar is one form of time-reckoning feminists might use and the ever-changing thirteen-month lunar calendar is another, both are simply examples of what nature oriented calendars might be like.[3] We wanted to stay with what is familiar to all of us while indicating the earth's rhythms by our time divisions.

Feminist food, in our case, is produced by a collective. That means each of us does what she can do best and that we learn from and teach each other. It means that, because we are working at what we want to be doing (which is to make a women's space, informed by women's values), we care very much about what we produce. Our food is our art. That means we are very particular, that continuity is important to us, that we all taste and discuss the final seasoning of a soup. It means we admire the simplicity of quick breads, puddings, or boiled greens and that we also appreciate the richness of a quiche or the elegance of an endive salad.

[3]Sample calendars include *Sister Heathenspinster's Lunation Calendar* from 809 Maggard, Iowa City, Iowa 52240, and *The Lunar Calendar* from Luna Press, Box 511, Kenmore Square, Boston, Mass. 62215. Be sure to see *Moon, Moon* by Rush, Anne Kent (Moon Books, P.O. Box 9223, Berkeley, Ca. 94709) for a fine chapter on timekeeping.

Because we think of cooking as an art form, some discussion of our thoughts concerning the connection of art and politics is necessary. We all are taught that art is special, beyond our daily lives, requiring the learning of an obscure code of communication taught by experts. Since both those experts and the artists themselves share the general misogyny of society[4] and the work of women artists has been ignored (as documented by Harris and Nochlin, Judy Chicago, Lucy Lippard, Eleanor Tufts, Germaine Greer[5]), a woman aspiring to learn how to make aesthetic judgments acquires an expertise that is irrelevant or negative regarding women's daily lives. Meanwhile other "lower" art forms bombard us with the violence of pornography and punk rock (as rape and wife beating increase), the lies of sentimentality and romanticism, and the excesses of consumerism. "Art" is used as justification for pornography in high fashion magazines or for the latest racism and woman hating in the galleries[6]; the lies of advertising are justified by the dollars they supposedly bring in. Somewhere the two merge and become a perversion we are not supposed to understand or evaluate. Both leave us numb and alienated.

Yet it seems obvious that art is communication about what we experience and what we believe, and is, therefore

[4] See Chicago, Judy, *Through the Flower* (Doubleday, Garden City, New York 1975) pp. 156 and 164. Also "Retrochic: Looking Back in Anger" by Lucy Lippard, *The Village Voice,* December 10, 1979.

[5] Harris and Nochlin, Women Artists: 1550–1950 (Knopf, N.Y.C., N.Y., 1976); Tufts, Eleanor, *Our Hidden Heritage: Five Centuries of Women Artists* (Paddington Press, N.Y.C., N.Y., 1974); Lippard, Lucy, *From the Center* (Dutton, New York City 1976); Chicago, Judy, *Through the Flower*, op. cit., Chicago, Judy, *The Dinner Party* (Doubleday, Garden City, N.Y. 1979); and Greer, Germaine, *The Obstacle Race-The Fortunes of Women Painters and Their Work* (Farrar, Straus and Giroux, N.Y.C., 1979).

[6] "Retrochic: Looking Back In Anger" by Lucy Lippard, cited above, is a discussion of current art as political expression.

inherently political. It is effective when it speaks to our real experiences, not to the phony responses we have been taught are appropriate. Working together daily in our own space, we are beginning to trust our intuition and our intelligence as we judge these forms of communication. It is much harder to do this when we are in offices, private homes, supermarkets. Because of the isolation of women in patriarchy, we find it hard to develop women's (feminist) judgement. The best a "liberated" woman can do is to learn their code and "think like a man". When we stop wanting to do that, when we start wanting women's values, women's art and women's politics, then we need new images, new words, new ways to think as Mary Daly, Adrienne Rich and others have written. We need new ways to live. As we and others begin finding these ways, we must remember that women have done this before and that much of the history of it has been ignored, not recorded, or destroyed.[7] We

[7]See Lerner, Gerda, *The Majority Finds Its Past: Placing Women in History* (Oxford University Press, 1979). Lerner argues that women's experiences have been trivialized or deleted from history altogether, since the building of service organizations, the establishment of schools and libraries are deemed less important than waging war and signing treaties. Two quotes: "The central question raised by women's history is: what would history be like if it were seen through the eyes of women and ordered by the values they define?" and "All history as we now know it is, for women, merely prehistory."

Also see "Female Support Networks and Political Activism: Lillian Wald, Crystal Eastman, Emma Goldman," by Blanche Weisen Cook in *Chrysalis,* No. 3. Cook also edited *Crystal Eastman on Women and Revolution,* (Oxford University Press, 1978). Her study of the women who were responsible for Workers' Compensation Laws, the founding of ACLU and WILPF is fascinating but embittering when we realize how well men such as Eastman's brother Max are remembered while the women are forgotten. More recently the work of Lillian Smith, Rosa Parks, Fannie Lou Hamer in their struggles with racism are being ignored and forgotten while men's names remain in the limelight. See "Pauli Murray" in *Ms.* Magazine, March 1980, to learn that it was a black woman's senior law thesis which was used as the main argument against separate but equal in *Brown vs. Board of Education* and who developed techniques of confidence and self restraint for student protests in the '40s which became the basis of non-violent civil rights action in the '60s.

cook as a way to survive economically, yet our cooking is part of our study, our living, and our politics. It seems to us that there is no separation between art and politics; there is integrity which requires judgments and a value system underlying our work and our lives. Everything we do is the result.

Many of our customers assume we are a health food restaurant. We don't think we are, though eating recently at a local hospital cafeteria and noting how oversalted and oversugared the food was (and how replete with additives) made us wonder. Our philosophy is vegetarian and seasonal. Yes, we do use sugar and salt, though a lot less than people are used to. We always have some sugar-free desserts on our menu and you will find both kinds of recipes in this book. We experiment to develop sugar-free, baking powder-free, and low salt dishes. We are extremely interested in soy protein for those who cannot or do not wish to eat dairy products. Much more remains to be done. Because our food must be (taste) wonderful, we make our pie crust of butter and white pastry flour. We make a whole wheat bread but also serve and enjoy other breads made with unbleached white flour in combination with whole grains. We do believe in eating whole grain foods, but in some dishes, white rice tastes better to us, and so that's what we use! You must decide to what degree health considerations enter your cooking.[8]

[8]See Dinaberg and Akel, *Nutrition Survival Kit* (Panjandrum Press/Aris Books, San Francisco, Ca., 1976) for a sensible and well written guide to the health aspects of a vegetarian diet.

More on political cooking can be found in William
Shurtleff's and Akiko Aoyagi's *Book of Tofu* and *Book of
Miso* from Autumn Press and *Book of Tempeh* from Harper
and Row. These books are about the misuse of the earth
that results in starvation and about cultures whose way of life
demand concern with balance and quality instead of the
tradition of excess typical in the West. They are well worth
reading for data on protein availability, even if you don't
want to learn about tofu, miso, or tempeh. They are truly
political books in the respect they show for eastern cultures
and their desire to appropriately inform us of the value of
our own efforts to live responsibly with concern for others.

Our interest in ethnic cooking means we love discovering
early New England recipes for "Indian" pudding or for
molasses-apple gingerbread. We also hope to learn much
more about non-meat eating cultures. It seems poor
peoples have had intuitive understanding of protein
complementarity while caring how to make food taste good.
While our heritage means we know most about American,
French-Italian ("continental") and eastern European
cooking, we want to learn more about Japanese cuisine with
its exceptional respect for the seasons and Indian cooking
with its exquisitely seasoned vegetarian dishes. We are
discovering Middle Eastern lentil and vegetable
combinations, Native American cooking, and the use of
peanuts and root vegetables in Africa and South America.
There is much to learn from other cultures and no need to
get confused with other woman-hating systems of thought
such as which foods are yin and which yang.

We must remember the continuity of recipes within any
given culture. We have experimented and changed to our
taste; however, all our recipes derive from others. Many of
our favorite dishes came from friends and customers (and

they will be duly noted) though we have, at times, made changes in them. Much of our cooking is derived or adapted from what we have learned from the best cookbook authors:[9] Paula Peck, Julia Child, Craig Claiborne, Michael Field, Elizabeth David, and the writers of *Gourmet* Magazine and the Time-Life *Foods of the World* series. And some of our best vegetarian soups are from Julie Jordan's *Wings of Life,* (Crossing Press), our favorite vegetarian cookbook. We don't believe in secret recipes. Our file is open to anyone who wants to copy, and we hope we have properly acknowledged where inspiration or recipe has come from.

We must warn you that our recipes assume the use of good equipment and good raw ingredients. We have a restaurant stove, a big Hobart mixer for kneading bread, and a large food processor for making pureés. Of course you can use a blender or a sieve and you can knead small quantities of bread by hand, but our recipes assume you will put the extra effort into doing the job adequately. And we believe there is no substitute for sweet butter, good-quality aged soy sauce, fresh herbs in certain dishes, Switzerland Swiss and Italian well-aged Parmesan, or real heavy cream when called for. We don't compromise quality. We hope you don't need to either.

As for counting calories and watching the waistline, we're not interested. Dieting has been an especially oppressive masochism expected of women in recent years. An obsession with slenderizing is supposed to give women the illusion of control over their lives—a rationale expressed by the anorexic as well as implicit in behavior modification or

---

[9]See the cookbook bibliography herein for a list of our favorite cookbooks.

other easy or hard diet regimes. It should be obvious that we come in all sizes, different shapes as well as different heights, and therefore enforced thinness is starvation and misery. It is an illness created by the attitude that the only beautiful or healthy size is thin.[10]

We are writing this "cookbook" for all the people who asked for it. When we began, we had little enthusiasm for the effort until we realized that to "feed" you, we had to tell you what feeds us. Without our best loved treasures—the resources in our bookstore to think about, talk about and try to live by—our long hours of cooking and cleaning are drudgery. The songs, poems, stories and ideas are necessary to our lives; we hope to awaken your interest in them, and that you will pursue them beyond the small tastes we offer here.[11]

[10]There is some feminist analysis of food in *A Woman's Conflict: The Special Relationship Between Women and Food,* by Jane Rachel Kaplan (Spectrum, Englewood Cliffs, N.J., 1980), in particular the Introduction, "A Woman's Body in a Man's World," "Working Up an Appetite," and "Farming Out the Home." Be careful of sexist presumptions in some articles, especially the acceptance of Desmond Morris' theories in "Venus as Endomorph" and the supposedly funny "Women in the Kitchen: the feminist boiling point."

Also see *The Fat Illusion* and *Fat Liberation - A Luxury?,* both by Aldeberan as well as other materials from Fat Liberation Front, P.O. Box 342, New Haven Ct., 06513; i.e., *The Calorie Controversy - Who's Cheating?* and *A Fat Women's Problem Solving Group: Radical Change.*

[11]See the feminist resource bibliography herein for a list of our bookstore favorites.

THE G. KNAPP HISTORICAL SOCIETY

"Thou shalt not suffer a witch to live" Exodus xxii 18

In 1653 Elizabeth Knapp, known as Goody Knapp, was hung for being a witch. She was the only woman executed in Fairfield County, Connecticut; others were accused, but not executed. She was hung from a tree in Try's Field, which is thought to be the present site of the Burrough's home for the elderly in Black Rock, Bridgeport, Connecticut. Little is known about the actual trial, but fragments of information concerning her imprisonment, execution, and burial are documented because of a development after her death.

On the day of execution, a group of appointed women went to the prison to search G. Knapp for "teat" marks[1] (arbitrarily decided marks of the Devil) and to persuade her to confess the names of other witches. She replied to the women that she would not say anything untrue, and she would not render evil for evil by naming a certain Goody Staplyes as a witch. Goody Staplyes had let it be known that she did not believe Elizabeth Knapp was a witch, thus setting herself up for suspicion in the community.

After the execution, Staplyes went with a group of women to the gravesite, pointed to the marks on Knapp's body and told the women, "If there be teats, here are no more than I have myself, or any other woman, or you, if you search your body"[2]. Some of the women refused to look, some of them claimed the marks were witch marks, and others saw nothing but what was common to other women.

entThe courage of Goody Staplyes was partially rewarded
when a year later, Roger Ludlow, deputy governor of
Connecticut and Massachusetts, and a man extremely
influential in bringing Knapp to trial, was sued for defaming
the character of Staplyes as a witch. Ludlow lost his trial and
left Connecticut, but had no problem securing appointment
as Commissioner for Administration of Justice in Dublin.

On Wednesday evenings, a feminist organization called the
G. Knapp Historical Society meets at Bloodroot to
commemorate the death of Elizabeth Knapp and all the
other women witches who have been tortured and died
before and after her. Elizabeth Knapp was a local witch and
her death, like 9 million others between the 14th and 17th
centuries, was an act of woman hating. To us the humorous
portrayal of witches at Halloween is comparable to
malicious concentration camp jokes about Jews. Every
woman must be conscious of her need to fight/survive in a
patriarchal "system of justice" which today encourages the
violent marking of women through such acts as unnecessary
hysterectomies, mastectomies, the epidemic of wife beating
and rape, and the proliferation of pornography. Today, as in
1653, some women refuse to look, some see our problems
as our own fault, but some see our "marks" as common to
all women. As feminists we must see these marks of violence
by patriarchy as an often invisible but always present reality.
Andrea Dworkin has said in reference to the genocide of
witches: "A lot of knowledge disappears with 9 million
people".[3] The G. Knapp Historical Society is an attempt
to remind women that such knowledge must not disappear
again.

[1]Russell Hope Robbins, *Encyclopedia of Witchcraft and Demonology* (New York: Crown Press, 1959), p. 6.

[2]Sally Smith Booth, *The Witches of Early America* (New York: Hasting House, 1975), p. 81.

[3]Andrea Dworkin, *Woman Hating* (New York: Dutton, 1974), p. 141.

SOME NOTES ON THE PASSAGE OF SEASONS . . .

Part of the necessity of survival is the need to reclaim the natural time-marked events of the earth. As the water in our women's bodies subtly responds to the daily changing high and low tides of the moon, so indeed some part of our spirits respond to the larger changes the seasons bring us. By observing the events of the seasons, the Spring and Fall Equinoxes, Summer and Winter Solstices, and cross quarter days, women can begin to claim their own sense of birth and death. In our need to reevaluate what food to eat or medicine to use, even to learn women's ways of loving, we can consciously try to realign ourselves with the earth's cycles. In this way, we may be able to discover the justice that exists in the real world of nature.

Seasonally a kind of justice takes place. Beginning with what is called witch's new year on Oct. 31 (November eve is a cross quarter day which marks the mid point between Fall Equinox and Winter Solstice), a certain direction is set for us. This cross quarter day gives clear indications that the light and temperature of the earth are changing. In late October, our bodies respond to the smell of decay and the chill of afternoons growing shorter. Our senses act as a guide. As the sun withdraws in early afternoon, this signals our anticipation of withdrawal for the winter as other cross quarter days (Feb. 2, May 1, Aug. 2) mark the anticipation of Spring, Summer, and Fall respectively.

Winter Solstice (Dec. 22) brings us to the "new moon of the sun" or the longest night of the year. It is a time when women particularly need to recognize that the

"destructiveness" of what takes place on earth naturally—
the newly frozen stilled earth enveloped in darkness—is the
opposite of the active evil of nuclear energy and nuclear
weapons. While some conscious women struggle to live in
the sometimes cold space of our truths underground, a
world above ground frantically celebrates the hollow
"holidays" of Christmas and New Years.

Spring Equinox (March 21) brings with it the strong winds
which remind us that the sun is traveling faster than any
other time of year.* It is a time to look closely at the earth's
beginning growths and to sense that the equality of day and
night gives us clues to the earth's secrets of balance.

Summer Solstice comes on June 21 and while the earth is
warming with the rays of the sun, we shed our clothing to
feel its power more directly. It is a good time to think about
the morality of women's love for each other and how the
power of that love quickens and moves our lives together.

Fall Equinox (Sept. 21) brings us to the fullness of the
harvest which is at one with the culmination of life cycles. To
the extent that we can live fulfilling lives, women are
reminded that we need to take death and dying into our own
hands—that life at any cost is as senseless an act against our
natures as any other victimization we might experience. . .

*"Storms that arise during an equinox are sometimes called equinoctial
gales, for a very good reason. At this time the sun travels north or south
faster than at any other time of the year. In a week it moves over 2½°, or
half the distance between the two pointers in the Big Dipper. This
change in the sun's position produces such variations in the pattern of
warm and cold air masses that violent storms are often caused."
p. 269, Vol 6. The World Book Encyclopedia, 1969.

Hecate

~~~~~~~~~~~~~~~~~~~~~~~

CHAPTER 1   LATE AUTUMN
Halloween, October 31, to Winter Solstice, December 22.

LIMA BEAN SQUASH SOUP

From our renovation carpenters. Katie Wolf and Don Stuart.

1) Soak **2 c. dried baby lima beans** overnight in **water** to cover.

2) In the morning cook beans in their liquid, adding more if necessary, with **1 large onion** peeled and cut up, and **3 carrots** scraped and cut into 1" pieces. When quite soft, puree in food processor, blender or through sieve.

3) Meanwhile, cut up **1 hubbard squash.** Scrape out seeds and stringy fiber with a spoon. (Seeds can be washed, dried and roasted with coarse salt and a little oil for a snack.) Steam or bake until soft. Scrape out and puree enough squash to measure 2½ c.*

4) Combine lima and squash puree. Season with ¼ **c. tamari.** Add **water** until you like the consistency of the soup. Chop **1 Tb. fresh sage, ½ Tb. fresh rosemary,** and add **salt, freshly ground pepper,** and **1–2 Tb. lemon juice** until seasoning is just right. Taste and judge.

5) Serve with **sour cream.**

Serves 6–8

* We have many other uses for the remaining squash. Store it in the refrigerator.

BEET AND CABBAGE SOUP

1) Finely chop **1 large onion** and shred or grate **5–6 beets** and **1 large parsnip**.

2) Saute the onion and **2** crushed **garlic cloves** in ½ **stick unsalted butter.** Add the beets and parsnips, **¼ c. wine vinegar** and **1½ c. water.** Add **2 c.** canned **tomatoes, ½ t. sugar, 1 Tb. caraway seeds, 2 Tb. tamari.** Simmer, covered, 45 minutes.

3) Peel and dice **3 medium Idaho potatoes.** Coarsely slice **½ large cabbage** and boil in **1½ qt. water** until potatoes and cabbage are just done.

4) Combine both mixtures in one pot and taste for seasoning. Despite the tamari, some salt may be necessary. A Russian soup like this one should be sweet, sour, and salty.

5) Serve with **sour cream** and chopped **dill.**

Serves 8–10

It's not for you to choose, either way you lose
Will you be a witch or a martyr?

Power to the witch and to the woman in me . . .

"The Witching Hour"
Debutante
Willie Tyson; Urana Records

CURRIED APPLE AND POTATO SOUP

From Samn Stockwell.

1) In a small pan over high heat roast **1 t. cumin seed** by shaking the pan until seeds are browned. Cool and crush with mortar and pestle.

2) Peel and dice **3 medium potatoes.** Put the potato cubes in small bowl, cover with **2 c. water,** set aside.

3) Peel and chop **2 medium onions.** Dice **1 carrot, 1½ large green peppers** and **1 stalk** of **celery** with **leaves.** Chop all vegetables uniformly in size.

4) In a large soup kettle over high heat, saute all vegetables except the potatoes in **2 Tb. vegetable oil.** As the vegetables are cooking, add **2 cloves** minced **garlic** and the following spices: **1 t. ground roasted cumin seed, 1½ t. whole mustard seed, ¼ t. turmeric, ¼ t. ground cloves, ¼ t. coriander, ½–1 Tb.** good quality **curry powder** and **1 bay leaf.** Continue to saute vegetables and spices until they are well browned. Scrape bottom of pot often. Add **2 Tb. tawny port** and scrape browned bits at bottom of pot.

5) Add the potatoes and their water, **1 Tb. tamari, 1 t. salt, ½ t. pepper, 1 c. heavy cream, 2 c. milk,** and **½ c. raisins.** Cook until the potatoes are done.

6) While the potatoes are cooking, peel and dice **1½ tart apples,** such as Baldwin or Winesap. Add the diced apple to the soup and heat through. Taste for salt, pepper and tamari. You may wish to make the soup spicier; if so, add more curry. Once the apples have been added, do not boil the soup or their texture and flavor will be lost. Reheat gently.

7) Garnish each serving of soup with **yoghurt, sunflower seeds** and **pomegranate seeds.** The seeds are an especially interesting finish to this soup.

Serves 8–10

In her bottled up is a woman peppery as curry,
a yam of a woman of butter and brass,
compounded of acid and sweet like a pineapple,
like a handgrenade set to explode,
like goldenrod ready to bloom.

"The woman in the ordinary"
To Be Of Use
Marge Piercy; Doubleday

CHESTNUT SOUP

1) Using a small sharp knife, cut an "X" in the flat side of **2½ lb. chestnuts.** Cover them with boiling water and bring to a boil again. Pick them out, one at a time, and pull off shell and inner brown skin simultaneously. You may have to reheat the chestnuts. It helps to have a friend or two to help peel.

2) Coarsely chop **5 carrots, 5 leeks,** split and well washed, **2½ small bunches celery,** including **leaves,** and **2½ onions.** Saute in **4 Tb. butter** in a pot. Chop **1 bunch straight leaf parsley** and add to pot. When vegetables begin to brown a little, add **10 c. water** and **1 Tb. salt.** Simmer 1 hour.

3) Pour cooked vegetables and their broth through a strainer into another pot or bowl, pressing down on the vegetables. Use about half the vegetable broth to simmer about ⅔ of the peeled chestnuts until they are quite tender. Puree in a food processor or blender or use a potato masher to coarsely crush chestnuts.

4) To finish the soup, add **1½ c. half and half** (or light cream) and **1 Tb. lemon juice.** Slice the remaining chestnuts into the pureed soup and add as much of the remaining vegetable broth as you like to thin the soup. Taste for salt.

5) Serve hot, and garnish soup with salted whipped cream: Whip **1 c. heavy cream** with **½ t. salt** until stiff.

Serves 8–10

TURNIP VICHYSSOISE

1) Split lengthwise and wash thoroughly **4 leeks.**
   Coarsely chop the leeks and **1 medium onion.** Peel
   and dice **6 medium Idaho potatoes** and add to a pot
   with **onions** and **leeks.** Add **8–9 white turnips,**
   diced, and **4 c. water.** Bring to a boil and simmer until
   all vegetables are tender.

2) Using a food processor or blender, puree the soup.
   Return to the pot and add **2 qt. milk, 2 t. salt,
   2 t. fresh grated nutmeg.** Bring to a boil and taste
   for seasoning.

3) Serve this soup hot or cold, garnished with scallions or
   chives. If you serve it cold, it will require more salt.

Serves 8–10

*One of the most pervasive myths regarding big
house publication is that the trade-off you get for
losing much control over your work is efficient,
wide distribution and promotion. Poopadoodle.*

The Passionate Perils of Publishing
Celeste West and Valerie Wheat; Booklegger Press

WALDORF SALAD

1) Prepare alfalfa sprouts* three to four days in advance, or buy sprouts.

2) Prepare **Mayonnaise:** Have ready in a small pitcher **1 c. vegetable oil.** In a food processor or with an electric mixer beat thoroughly **2 egg yolks.** Keeping the machine on, add **1 Tb. lemon juice,** ½ **t. salt,** a grating of **nutmeg,** a pinch of **pepper** and ¼ **t.** good quality **prepared mustard.** Then add the oil (machine still on) in a slow dribble at first and then more quickly at the end. Turn machine off. Add ½ **c. sour cream,** turn machine on and mix thoroughly into the mayonnaise. Set aside.

3) Core (do not peel) 3 large firm apples and dice into ½" pieces to make **4 c. chopped apples.** Toss with **2 Tb. lemon juice.** Dice **celery** to yield **1½ c.** and add to apples together with **2 c.** chopped **walnuts.**

4) Fold mayonnaise into apple-walnut-celery mix. Taste for salt, pepper and lemon. Chill until ready to serve.

5) Arrange the waldorf salad on a bed of **Boston** or **Bibb lettuce,** garnish with **avocado slices, alfalfa sprouts.**

* **Alfalfa sprouts:** Put **2 Tb. alfalfa seeds** in a jar with a screen or cheesecloth lid. Soak them in **water** for a minimum of 1 hour and not longer than overnight. Drain the water off and set the jar in a dark spot. Rinse the seeds at least once every day. When the sprouts are grown to about 1" they may be refrigerated until ready for use.

FENNEL SALAD

1) Slice **2 "bulbs"** of **fennel** in half lengthwise discarding any discolored outer stalks and the feathery leaves. Crisp several hours in **water** in refrigerator.

2) On beds of mixed **escarole** and **romaine lettuce,** arrange slices of the fennel, thin slices of **salt** or **"table" ricotta cheese** and a few **Italian olives.** Both olives and cheese are available in Italian delicatessens. About **½ lb.** of cheese and **¼ lb.** olives should be adequate.

3) Drizzle with **vinaigrette** (see following recipe).

Serves 8

VINAIGRETTE

1) In a jar or bowl combine **⅓ c.** good quality **wine vinegar, ½ t. salt** and ½ t. good quality **prepared mustard** (we use Kosciusko). Shake or whisk together thoroughly.

2) Add **1½ c. oil** (we use a blend which is 25% olive oil, 75% pure vegetable oil) and fresh ground **pepper.** Shake or whisk again until well blended.

AVOCADO PERSIMMON SALAD

Persimmons are available in November. Unless they are fully ripe (very soft to the touch), they will taste puckery instead of sweetly luscious as they should.

1) For each serving, make a bed of **lettuce greens** on a plate, using **Boston, chicory** or/and other favorite combinations.

2) Arrange on top of lettuce in a pinwheel pattern peeled **grapefruit** sections, **avocado** slices, and **persimmon** slices. Top with **Bermuda onion** rings.

3) In a small jar, shake together ½ **c. oil,** ¼ **c. lemon juice,** and **salt** and **pepper** to taste. Spoon dressing on salad. This is enough dressing for 6 salads.

Dawning of a new beginning
Ancient anger goes on living
Through the souls of women who have touched

"Family of Woman"
A Lesbian Portrait
Linda Shear; Old Lady Blue Jeans

BRUSSEL SPROUTS AND GRAPE SALAD
WITH SOUR CREAM SAUCE

1) For each diner, trim bottom and slice in half lengthwise
   6 brussel sprouts. Steam until barely tender. Slice
   about **8 red** or **purple grapes** in half lengthwise and
   remove seeds. Scatter sprouts and grapes on a bed of
   Boston lettuce. Drizzle a little **vinaigrette** (see recipe
   index) over lettuce and top sprouts and grapes with a
   spoonful or two of **sour cream sauce.**

2) **Sour Cream Sauce:** Mix together **1 c. sour cream, 1
   Tb. tamari** or good soy sauce, **½ t. lemon juice, 1
   Tb. finely chopped fresh herbs** (such as scallions,
   dill, burnet or parsley), fresh **ground pepper,** and
   1 Tb. gomahsio (see recipe index). Taste sauce and
   adjust it. This sauce is good with broccoli or as a dip for
   raw vegetables, too.

Dressing is enough for 6–8

*Learning about (Amazons) has given me a new feeling
about the term "battle-ax" and when I hear it, I think it
must be in reference to that labyris of old, wielded in the
struggle to maintain women's independence.*

God Herself
Geraldine Thorsten; Doubleday

HALUSHKIN

From Ira Novsam.

1) Open **two 1 lb. cans sauerkraut.** Drain, reserving
   liquid*, if desired, and squeeze kraut dry. Saute until
   well browned in a fry pan in ¾ **stick sweet butter**
   (unsalted). Turn out into a casserole.

2) Coarsely cut ¼ **cabbage** into 1″ squares and saute in
   the same fry pan in ½ **stick sweet butter.** Add
   cabbage to sauerkraut.

3) Cook **6–7 c. egg noodles** in **boiling water** until
   done. Drain and add to sauerkraut and cabbage. Add
   1 Tb. poppy seeds and about **1 t. salt** (taste to see if it
   is needed) and another **3 Tb. butter.** Cover with foil
   and reheat in oven before serving.

4) Serve with cucumber salad (see following recipe) and
   Applesauce: Peel, core, and slice **8 apples.** Stew in
   ⅓ **c. apple juice** with **2 Tb. brown sugar** and
   ¼ **t. cinnamon.**

Serves 6–8

* Sauerkraut juice is needed to make Hupi Pollivka. It will
keep for at least 2 weeks in the refrigerator.

CUCUMBER SALAD

From Menga Thurm.

1) Peel and slice **5 thin cucumbers.** Sprinkle with
   coarse salt and let stand 1 hour.

2) Rinse cucumbers thoroughly in cold water. Turn into a
   dish towel and roll up and squeeze until cucumber slices
   are very dry. Turn into bowl and add **3 Tb. chopped
   fresh dill, ½ c. sour cream, 2 Tb. vinegar** and **fresh
   ground pepper.** Taste to see if salt is needed.

*As she thought about the gussaks she suddenly
knew why the brown bear was awake. The
Americans' hunting season had begun! Her wolves
were in danger! The gussaks were paid to shoot
them . . . . "When the wolves are gone there will be
too many caribou grazing the grass and the
lemmings will starve. Without the lemmings the
foxes and birds and weasels will die. Their passing
will end smaller lives upon which even man
depends . . . and the top of the world will pass into
silence."*

Julie Of The Wolves
Jean Craighead George; Harper & Row

SOLIANKA

This Russian Dish was adapted from Rosetta Reitz'
Mushroom Cookery. Solianka gets better on reheating.

1) Core and slice **1 cabbage.** Slice **3 medium onions.**
   Using ½ **stick sweet butter,** first fry the cabbage slices
   until lightly browned. Remove to a large bowl, then fry
   onions adding more butter if needed. Saute until light
   brown.

2) Soak **1 oz. dried mushrooms** (boletus edulis) in hot
   water to cover.

3) Using a large shallow pan, layer half the cooked
   cabbage on the bottom. Place the onions on top. Now
   peel and slice **2 small cucumbers** and add them. Slice
   ½ **lb. fresh mushrooms** on top of the cucumbers. Peel
   and slice **2 apples** and arrange on top. Drain and chop
   dried mushrooms, saving the liquid, and add them to the
   casserole. Top pan with remaining cabbage.

4) Make sauce: Melt **3 Tb. sweet butter** in a pot and
   saute **1 crushed clove garlic.** Add **1½ Tb. flour** and
   cook together a minute. Add **15 oz.** canned **tomato
   sauce.** Add ¼ c. **brown sugar, 1½ Tb. tamari,
   fresh ground pepper, juice** of ½ **lemon** and dried
   mushroom liquid, being careful not to add grit or sand
   that may be at the bottom. Add ½ **c. water** to the sauce
   and taste for seasoning. Sauce must be very
   overseasoned, sweet, sour and salt to compensate for
   no seasoning at all in the solianka.

5) Carefully pour as much sauce as you can over casserole, cover with foil, and bake at 375° for 1 hour. Uncover and bake 10 minutes to brown.

6) Cook **2 c. whole buckwheat groats** in **boiling salted water** until barely tender. Drain in a colander.

7) Cut solianka into squares and serve with buckwheat groats. Spoon remaining sauce over both.

Serves 8–10

. . . two soft mounds, as gentle as the breasts of a woman, and if you wanted red apples, you shoveled through the snow at the edge of one of the mounds, through the soft earth beneath until you struck layers of them, separated by layers of yellow straw. Or, if you wanted cabbage or potatoes, you dug into the other mound. The crib in the barn was heaped with corn that slipped between your fingers in a rain of yellow gold. Above, the hayloft was stuffed to the roof with sweet-smelling, dusty hay. Up there it was always soft as twilight, and one could dream strange, formless dreams.

Daughter of Earth
Agnes Smedley; The Feminist Press

CAULIFLOWER FRITTERS

Fritter recipe from Janet Habansky.

1) Cut out core of **1 cauliflower** and separate into flowerets. Parboil and let cool, reserving water. Measure **water** and add enough to make **2 c.** When lukewarm, add **1 Tb. yeast, 1 Tb. salt, 1 t. pepper,** and **1 clove garlic,** crushed. Leave 15 minutes. Add cauliflower pieces, cut up, and add enough **unbleached white flour** to make batter difficult to stir, about **2 c.** Let stand 15 minutes.

2) Steam **1 c. brown rice** to serve with fritters.

3) Optional: make an **Indonesian Peanut Sauce** to serve on the side: Saute **1 c. peanuts** in **1 Tb. oil.** When light brown, add **¼ c. chopped onion** and **1 clove garlic,** crushed. Saute gently, don't burn. Add **½ c. water, ½ Tb. honey** and simmer a minute. Let cool a little. Puree in food processor or blender, adding **⅓ c. miso, 3 Tb. dried coconut, 1 t. Chinese chili paste with garlic** (or ½ t. Cayenne pepper). Add **2 Tb. tamari** and **1 Tb. lemon juice.** Taste sauce. If it seems too thick to your liking, thin with **water** or **beer.**

4) Heat **2 c. oil** in a wok and fry fritters by tablespoonsful in the oil. When done, they can be sprinkled with **gomahsio** (see recipe index) or **salt.**

5) Serve on rice with the peanut sauce, if desired.

Serves 6–8

HARVEST VEGETABLE PLATTER

The inspiration for this Harvest Vegetable platter came
from an editorial in *Womanspirit*, Wolf Creek, Oregon,
1975 Fall Equinox issue. Written by Christina Pacosz of
Eagle Creek, Oregon, the editorial points out that we
should celebrate the harvest without reference to the
patriarchal Puritans and their condescension and
exploitation of "Indians," nor do we need dead turkeys to
commemorate the fruits of the earth. Christina Pacosz
suggests stuffing womblike squashes, and using roots,
seeds, and cranberries, as we have. The roasted parsnip
and carrot recipe comes from our renovation carpenters,
Katie Wolf and Don Stuart.

1) Make **Rutabaga-Potato Puree:** Peel and cut into
   chunks **1 medium sized rutabaga** (yellow turnip).
   Cook in boiling **salted water** about 10 minutes. Add **2
   medium potatoes,** peeled and cut into chunks. When
   both are cooked, drain and puree in food processor or
   mixer while still hot. In a small pot, saute **1 clove garlic,**
   crushed, in **2 Tb. sweet butter.** Add to puree together
   with **¾ stick sweet butter.** Season to taste with
   salt and **pepper.** Can be reheated, uncovered, in
   a 350° oven.

2) Make **Roasted Parsnips and Carrots:** Preheat oven
   to 450.° Thinly slice **1 bunch peeled parsnips, 1
   medium onion, 1 bunch scraped carrots.** Put into
   shallow roasting pan and moisten with a little **oil.** Roast,
   stirring often, until browned. When almost done, add
   ¼–½ c. sunflower seeds. When well cooked, add
   ¼ c. water and **1 Tb. tamari.** Cover with foil to keep
   warm or reheat covered.

3) Prepare **Acorn Squash:** Slice **4 acorn squash** in half
lengthwise and scrape out seeds. (Discard seeds or roast
in oven, sprinkled with a little oil and coarse salt). Now
either slice squash crosswise in scalloped slices, or for a
more elaborate dinner, stuff them with chestnut stuffing
(see below). If you are simply slicing them, put them in a
roasting pan, add **1 c. water,** cover with foil and bake
at 350° until they are just soft. Don't overcook.

4) Make **Chestnut Stuffing,** if you are using it for the
squash: Dry enough **homemade bread** and chop by
hand or in blender or food processor to get **2 c.** Cut an
X in **20 chestnuts,** cover with **water** and bring to a
boil. Peel one at a time while still hot so that inner skin
comes off together with shell. Finely chop **½ c. onions**
and **¼ c. shallots** and saute in **2 Tb. sweet butter** in
large fry pan. Add bread crumbs, **½ t. dry thyme, 2 Tb.**
chopped **celery leaves, 3 Tb. straight leaf parsley,**
chopped, **1 t. salt, fresh ground pepper, 1 t. lemon
juice** and a **splash** of **brandy.** Slice the chestnuts into
the mixture, which should be slightly moist. Add **cream**
if needed. **Salt** and **pepper** the insides of the squash
halves and dot with **butter.** Heap stuffing into squash
halves and place in pan. Add ½" of water to pan, cover
with foil and bake until squash are done, about 45
minutes, at 350.° To reheat, uncover pan.

5) Make **Apple Cranberry Sauce:** Peel, core, and slice
6 apples. Put in a pot with **½ lb. cranberries.** Add
½ c. apple juice or **cider, ¼ t. cinnamon** and cook
covered until cranberries are popped and apples are
soft. Now add enough **honey** to sweeten.

6) Make **Miso Gravy:** see following recipe.

7) When ready to serve, steam 1 head of **broccoli flowerets** until barely done.

8) Serve rutabaga-potato puree and the acorn squash with miso gravy. The roasted parsnips and carrots, broccoli and apple cranberry sauce all make a very pretty platter.

Serves 8

MISO GRAVY

1) Finely chop **2 Tb. onion** and saute in sauce pan in **1 stick sweet butter** or **½ c. vegetable oil** together with **2 cloves crushed garlic** and **6 minced mushrooms.** While sauteing, add **½ t. dried thyme** and **½ t. dried basil.** Cook slowly until browned.

2) Add **½ c. unbleached white flour.** Cook several minutes, stirring. Add **6 oz. beer** and enough **water** to make gravy (vegetable water is best if you have it). Add **3 Tb. miso, 1 Tb. tomato paste, 2 Tb. dry sherry** and **1 Tb. tamari.**

3) Simmer slowly ½ hour and correct seasoning.

STUFFED BROILED MUSHROOMS

A fancy appetizer before a harvest meal. From Martha Aasen.

1) Use a fork to mash together **8 oz. cream cheese, 1 t. anchovy paste,** and **1 t. lemon juice.**

2) Remove the stems from **1½ dozen mushrooms** by using an unscrewing motion. Save stems to flavor soups or for miso gravy.

3) Use the fork to roughly fill mushrooms, leaving cheese mixture slightly mounded. Place in baking pan and sprinkle tops with **paprika.** Refrigerate until dinnertime.

4) When ready to serve, preheat broiler and then broil mushrooms until cheese melts but mushrooms remain uncooked.

Serves 6

A major difference between witches and psychotherapists is that witches see the mental health of women as having important political consequences.

Changing of the Gods
Naomi R. Goldenberg; Beacon Press

WITCHES' FROTH (APPLE CREAM)

1) Peel, core, and slice **4–6 apples.** Stew in covered saucepan in a little **apple juice** (or cider) until fruit is soft enough to mash to apple sauce. You need **2 c.** apple sauce.

2) Beat **6 egg whites** (about ½c.) until stiff.

3) Stir about ¼ **c. honey** into the apple sauce and add about **3 Tb. rum** or applejack. Use as much sweetening and liquor as pleases your taste.

4) Fold stiff beaten whites into the apple sauce. Chill.

5) Serve in glass dessert dishes. Witches' Froth won't keep more than a day.

Serves 8

*Nobody can stop a woman from feelin' she has to
rise up like the sun.
Somebody may change the words we're sayin' but
the truth will live on and on.
You can't kill the spirit. It's like a mountain,
Old and strong. It lives on and on.*

"Like a Mountain"
Izquierda
© *1977 by Naomi Littlebear*

MOLASSES APPLE GINGERBREAD

1) Butter an 8″ square pan. Preheat oven to 325°.

2) Peel, core and slice **3 or 4** Baldwin or Stayman Winesap **apples** and stew in a little **apple juice** in a covered pot. Line buttered pan with cooked apple slices. About ⅓ cup should remain and should be mashed with a fork to applesauce. Reserve.

3) In a pot melt together ⅔ **stick sweet butter** and ⅔ **c. molasses.** When melted, let cool.

4) In a bowl, use a whisk to stir together **1⅓ c. white unbleached flour, 1 t. baking soda, 1 t. ginger, ⅓ t. salt, ½ t. nutmeg, ½ t. cinnamon.**

5) In a separate bowl, beat **1 egg.** Add ⅓ **c. buttermilk** and the cooled butter and molasses. Stir together with flour mix and the reserved ⅓ **cup applesauce.** Do not stir too much. Turn into pan over apple slices and bake until cake pulls away from sides of pan.

6) Serve this cake warm with whipped cream melting over it: Beat together until stiff **1 c. heavy cream, 1 t. honey, ½ t. vanilla.**

CRANBERRY KISSL

The New England name for fruit juice pudding is flummery; the Russian name is kissl.

1) Simmer **1 pkg** (4 c.) **cranberries** in **2 c. juice.** (We use an organically grown juice, L & A brand apple boysenberry, and consider it excellently flavored and without undesirable additives, such as sugar. Perhaps local fresh apple cider will do as well.)

2) Put cranberries and juice through a foley food mill or a similar sieve. Return to pot. Add scant **1 c. water, ¾ c. honey, pinch** of **salt** and bring back to a simmer.

3) Stir **¼ c. potato starch** into **½ c. cold water.** Combine thoroughly, then add to simmering pot while stirring or whisking well. Kissl should thicken immediately. If it doesn't, stir together another 1½ Tb. potato starch with a few tablespoons cold water, and add.

4) Cool in pot about 10 minutes. Stir again and turn into glass dessert dishes. Chill until kissl "sets up." Serve with **heavy cream** and **slivered almonds.**

Serves 6–8

CRANBERRY COBBLER

From Barbara Butler.

1) Preheat oven to 325°. Butter a 7" x 11" or 8" square
   pyrex pan. Spread **1½ c. cranberries** in pan. Sprinkle
   with **⅓ c. sugar** and **¼ c. chopped walnuts.**

2) Beat **1 egg** with **⅓ c. sugar** and **¼ t. cardamom** very
   thoroughly.

3) Melt **6 Tb. sweet butter.** Stir egg mixture together
   with butter and **½ c. unbleached white flour.** Spoon
   batter over cranberries.

4) Bake until light brown. Cool. Serve with unsweetened
   whipped cream.

Serves 9–10

for the bond between women is returning
we are endlessly within it
and endlessly apart within it.

"plainsong from a younger woman to an older woman"
The Work of A Common Woman
Judy Grahn; St. Martin's Press

MAPLE APRICOT RICE PUDDING

1) In a large shallow baking pan, combine **⅓ c. brown rice** (we prefer short grain), **2½ Tb. maple syrup, dash salt, ½ c.** chopped or snipped **dried apricots, ¼ t. almond extract,** and **1 qt. milk.***

2) Bake at 325° for 1½ to 2, hours, stirring occasionally. The pudding will repeatedly get a brown skin which should be stirred in.

3) Remove from oven when pudding still seems soft and loose. It will thicken up as it cools. Serve with **heavy cream.**

Serves 6–8

* For a richer pudding, substitute **1 c. heavy cream** and **3 c. milk** for the 1 qt. milk.

*Well you want to see some sweetness, not just
Streams of angry words,
You really dig the music but the message is too tough,
It's not that we've forgotten about happiness and love
But until the times have changed, it's not enough.*

"All Our Lives" Words and music © 1974 D. Silverstein
"...And Ain't I A Woman?"
New Harmony Sisterhood Band; Paredon Records

SOUR CREAM PUMPKIN PIE

You can use pumpkin if you like, but we use Hubbard squash.

1) Cut up **1 Hubbard squash.** Scrape out seeds and stringy fiber with spoon. Steam or bake until soft.

2) Measure out **1½ c.** cooked **squash.** In a food processor or blender, mix squash together with **scant ½ c. sugar, 1 t. cinnamon, ½ t. ginger, ¼ t. nutmeg, ⅛ t. cloves,** and **¼ t. salt.** When well mixed, add **1 c. sour cream** and **3 egg yolks,** reserving whites in a mixer bowl. Preheat oven to 375°.

3) Roll out crust to fit pie (see following recipe).

4) Turn squash and sour cream mix into a pot and cook gently, stirring well, until slightly thickened. Beat **egg whites** until they form soft peaks, then sprinkle in **¼ c. sugar** and beat until stiff but not dry. Fold egg whites into squash mixture; turn into unbaked pie shell. Bake 40–45 minutes or till puffed and brown. Let cool.

5) Serve topped with whipped cream: Beat together until stiff **1½ c. heavy cream, 1½ Tb. sugar** and **½ t. vanilla.**

PIE CRUST

It is convenient to have pie crust dough waiting in the refrigerator to be used when you want to make a pie. Wrapped in foil, pie crust will keep 2 weeks refrigerated. So double, triple or quadruple this recipe to be well supplied.

1) For each single crust pie shell (with scraps left over), mix together **2 c. flour** and **½ t. salt.** Cut **1 stick sweet butter** into small bits and place in bowl with flour. Also add **3 Tb. vegetable shortening.** Use the flat beater of a Kitchenaid mixer, a pastry blender or fingertips to cut fat and flour together until the mixture looks like flakes of oatmeal.

2) Add **⅓ c.** very cold **water.** Mix in thoroughly but as briefly as possible. This may be accomplished best by using the heel of your hand to very briefly knead the dough on a floured board.

3) Wrap in foil and chill 2 hours before you roll out the dough.

4) Roll out pie crust on a well floured counter or board. Roll crust as thinly as possible. Place in pie pan by first folding dough in half and then gently lifting it into the pie pan. We like removable bottomed quiche pans. Since pie crust will shrink in baking, be sure not to stretch it. If recipe calls for unbaked shell refrigerate crust until ready to use; otherwise, preheat oven to 400°. Prick shell at juncture of rim and bottom with a fork. Line shell with aluminum foil and something to weigh the foil down such as lentils or beans.

5) Bake about 5 minutes. Carefully remove foil and beans and add whatever filling needs cooking. Or, for a fully baked shell, turn oven down to 375° after removing the foil and bake another 5–10 minutes until evenly browned and done.

6) Scraps of crust can be rolled in cinnamon-sugar, cut with a pastry wheel into strips, the strips then twisted and placed on a cookie sheet. Bake at 375° for a lovely cookie.

. . . the memory of another voice, the voice of Dunyazad, Shahrazad's sister, that mad, dead, haunted woman who could not tell stories, who could not save herself. It is the voicelessness of Dunyazad that passes like a sigh from wall to wall of the valley of dry bones and shivers faintly over the multitude of the dead . . . From autumn leaf to autumn leaf goes the message: something, nothing, everything. Something is coming out of nothing. For the first time, something will be created out of nothing. There is not a drop of water, not a blade of grass, not a single word.

   But they move.
   And they rise.

The Two Of Them
Joanna Russ; Berkley

PEARS ISABEL

Named for Isabel Brach who inspired this adaptation of
Zabaglione.

1) In the top of a double boiler (or in a stainless steel bowl
   that will fit on the rim of a pot as a double boiler does)
   place **5 egg yolks** and **¼ cup honey.** The bowl or
   double boiler top must be stainless steel or enamel or
   the sauce will discolor. Put enough water in bottom pan
   to last 10–15 minutes without touching upper bowl.

2) Beat and/or stir constantly with whisk over low-medium
   heat until sauce becomes quite thick and sticks to sides
   of bowl (about 10–15 minutes).

3) Remove from heat and add a **scant ½ c. Grand
   Marnier liqueur,** whisking until sauce is smooth.

4) Place in refrigerator until sauce is very cold.

5) Whip **1 c. heavy cream** stiff and fold into sauce until
   mixture is smooth and even. Fold, do not stir.

6) Fill a glass serving bowl with 5–6 sliced comice **pears.**
   Top with the sauce.

Serves 6–8

CHENOPODIUM GEMS

From Gary Lincoff, an exceptionally fine teacher of wild
mushroom and wild foods courses.

1) In early November gather **1 c.** plus **3 Tb.
   chenopodium seeds.** Shake them through a strainer
   to remove any leaves or twigs.

2) Preheat oven to 425°. Butter muffin tins or line with
   papers.

3) Melt ½ **stick sweet butter.**

4) Mix together (whisk works well) chenopodium seeds,
   1 c. plus **3 Tb. unbleached white flour, ¼ c. sugar,
   1 Tb. baking powder, ½ t. salt.**

5) In a small bowl beat **1 egg.** Add **1 c. milk** and the
   melted butter. Stir.

6) Combine the liquid and dry mixtures. Stir briefly; do not
   overmix.

7) Spoon the batter into muffin tins and bake in
   pre-heated oven until muffins have risen, about 5–10
   minutes. Reduce heat to 400° and continue baking until
   light brown. (Total baking time about 20–25 minutes.)

Yields 10–12 muffins

Note: The chenopodium seeds referred to come from a kind of wild spinach known commonly as lamb's quarters. A good field guide to wild herbs will help in identification. The small leaves are good to eat too, either raw or cooked, earlier in the year. The seeds are best after the first frost. Be sure you know your wild plants before you eat them.

. . . there are a few things I'd like to preserve for future generations.

Such as, Gertrude? the other prompts, severely.

Recipes, Mrs. Baxter defensively murmurs, recipes and things.

Recipes! Recipes is hardly the kind of thing Jo Ellen would want to hear about, Mrs. Biehler is driven to explain. I did not tell her I write about my flowers . . . Aren't you aware that this is what they think is wrong with us, that we spent too much time cooking and cleaning and having babies? . . .

Mrs. Biehler regards her disapprovingly. I'm seventy-seven and still not ready to die.

You might tell her I will give her some additional information, if only she will record my recipes, Mrs. Baxter insists.

"Yellow Jackets"
Mother, Sister, Daughter, Lover
Jan Clausen; Crossing Press

HUBBARD SQUASH BREAD

From Edna Priest.

1) You will need **2 c. steamed and pureed winter squash.** (See Lima Bean Squash Soup recipe). Preheat oven to 350°.

2) Warm **4 eggs** in a bowl in their shells, in warm tap water.

3) Butter and flour 3 small loaf tins. Sift or whisk together **3⅓ c. unbleached white flour, 1¼ c. sugar, 2 t. baking soda, 1½ t. salt, 1 t. cinnamon, 1 t. nutmeg,** a **pinch** of **cloves**.

4) Break warmed eggs into mixer and beat with **1¼ c. sugar,** until thick and light yellow. On low speed, add **1 c. oil** and the squash puree. Don't overbeat. Add **1 c. chopped walnuts** or **pecans.**

5) Fold in dry ingredients. Bake 1 hour or until breads pull away slightly from sides of pans. Cool in pans on racks and then turn out. Slice thinly and serve with **whipped cream cheese** or **butter.**

Yields 3 small loaves

MULLED WINE CIDER

1) In a large pot combine **4 c. cider, 2 t. honey, rind** of **1 orange** (try to peel off rind with as little of the bitter white pith as possible), **3 sticks cinnamon** and **5** whole **cloves.** Bring slowly to a boil.

2) Add **2 c. red wine.** Skim out cloves and orange peel and ladle into mugs or glasses.

Serves 6–8

May I never remember reasons
for my spirit's safety
may I never forget
the warning of my woman's flesh
weeping at the new moon
may I never lose
that terror
that keeps me brave
May I owe nothing
that I cannot repay.

"Solstice"
The Black Unicorn
Audre Lorde; Norton

CHAPTER 2   EARLY WINTER
Winter Solstice, December 22, to February 2.

HUPI POLLIVKA

Slavic Mushroom soup from Joe Knapik, who tells us this is
a traditional December (solstice) dish.

1) Soak **4 oz. dried mushrooms** (boletus edulis) in
   water to cover for 2–3 hours. Squeeze them to be sure
   they are clean, and slice. Any tough portions should be
   discarded. Save mushroom liquid.

2) Chop **2 small onions** and saute in ½ **stick unsalted
   butter** until medium brown. Add the prepared dried
   mushrooms and their soaking liquid, being careful not
   to add any sand or dirt that may be at the bottom of the
   bowl. Add **1 qt. sauerkraut juice*** and simmer for
   about 1 hour.

3) Slice **1 lb. fresh mushrooms** (Agaricus) and add to
   pot. Cook a few minutes until they are done. Then add
   about **1 qt. water** to dilute the strong sauerkraut juice
   flavor to your taste. Season with **fresh ground
   pepper.**

4) Separately cook **1 c. orzo,** a rice shaped pasta, in water
   until tender. Drain and add to soup.

5) Serve with grated **parmesan,** if desired.

Serves 8

* Canned sauerkraut juice is often hard to find. We drain canned sauerkraut to use in S'chee or Halushkin and save the liquid for Hupi soup.

> *Since many women confide to their gynecologists and therapists private matters which they do not share with any woman, the team of holy ghosts keeps women from sharing secrets with each other . . . A woman seduced into treatment is "inspired" with dis-ease she had never before even suspected . . . The multiplicity of therapies feeds into this dis-ease . . . invasion continues unchecked because it fixes women's attention in the wrong direction, fragmenting and privatizing perception of problems . . . While the body doctors offer their faithful The Pill as daily holy communion, the mind doctors offer weekly confession.*
>
> **Gyn/Ecology**
> *Mary Daly; Beacon Press*

ONION SOUP

1) Thinly slice enough **onions** to yield **6 c.** Put them in a
   soup kettle with **½ stick unsalted butter** and **1 Tb.
   oil.** Cover pot and simmer 20 minutes. Uncover pot,
   add **½ t. crushed dried thyme, 1½ t. salt** and
   ¼ t. sugar. Raise heat slightly and cook onions, stirring
   occasionally with wooden spoon, until they are a rich
   medium brown color. It will take at least 45 minutes,
   and is the secret to the good flavor of this soup.

2) Stir in **¼ c. unbleached white flour** and cook a few
   minutes more, stirring. Add **2½ qt. water** and bring to
   a boil, stirring up browned particles. Add **⅓ c. tamari,**
   or good quality soy sauce, and **½ c. dry white wine.**
   Simmer another half hour and taste. Add **salt** and
   pepper as you need it.

3) Dry out stale pieces of **French bread** in a 300° oven
   and rub the crisped surfaces with a peeled clove of
   garlic.

4) When ready to serve, put **1 Tb.** each **grated Swiss
   cheese** and **grated parmesan** in each bowl—you will
   need **½ c.** of each cheese. A splash of **brandy** is nice
   too, if you like. Ladle soup into bowls, stir, and top with
   garlic crouts.

Serves 8

BLACK BEAN SOUP

From *Wings of Life* by Julie Jordan, Crossing Press, and used with their permission.

1) Soak **2 cups dried black beans** overnight.* When ready to cook, bring the beans to a boil in a soup pot with **5 c. water** and turn down to a simmer. Cook the beans until done and set aside. (Allow 1 hour or more.)

2) Chop **4 medium onions** and start to fry them on high heat in **4 Tb. vegetable oil**. Add **1 green pepper,** finely chopped, **3 cloves garlic,** crushed, **1 t. oregano, ½ t. dry mustard** and **1 t. whole cumin seed.** Stir the bottom of the soup pot frequently making sure the vegetables don't burn but brown evenly.

3) When the vegetables are browned, add the cooked beans to the soup pot, mashing some of the black beans with a spoon. Add as much **water** as necessary to the soup so it is not too thick.

4) Turn the heat on high and add **1 c.** canned **tomatoes** and **2 t. salt.** Let the soup come to a boil, turn down to a simmer, and let cook ½ hour or more to develop flavor. Taste for seasoning and add the **juice** of **1 lemon** before serving. Serve with a dollop of **sour cream.**

Serves 8

* If beans cannot be soaked overnight, they can be brought to a boil in water, removed from heat for 1 hour and then returned to stove and cooked until tender.

S'CHEE

A wonderful Russian cabbage soup that never misses meat. Time consuming to prepare, but will feed ten people. It helps having at least 2 cooks to fry vegetables and to judge seasoning properly.

1) Prepare vegetable broth: Preheat oven to 500.° In a roasting pan place **1 large** peeled and quartered **onion, 2 carrots, 1 parsnip,** and **1 white turnip.** Drizzle with **oil** and roast, turning often, until well browned. Remove roasted vegetables to a large soup kettle. Use boiling water to deglaze roasting pan, scraping up browned bits. Add this water to soup kettle with enough additional **water** to cover. Cut **celery tops** from **1 bunch celery** and add. Add **2 bay leaves** and **2** well-washed **leeks.** Simmer at least 1 hour. Then put broth through strainer into another large soup kettle or bowl. Press down on vegetables to get as much of their juices as possible. Discard remaining pulp.

2) Chop and saute in **2 Tb. oil** in frying pan: **1 c. onions, ½ c. celery, ½ c. carrots.** When slightly browned, add **2 cloves garlic,** crushed. Turn off fire. Rinse **1 lb. sauerkraut** in a colander. Squeeze dry and coarsely chop. Add to fry pan and saute till kraut starts to brown, adding more oil if necessary. Turn contents of frying pan into the pot of vegetable broth.

3) Shred **1 cabbage** (about 2 lb. or 2 qt. shredded) and
    saute it in the same frying pan, again adding **oil** if
    necessary, until cabbage is wilted. Turn into soup kettle
    with a **2 lb.** can **Italian plum tomatoes,** chopped a
    little with a spoon, **2 Tb. tomato paste, 2 Tb. honey,**
    and **⅓–½ c. tamari.** Add **water** as necessary.

4) Simmer at least one hour more. Add juice of **1½–2
    lemons** and begin to taste. Soup will likely need more
    water and possibly up to **1 Tb. salt.** It should taste
    sweet and sour, as well as salty. Add more lemon juice
    or tamari, if needed. Chop **one small bunch dill** and
    add. Serve topped with a dollop of **sour cream.**

Serves 8–10

What price for a woman
You can buy her for a ring of gold
To love and obey without any pay . . . .

"I'm Gonna Be An Engineer"
At The Present Moment
Peggy Seeger; Shelter Music

POTATO KNISHES

Perfect as appetizers or soup accompaniments.

1) Cook **3** large **potatoes** in boiling **water** till done.

2) Meanwhile, chop **4 medium onions** and saute in a fry pan in ¾ **stick unsalted butter.**

3) Put drained cooked potatoes in a mixer and beat well. Add **salt** and **pepper,** the onions and butter, and **2 eggs.** Beat again. Mixture will be soft. Turn into bowl and refrigerate.

4) Make noodle dough: In mixer put **3 c. unbleached white flour,** ½ **t. salt** and **2 Tb. oil.** Add **2 small eggs** and **1 egg white** and beat well on low speed. Add **warm water** if necessary to make dough. If mixer doesn't work well, it will be necessary to knead dough by hand until smooth and silky. Cover with towel and let rest 15 minutes.

5) Divide noodle dough into two parts. Roll and stretch one piece on a large flour covered dishcloth or small tablecloth until it is a thin rectangle. Melt **1 stick sweet butter** and use a pastry brush to lightly butter dough and a cookie sheet. Place a thin line of potato filling along one end of the dough—it can be about as thick as your thumb—and lift cloth to roll dough two turns.

Carefully cut the long line off from the larger piece and cut individual slices about 1½" each. Place filling side up on cookie sheet and flatten slightly with a fork. Repeat with the rest of the rolled-out dough and more filling, and then roll out rest of dough and repeat again.

6) Knishes can be covered with plastic wrap and refrigerated or frozen until you are ready to serve them. Bake at 350° until they are browned, 45 minutes to 1 hour.

Makes about 60 small knishes

Dieting is a personal solution not too different from suicide: remove the offending body.

"Fat Woman"
Aldebaran

CURRIED LENTIL SOUP

From *Wings of Life* by Julie Jordan, Crossing Press, and used with their permission.

1) Soak **1 cup dried lentils** overnight.* When ready to use, bring the beans to a boil in a small pot with **3 cups water** and turn down to a simmer. Cook the beans until done and set aside. (Allow 1 hour or more.)

2) Chop **4 medium onions** and start to fry them on high heat in a soup pot with **4 Tb. vegetable oil.** Add **2 green peppers,** coarsely chopped, **3 cloves garlic,** crushed, **½ t. dry ginger, 1 t. ground turmeric, 1 t. ground coriander, ¼ t. ground cloves, 1 t. chili powder,** and **1 t. ground cumin** (we pan roast whole cumin seeds first and then crush them in a mortar and pestle). Stir the bottom of the soup pot frequently making sure the vegetables don't burn but brown evenly.

3) When vegetables are browned, add the cooked lentils to the soup pot, adding as much **water** as necessary for the soup to be somewhat thin. (As lentils go on cooking they absorb water.)

4) Turn heat on high and add **1 qt.** canned **tomatoes,
   1 t. salt,** and ¼ **cup raisins.** Let the lentil soup come
   to a boil, turn down to a simmer and let cook ½ hour or
   more to develop flavor. Taste for seasoning and add
   the juice of **1 lemon** just before serving. Serve with a
   dollop of **yogurt** on top and a thin slice of **apple.**

* If beans cannot be soaked overnight, they can be brought
  to a boil in water, removed from heat for 1 hour and then
  returned to stove and cooked until tender.

*The nineteenth century produced many other
vegetarian feminists—Margaret Fuller, Louisa
May Alcott, Victoria Woodhull, Mary Shelley, and
the Grimke sisters. The Vegetarian Society held
huge feasts during the 1850's, with honored
feminist guests such as Lucy Stone, Amelia
Bloomer, and Susan B. Anthony.*

"The Oedible Complex: Feminism and Vegetarianism"
The Lesbian Reader
Carol Adams; Ed: Gina Covina and Laurel Galana;
Amazon Press

POTATO CELERY SEED SOUP

1) Dice ½ **bunch celery** and **3 carrots**. Save the **celery leaves** and chop. Chop **1 large onion**.

2) In a soup pot, saute all the vegetables in ½ **stick sweet butter**. As the vegetables are browning, the bottom of the pot must be scraped vigorously. Add **3 cloves garlic,** coarsely chopped. Cook long enough for the garlic to be incorporated.

3) Wash, peel, and dice by hand **5 medium potatoes**. Add to the soup pot with enough **water** to cover the vegetables. Add ¾ **t. celery seed, 1 Tb. salt, ½ t. pepper.** Bring to a boil and simmer till potatoes are soft.

4) Add ¾ **c. heavy cream, 2 t. tamari,** and a **dash** of **Tabasco**. Taste for seasoning. If soup is too thick, add milk or water. Warm over low heat and do not boil when reheating. Garnish with **scallion slices**.

Serves 6–8

I am still caught unawares
By ghosts lurking in my nightmares
That mock our revolution.

"Scars"
I know you know
© *1974 Meg Christian; Olivia; Thumbelina Music (BMI)*

CABBAGE SALAD

1) Cut into quarters and finely slice **1 medium cabbage.**
   (Red cabbage is beautiful in this salad.) Grate **3 carrots**
   and marinate them in ½ **c. vinaigrette** (see recipe
   index). Soak ½ **c. raisins** in warm water to plump
   them.

2) Finely chop **1 small bunch parsley.** Set aside.

3) Make mayonnaise using a food processor or mixer.
   Have ready in small pitcher **1¾ c. vegetable oil.** In
   the processor or mixer beat thoroughly **3 egg yolks.**
   Then add **1½ t. lemon juice, 1½ t. mustard,** a **dash**
   of **Tabasco,** ½ **t. salt** and **pepper.** Keep the
   processor on, or mixer running at moderate to high
   speed, and add the oil in a slow dribble at first and more
   quickly at the end. Turn the machine off when the oil is
   thoroughly mixed in and mayonnaise has thickened.

5) Add ½ **c. yoghurt** and the chopped parsley to the
   mayonnaise. Mix thoroughly.

6) In a large bowl combine the cabbage, carrots and raisins
   with the yoghurt mayonnaise. Taste for salt, pepper and
   lemon juice.

7) Assemble the cabbage salad on a lettuce leaf and top
   with thin slices of **Bermuda onion** and **diced apples.**

Serves 6–8

ORANGE ESCAROLE SALAD

1) Thoroughly wash and dry **1 large head escarole.**
   Chill.

2) Use a small knife to peel the skins and white pith from
   3 large California oranges, cutting pith and skin off
   simultaneously. Use a large sharp knife to cut oranges
   into slices.

3) Arrange escarole on 6 plates and place overlapping
   slices of oranges on each one.

4) Mix **1 c. vinaigrette** (see recipe index) with **2 Tb. sour
   cream.** Pour over prepared salads and top each one
   with **Bermuda onion slices** and a little **gomahsio**
   (see following recipe).

                                              Serves 6

*The Christian emphasis on pain and suffering as
the path to transcendence and salvation is the very
meat of most sadomasochistic pornography, just
as the Christian definition of woman is its
justification.*

Woman Hating
Andrea Dworkin; E. P. Dutton

GOMAHSIO

1) In a heavy skillet over medium-high heat roast
    2 Tb. sea salt stirring constantly until the chlorine odor
    is released. This takes about one minute. Transfer the
    salt to a stainless steel bowl.

2) In the same pan over medium high heat roast
    1 c. sesame seeds stirring often till light brown and
    fragrant.

3) Grind the salt and roasted seeds together with a mortar
    and pestle or by machine. We use a small electric coffee
    mill. Do not overgrind or you'll have sesame butter.

                                        Makes about 1 cup

*Goddesses never die. They slip in and out of the
world's cities, in and out of our dreams, century
after century, answering to different names,
dressed differently, perhaps even disguised,
perhaps idle and unemployed, their official altars
abandoned, their temples feared or simply forgotten . . .*

Women And Madness
Phyllis Chesler; Avon

ROQUEFORT, GRAPEFRUIT AND AVOCADO SALAD

1) Peel **4 large grapefruits** and separate into segments.
   Arrange on beds of **Boston lettuce** in pinwheel
   pattern alternating with slices of **avocado** (you will
   need 1 very large avocado).

2) Cut about **6 oz. roquefort cheese** into 6 wedges and
   center each salad with the cheese.

3) Top with **onion rings** and **vinaigrette** (see recipe
   index).

Serves 6

*They've got the power won't you please realize
to make the battered woman the very one who denies.
When I see a woman betray her own side
it hurts so much, my rage kills me inside.
The goddamn man, he's done it again!*

"man-hater"
witch is witch
Monika Jaeckel and Barbara Bauermeister

AVOCADO STUFFED WITH SHREDDED PARSNIPS AND CURRIED MAYONNAISE

1) Prepare **Mayonnaise:** Place **2 egg yolks** in a food processor or electric mixer. Add **1 Tb. lemon juice, ½ t. salt, ½ t.** good quality prepared **mustard** and turn machine on. Add **1 c. vegetable oil** drop by drop until mayonnaise begins to thicken. When mayonnaise is smooth and well thickened, turn machine off. Add **1½ Tb. tomato puree** or **catsup** (we prefer Johnson's table sauce), **2½ t.** good quality **curry powder** and **1–2 drops Tabasco.** Blend well.

2) Shred enough **parsnips** to yield **3 c.** Chop **1½ c. celery** very fine. Mince **⅓ c. scallions** or **onion.** Combine parsnips, celery, and scallions with enough of the prepared mayonnaise to moisten the mixture. Taste for seasoning. More lemon juice, salt, or curry powder may be necessary. You may add **⅔ c.** chopped **black olives** or **½ c.** finely chopped **walnuts** if you like. Refrigerate, covered, until ready to serve.

3) Cut **4 small avocados** in half. Peel and remove pits. Place each half on a bed of lettuce and fill with parsnip mixture. Drizzle **vinaigrette** over lettuce and sprinkle top of salad with **gomahsio** (see recipe index).

Serves 8

POTATO LATKES

1) Prepare **applesauce** (see recipe index) to serve with latkes.

2) Grate **3 large potatoes,** peeled and washed, and **1 small onion** in a food processor or by hand (blender yields inferior results) into a colander over a bowl. Set aside and let mixture drain into the bowl.

3) In a larger bowl beat **2 eggs.** Add **2 Tb. potato starch, 1 t. salt, ½ bunch parsley,** fresh chopped, and a little grated **pepper.**

4) Go back to the grated potato-onion mixture and squeeze it directly over the colander so the bowl beneath catches all the liquid. Put the squeezed mixture into the larger bowl of mixed eggs, etc. Mix them together well.

5) Lift off the colander. In the bottom bowl will be a layer of liquid on top of some **potato starch.** Pour off the liquid and discard. Using a scraper, add this residual starch to the larger bowl of mixed eggs, potato and onion. Make sure the starch is mixed well into the batter. This batter should be stored in the refrigerator in a narrow container with a tight lid. The top of the batter may turn a greyish/black color—it is only potato discoloring and is not harmful. It may be lifted off and thrown away or stirred in.

6) When ready to cook, preheat a large skillet or frying pan with **vegetable oil.** Use a fork to lift and place the batter into the hot skillet or fry pan, patting the individual latke (about 4 inches wide) down with the fork. Repeat this procedure until desired amount of latkes are formed in the pan, carefully noting if more oil is needed. For best browning use as little oil as possible. Watch until the bottom side of the latkes are brown and with a spatula flip them over to cook on their other side. Press lightly with spatula. End result should be flat, brown, lacy pancakes. Serve immediately with **sour cream** and **apple sauce.**

Serves 6

. . . but who are the daughters of Rachel and Ruth and Sarah and Rebekah the rest we do not know the daughters never had any daughters . . . If you recognized an aspect of yourself that you love in these ancient new womens heads I too have recognized an admirable aspect of myself in your willingness to be as beautiful as you are who you are . . . On A Clear Day You Can See Your Mother.

Lesbian Nation
Jill Johnston; Simon and Schuster

SPINACH NOODLES WITH GARLIC VERMOUTH SAUCE

1) Make **Garlic Vermouth Sauce:** Melt **1 stick sweet butter.** Saute **4** crushed **cloves garlic.** Add ½ **t. dried basil,** crumbled well in your hand. When cooked but not browned, add ½ **c. unbleached white flour.** Cook gently a few minutes. Add ⅓ **c. dry vermouth, juice** of ½ **lemon, 1 c. heavy cream.** Let sauce thicken a little, then add up to **1 qt. milk.** Finally, season with **1–2 Tb. tamari,** a **dash** of **Tabasco** and **1½ Tb. pesto.*** Taste. You may want to add ½ **t. salt.** Simmer ½ hour.

2) Prepare **pignoli nuts:** Use a rolling pin to crush about **1 c.** of them on a counter. Then toast them, stirring, in an oven (350°) or toaster oven till light-medium brown. Be careful, they burn easily.

3) Cook **spinach ribbons** (noodles) or **artichoke ribbons** in boiling salted water. Drain and toss with a little **olive oil** and **salt.**

4) Serve noodles with sauce, fresh grated **parmesan,** a sprinkling of pignoli nuts and fresh ground **pepper.**

* **PESTO:** We grow **basil** in the summer, then chop the leaves in a food processor together with **garlic** and enough **olive oil** to make the machine efficient. Traditionally, the nuts (pignoli, walnuts, almonds) are ground together with the basil. We prefer the nuts as a toasted topping instead. The pesto is frozen and removed from the freezer when we begin making the sauce. After ½ hour, it has softened enough so that we can scrape out a nice piece to season with; the rest is returned to the freezer. Lacking pesto, add 1 Tb. more crushed **basil**.

It is like sex, this life process. The idea of being satisfied is inconceivable . . . . What I love about sex is that it is never completed . . . I think of a prism. Every time something opens up, something else appears . . . Life to me is like the inside of a vagina, an open tunnel that has no end. On the other side of one cave is another cave and its darkness keeps you from seeing the end.

"Anica Vesel Mander"
Interview With The Muse
Nina Winter; Moon Books

SWISS CHEESE FONDUE

You will need a table burner and a casserole to cook the
fondue in. The flameproof pottery casseroles specially
made for fondue cooking are best.

1) Prepare bread and vegetables: Cut **1 whole French** or
   Italian bread into 1″ cubes, being sure each piece has
   crust on it. Arrange in a large bowl. Add **3 carrots,**
   scraped and cut into sticks, **1 bunch broccoli** cut into
   flowerets with about 1″ of stem, **18** whole or halved
   fresh mushrooms, 2 apples cut into wedges and
   cored but not peeled.

2) Using a blender or food processor, shred **1 lb.**
   Switzerland Swiss cheese. Toss with ¼ c.
   unbleached white flour.

3) Put flameproof casserole on stove and add **2 c. white**
   wine. Spear **1 clove garlic,** peeled, on a fondue
   fork and bring wine and garlic to a simmer. Now add
   cheese handful by handful, stirring with a kitchen fork.
   Season to taste with **salt** and **pepper.** When cheese
   and wine are well blended and color and texture are
   smooth, add ¼ c. **Kirschwasser.** Don't subsititute
   other liqueur if you don't have **Kirsch.** Discard garlic
   clove.

4) Bring casserole to table with bread and vegetables and give each diner a fondue fork, a plate, and a small salad. As the fondue cooks down, use fondue forks to scrape up the crust of toasting cheese at the bottom. Some of us think that part is best.

Serves 4

When walkin in the winter time
bare trees told me about inner rhyme
Some days I sleep and dream that nothing will be left for
green and walls will be garnished with a guard
When I awake those days I collect my emotion-pay
and pour it on a tree outside the yard.

"in retrospect"
Ferron
Ferron; Lucy Records

CRAB CREPES SOUFFLE

A fancy dish for a special dinner. Obviously, the souffle can be done in a buttered souffle casserole without the crepes and with or without the sauce.

1) Prepare **Crepes:** Melt ½ **stick sweet butter.** Put the following ingredients into a blender: **¾ c. milk, ¾ c. cold water, 4 eggs, 3 egg yolks** (reserve whites), **1½ c. unbleached white flour, ½ t. salt** and the melted butter. Blend well, scrape down sides, and blend again. Refrigerate for an hour or two.

2) You will need a crepe pan to make crepes, that is, a heavy pan you use for no other purpose and which is "seasoned" (heated slowly for 15 minutes with a little oil, then wiped clean) and never washed. It's easiest having 3 crepe pans so that you can make 3 crepes at a time. Heat the pan, wipe with an oily piece of absorbent paper, stir the crepe batter once again, and pour a little batter into the hot pan. Swirl the pan and immediately return excess batter to the blender or pitcher. When crepe turns brown at the edges, use a spatula to loosen it around the rim and the spatula and your fingers to turn it over to cook the other side a few seconds. Knock out onto a wooden board and repeat. Stack the crepes and cover with plastic wrap until ready to use. They will keep, refrigerated, for a week.

3) Make the **Souffle** mixture: Melt **4 Tb. butter,** add
   4½ Tb. flour and cook together a minute or two. Add
   1½ c. milk, ¾ t. salt, ¼ t. fresh ground pepper,
   ¼ t. dry mustard, and bring to a boil, stirring well until
   smooth. Remove from heat. Separate **6 eggs** (saving
   whites) and whisk yolks into white sauce, one at a time.

4) Pick over **1½ c. crabmeat,** fresh, frozen, or canned,
   to remove any bits of cartilage or shell. Add crabmeat to
   souffle mixture with **⅓ c. grated Swiss cheese.** Taste
   for seasoning. Refrigerate until ready to serve.

5) Prepare the **Wine and Shallot Hollandaise** up to an
   hour before ready to serve. Saute **1 Tb. shallots,**
   minced, in **2 Tb. butter** until soft. Add **½ c. white**
   wine and reduce (boil down) to ¼ c. Remove from heat
   and cool two minutes, then whisk in **3 egg yolks.** Melt
   1½ sticks butter. Whisk the yolk and wine mixture
   over low heat until it thickens slightly, then add melted
   butter very slowly until sauce thickens like a hollandaise.
   Remove from heat. Add **salt** and **pepper** to taste, and
   a few drops of **lemon juice.** Cover and leave near the
   stove, but not over heat where it would curdle.

6) When ready to serve, preheat oven to 400°. Stiffly beat
   7–8 reserved **egg whites** (¾ c.) with a **dash** of **salt.**
   Stir ⅓ of the whites into the souffle mixture thoroughly.
   Then fold in the remainder of the whites. Place a
   spoonful of this mixture on each crepe and fold in
   quarters. Since souffle will puff, don't overfill them.
   Butter a cookie sheet (or two) and place crepes on the
   pan. Place in oven and reduce heat to 375°. Bake until
   puffed and browned, about 10 minutes.

7) Immediately serve 3 crepes per diner, with wine and shallot hollandaise over the top. A green salad served separately completes this elegant dinner.

Serves 8

someday. Meantime here is your cracked plate
with spaghetti. Wash your hands &
touch me, praise
my cooking. I shall praise your calluses.
we shall dance in the kitchen
of our imagination.

"Confrontations With The Devil In The Form Of Love"
The Work of A Common Woman
Judy Grahn; St. Martin's Press

COLLARD GREENS, BLACK-EYED PEAS AND CORNBREAD

Marvalene Styles, in "Soul, Black Women and Food"*, writes that soul food is a means of preservation of Black identity. Abducted slaves managed to bring seeds of yams, okra, greens, watermelon, black-eyed peas and sesame with them from Africa, thereby maintaining an African identity. Although Black women working as slaves and kitchen maids were forced to learn European techniques in white kitchens, they nevertheless maintained their own cultural forms and passed them on in the Black oral tradition. Styles notes that roots are basic to the meaning of soul food and the choice of root plants such as yams or sweet potatoes can be traced to an African tradition. Furthermore, Black food, such as black-eyed peas, is inherently soulful whether prepared in a Black person's kitchen, white kitchen or Jewish kitchen. It's necessary to understand the political and cultural context of the foods we prepare to show proper respect for our varied histories.

1) Prepare **Greens:** With a sharp knife remove stems from **3 bunches collard, turnip,** or **mustard greens** (or any combination). Wash in cold water, discarding stems and any discolored leaves. Coarsely chop **1½ medium onions** and fry in **⅓ c. olive oil** in a 3 qt. pot together with **4 cloves garlic,** crushed, and **½ t. hot pepper flakes.** Cook the onions till slightly brown. Break the greens into smaller pieces and put them in the pot with onions. Add **1 Tb. salt, 1½ Tb. tamari** and enough **water** to cover. Bring to a boil, then turn down and simmer for 1½ hours. Add more salt if necessary and some fresh grated **black pepper.**

2) Prepare **Black-eyed Peas:** Bring **1½ c. dried black-eyed peas** to a boil with **4 c. water** in a small pot. Simmer covered ½ hour. Coarsely chop **1½ medium onions** and fry in **3 Tb. olive oil** together with **2 cloves garlic,** crushed, and **½ t. hot pepper flakes.** Fry till slightly brown. After the peas have simmered ½ hr., add the fried onions, **1½ c. white rice** and **1½ Tb. salt** to the peas. Add **water** to cover rice and peas. Cook over low flame till done (25 minutes). Sprinkle with **tamari.**

3) Prepare **Cornbread** (see following recipe).

4) Wash **6–8** small **sweet potatoes** or **yams** and bake in oven with cornbread till done (about ½ hr.).

5) Serve a portion of the greens on a plate with black-eyed peas, sweet potato or yam, and hot cornbread. Spoon some of the "pot likker" over the greens and soak/mop up the broth with the cornbread.

Serves 6–8

* Styles, Marvalene, "Soul, Black Women and Food" in *A Woman's Conflict,* edited by Jane Rachel Kaplan (Prentice Hall, New Jersey, 1980).

CORN BREAD

1) Butter an 8″ x 8″ x 2″ pyrex baking dish. Preheat oven to 400°. Melt **½ stick sweet butter.**

2) Whisk together **1¼ c. unbleached white flour, 1 Tb. baking powder, 1 t. salt, 1 c. cornmeal** and **2 Tb. sugar.**

3) In a small bowl, beat well **2 eggs.** Stir in **1¼ c. buttermilk** and the melted butter.

4) Combine wet and dry mixtures until just blended. Do not overmix. Turn into pan and bake until lightly browned (about 20–25 minutes).

Take the blues. Study it as a coded language of resistance. In response to questions from classmembers about whether Feminism has ever had anything to do with Black women, play Ma Rainey singing "I won't be your dog no more."

Michele Russell
"Black Eyed Blues Connections: From the Inside Out"
Heresies: A Feminist Publication on Art and Politics *Vol 2., No. 4, Issue 8: Third World Women.*

POTATO COTTAGE CHEESE DUMPLINGS WITH CABBAGE SAUCE

1) Make **Cabbage Sauce:** Peel **1 medium onion** and chop coarsely. Saute in a large sauce pan over moderately high heat in **1 Tb. vegetable oil.** Meanwhile, coarsely chop ½ **head** of **cabbage** (¾ lb.) and add to the onions when they are soft but not brown. Add more oil if necessary to cook the cabbage. Turn cabbage till somewhat browned. Add **1 qt. water, 1 Tb. salt, ½ t. pepper, ¼ t. caraway seed, 2 t. vinegar, 1½ Tb. honey** and **1 Tb. tamari,** or soy sauce. Add ½ **c.** canned **tomatoes.** Bring to a boil adding more water if necessary to cover the cabbage. Turn down heat to a simmer. It should now cook for at least 2 hours.

2) Make **Dumplings:** Wash and boil **3 small potatoes** (¾ lb.) in their skins until soft. Peel and mash potatoes in a mixer while they are hot. Add to the mixer in this order: ½ **stick sweet butter, 1½ t. salt,** grating of fresh **nutmeg, 2 Tb.** freshly grated **parmesan cheese, 1½ c. cottage cheese, ¼ t. pepper, 2** or **3 Tb.** chopped fresh **dill,** and **1 egg.** Add **1½ c. unbleached white flour** and mix well. (Mixture should be moist but with enough flour to be slightly stiff. Do not add too much flour or dumplings will be heavy.) Refrigerate dumpling batter till ready to use.

3) Taste cabbage sauce for seasoning. If it is too sweet, add a little **lemon juice**; if too sour, more **honey.** Salt and tamari may also be needed to develop flavor. If still not satisfactory, add a **splash** of **dry red wine** and let cook another hour or until it cooks into a well developed sweet and sour flavor.

4) When ready to serve, fill a large pot ⅓ full of **water** and add **1 Tb. salt.** Bring to a boil. Dip a large spoon into the boiling water then into the dumpling mix to lift out an oval shape. Dip spoon into the pot and dumpling will slip off the spoon. Repeat. Plan about 5–6 dumplings per serving. Cover pot and turn down heat to lowest simmer. Cook 12 to 15 minutes or until dumplings have risen to the top and are puffed but are not beginning to fall apart. Use a slotted spoon over some absorbent paper to drain each dumpling before placing them in shallow soup bowls. Lightly **butter** dumplings. Spoon cabbage sauce around them and serve **sour cream** on the side.

Note: Cabbage sauce is easy to make but requires a good 3 hrs. of simmering before it develops its full flavor).

It can kill you slow in a life time
or get you fast in a nuclear war.

"Ain't No Where You Can Run"
Holly Near; Redwood Records

GATEAU GRAND MARNIER

1) Preheat oven to 300°. Grease kugelhof or any 10″ tube
   pan thoroughly, and dust with flour. Grate rind of **2
   California oranges** and set aside.

2) Whisk or sift together **2½ c. unbleached white flour,
   1 t. baking powder, 1 t. baking soda, ½ t. salt.**

3) In mixer, cream **2 sticks unsalted butter.** Add **scant
   1 c. sugar** and reserved orange rind and mix well. Add
   2 eggs and beat well. Add **1 Tb. Grand Marnier
   liqueur.** Now stir in about ¼ of flour mix. Measure out
   1 c. buttermilk and stir in about ⅓ of it. Continue
   alternating wet and dry ingredients, ending with dry,
   and finally gently stir in **⅓ c. chopped walnuts.**

4) Turn batter into prepared pan and bake 1 hour 20
   minutes or until cake withdraws slightly from sides.
   Cool thoroughly in pan on rack.

5) Meanwhile, squeeze oranges and measure juice. You
   will need **¾ c. orange juice.** Combine with
   ⅓ c. sugar in a pot and simmer 5 minutes. Remove
   from stove and add **¼ c. Grand Marnier.**

6) Turn cake out onto dish and pour syrup over cake and
   into well in center. It will be absorbed by the cake.

7) Optional: Beat **2 c. heavy cream** stiff with
   2 Tb. Grand Marnier and serve as a topping.

PECAN PIE

1) Preheat oven to 425°. Roll out **pie crust** (see recipe index) to fit one large pie plate. Prick at bottom rim, line with foil and weight with dried beans. Bake 5–8 minutes until lightly browned.

2) In mixer, cream **3 Tb. sweet butter.** Add ¾ **c. sugar** and beat well. Add **3 eggs** and mix again, scraping sides of bowl. Add **1 t. vanilla extract, pinch salt,** and **1 c. dark corn syrup.** Be sure mixture is well blended.

3) Pour mixture into partially baked pie crust and top with **pecans,** closely placed. You will need **1–2 c.** of them. Lower oven temperature to 325° and bake until pie has puffed and is barely set.

4) Serve with **vanilla ice cream.**

It is not fair that I've been given this thorough, comprehensive education in how to acquire a man and keep him, and not a clue as to how to leave him.

Give Me Your Good Ear
Maureen Brady; Spinsters, Ink

PRALINE CHEESECAKE

1) Soften **1½ lb. cream cheese.**

2) Make **Praline:** Put **3 c. almonds or pecans** in a 350°
   oven and toast until walnut colored. Lightly oil a cookie
   sheet. Combine **3 c. sugar** and **1¼ c. water** in a pot
   and bring to a boil without stirring. Swirl pot to melt
   sugar crystals. When syrup is clear, cover pot and boil
   several minutes. Uncover and continue boiling until
   syrup turns caramel brown. Immediately add roasted
   nuts and turn out onto greased cookie sheet. Be very
   careful, since pot and cookie sheet are very hot! Let
   praline cool 20 minutes and then grind it in food
   processor or blender. This amount makes much more
   than you will need for this cheesecake. It stores well in a
   covered container.

3) Melt ¼ **stick sweet butter.** Crush enough **graham
   crackers** to yield ½ **c.** and mix together butter,
   crackers, and ½ **c. praline powder.** Butter a 12"
   springform pan or one that holds 14 c. dry volume.*
   Use praline and cracker mix for a bottom crust. Pat it
   into the pan. Preheat oven to 325.°

4) Separate **6 eggs,** whites into mixer and yolks into small
   bowl. Add **2** more **whites** to mixer with a **pinch** each
   salt and **cream of tartar.** Beat until stiff. Turn out into
   a large bowl.

5) In mixer, beat **1 c. heavy cream** stiff and turn out into
   another bowl.

6) Beat softened cream cheese in mixer. Add **1¼ c. sugar, 1 t. vanilla extract, 1 Tb. lemon juice, 1 Tb. cornstarch.** While mixing, add yolks one at a time. Beat well, scrape down and beat again.

7) Fold whipped cream into cream cheese mixture, then fold in beaten whites. Turn into prepared pan and bake 1 hour. Cake should be fully puffed and not at all brown. Now bake 1 hour at 275°. Cake should be a light tan. Turn off oven and open door. Let cake stay like this 2 hours. Sprinkle top heavily with praline powder.

8) Chill at least 3 hours before serving.

* Use rice or beans to determine dry volume.

And who is sure to give you courage
And who will surely make you strong
Who will bear all the joy that is coming to you
If not the woman in your life . . .
Because the woman in your life is you.

"The Woman In Your Life Is You"
Lavender Jane Loves Women
Alix Dobkin; Women's Wax Works

BAKED ORANGE CUSTARD

1) Preheat oven to 325°. In mixer combine **3 eggs, 1 c. heavy cream,** grated **rind** of **2 oranges, 1 c.** fresh squeezed **orange juice, 2½ Tb. honey,** and **⅛ t. salt.** Mix enough to blend eggs and honey but don't overbeat.

2) Pour into 5 or 6 custard cups and place in baking pan. Place in oven and add enough water to the pan to come halfway up the sides of the custard cups.

3) Bake until knife tip comes out clean, about 40–45 minutes. Cool and refrigerate. Serve with **heavy cream.**

Serves 5–6

Women need not literally have a daughter to bear witness to the mystery of continuity—just as, I suppose, you needn't bleed for four days to know the hold periodicity has on you. A child is as much the offspring of the body of your imagination, the treasure hard to attain, as it is the bloodfruit of your womb.

Mothers and Daughters
Nor Hall; Rusoff Books

PINEAPPLE ISABEL

Named for Isabel Brach who gave us this adaptation of
Zabaglione.

1) In the top of a double boiler (or in a stainless steel bowl
   that will fit on the rim of a pot as a double boiler does)
   place **5 egg yolks** and ¼ **c. honey.** The bowl or
   double boiler top must be enamel or stainless steel or
   the sauce will discolor. Put enough water in bottom pan
   to last 15 minutes without touching upper bowl.

2) Beat and/or stir constantly with whisk over low-medium
   heat until sauce becomes quite thick and sticks to sides
   of bowl (about 10–15 minutes).

3) Remove from heat and add a scant ½ **c. Grand
   Marnier liqueur,** whisking until sauce is smooth.

4) Place in refrigerator until sauce is very cold.

5) Whip **1 c. heavy cream** stiff and fold into sauce until
   mixture is blended. Fold, do not stir.

6) Quarter a **pineapple** lengthwise; cut away the hard
   center core and cut each piece in half again lengthwise.
   Use a sharp knife to remove the skin. Cut the pineapple
   into small pieces and place in bowls. Top with sauce.

Serves 6–8

CHOCOLATE MOUSSE

Note that no added sugar is needed for this mousse.

1) Melt **8 oz. sweet chocolate** in **1 Tb. coffee** in a small
   covered pot over low heat. Use good quality chocolate
   for a good mousse. Let cool.

2) Separate **6 eggs,** whites into mixer and yolks into a
   stainless steel pot. Add **2½ Tb. coffee** to yolks and
   using a whisk, beat over low heat until it begins to
   thicken slightly. Then add ½ c. **Grand Marnier
   liqueur.** Beat over low heat until moderately thick.
   Don't let yolks curdle. Whisk melted chocolate and yolk
   mixture together. Scrape into bowl and let cool at least
   30 minutes. While you wait, you can make creme
   anglaise (see below).

3) Beat the **6 whites** until stiff but not dry. Turn out into
   bowl. Beat **2 c. heavy cream** stiff. Fold whipped cream
   into cooled chocolate yolk mix and then fold in egg
   whites. Fold gently and thoroughly. Chill. Serve with
   creme anglaise or **heavy cream.**

4) To make creme anglaise: Bring ⅞ **c. milk** to boil in a
   stainless steel pot. Meanwhile whisk **2 yolks,**
   2½ Tb. sugar and ¾ **t. cornstarch** together in a
   bowl. Slowly beat hot milk into yolks. Return to pot and
   cook carefully till slightly thickened into a cream. Add
   ½ **t. vanilla** and ½ **Tb. Grand Marnier.** Chill.

Serves 8–10

CRANBERRY WALNUT MUFFINS

1) Preheat oven to 425°. Butter or line muffin tins with papers.

2) Melt ½ **stick sweet butter.**

3) Chop fine, by hand or in food processor, **1¼ c. cranberries.** (They can be frozen whole and chopped, still frozen, in food processor.)

4) Use a whisk to stir together **2½ c. unbleached white flour, ¾ c. sugar, ½ Tb. baking powder, ½ t. baking soda, ½ t. salt.**

5) Beat **1 egg.** Grate the **rind** of **1½ oranges** into the beaten egg. Squeeze enough juice to make **1¼ c. orange juice.** (You may use up to ¼ c. water to make up the whole amount if necessary.)

6) Combine melted butter, eggs and orange juice. Mix this liquid mixture together with the dry ingredients and the chopped cranberries and **½ c. chopped walnuts.** Don't overmix.

7) Spoon mix into muffin tins and bake in pre-heated oven until lightly brown (about 20–25 minutes).

Yields about 15 muffins

CREAM CHEESE COOKIES

From Fay Davidson.

1) Use a mixer, a pastry blender or your fingertips to thoroughly blend **1 stick sweet butter, 3 oz. cream cheese,** and **1 c. flour.** When well integrated but not overmixed, wrap in waxed paper or foil and refrigerate.

2) Fillings for these cookies can be any jam or preserve or chopped nuts. Try to find **honey sweetened strawberry** or **raspberry preserves,** or cook **dried apricots** and sweeten them with **honey** and puree for a filling. Or chop **walnuts** and **almonds,** flavor with **cinnamon** and mix with enough **honey** to a pasty consistency. Preheat oven to 375°.

3) Roll out small portions of the dough on a floured board. Keep remaining dough refrigerated. Cut out circles using a floured glass or large round cookie cutter and place a dab of fruit preserves on each round. Pinch edges together to make a three cornered cookie. Press edges together to prevent cookies from opening in the oven. If you are using the nut mixture, roll out dough into a long narrow rectangle and place filling along the edge in a thick pencil line. Roll dough over two times like a jelly roll and cut off 1″ sized cookies. Save scraps of dough to re-roll. This dough gets tough with too much re-working, so try to keep re-working at a minimum.

4) Bake cookies until light brown at 375°.

Makes 4–5 dozen

COQUIDA

A Puerto Rican party punch.

1) Use a hammer and screwdriver to punch holes in the "eyes" of a large **coconut** that sounds as if it has a lot of liquid in it when you shake it. Drain the liquid into a bowl. Break up the coconut with the hammer, pry off shell and peel inner skin off with potato peeler.

2) Warm **2 c. heavy cream** and put in a blender with coconut pieces and reserved coconut liquid. Blend.

3) In mixer, beat **6 eggs** for 20 minutes. While eggs are beating, add **1 t. cinnamon, 1 t. nutmeg** and **1 Tb. vanilla extract.**

4) Strain coconut cream into eggs, pressing down onto the strainer to squeeze out all the liquid. Also add **1½ c. half and half** (coffee cream). You may also add a can of concentrated coconut cream, for intensified coconut flavor. Beat another 15 minutes.

5) Add **a fifth** bottle of **golden rum,** Don Q is the recommended brand, and chill for several hours before serving.

~~~~~~

CHAPTER 3   LATE WINTER
February 2 to Spring Equinox, March 22.

SPLIT PEA AND CARROT SOUP

1) Soak **1 lb. split peas** overnight in water, or cover with water in soup kettle, bring to a boil, turn heat off and leave 1 hour. Either way, simmer them until just done, adding more water, if necessary. Do not add salt at this time.

2) Chop **3 medium onions, ½ bunch celery** (including leaves) and saute in **2 Tb. oil** in a frying pan. When medium brown, add **2 large cloves garlic,** crushed, **¾ t. marjoram, 2 bay leaves.** Stir till well browned.

3) Turn vegetables into kettle of cooked split peas. Deglaze frying pan by adding **½ c. red wine,** bring to a simmer, scraping up brown bits, and add to soup kettle.

4) Simmer soup at least ½ hour or until it seems done. Now season with about **1 Tb. salt** and lots of **fresh ground pepper.** Any lentil or dried bean soup must be salted after the beans are cooked to avoid toughness.

5) When soup is about done, peel, quarter, and dice **1 bunch** of **carrots.** Add to soup and continue cooking until carrots are just done.

6) Serve soup with a splash of **port wine** in each bowl.

Serves 8–10

CREAM OF BARLEY SOUP

1) Finely chop **3 carrots, 2 medium onions** and
   4 stalks celery. Slit **8 leeks** lengthwise , wash well
   and slice. Saute these vegetables in soup pot in **3 Tb.
   sweet butter** and **½ t. dried thyme.** Cook over high
   heat until vegetables are medium brown, scraping the
   bottom of pot when necessary.

2) Turn down heat and add **2½ qt. water, ¼ c. tamari,
   1 c. pearl barley, a dash** of **Tabasco, fresh ground
   pepper** and **1 t. salt.** Simmer uncovered over low
   heat for 1 hour or until barley is done. Remove from
   heat.

3) Beat thoroughly together in large mixing bowl **6 egg
   yolks** and **1 c. heavy cream.** Stirring egg mixture with
   whisk, add a ladle of soup at a time until about ½ the
   soup is in the bowl. Return the mixture to the pot and
   stir. Add the **grated rind** of **1 lemon** and taste for **salt**
   and **tamari.**

4) Reheat soup before serving but do not boil. Serve
   topped with chopped **scallions.**

                                     Serves approximately 10

WINTER MISO SOUP

1) Soak **1 c. soybeans** overnight. (This is essential).

2) Peel, quarter, and slice **2 very large onions.** Cut
   2 carrots in half lengthwise and then slice thinly. If you
   like, **2 parsnips** or **a small turnip** can be added also.
   Slice **6 mushrooms** and peel, quarter, and thinly
   slice **1 large sweet potato.** Place **1 cake** of **tofu**
   (about 5 oz.) on absorbent paper. Top with more paper,
   a plate, and a weight.

3) Put **2 Tb. oil** in a soup kettle and fry all the above
   vegetables, but not the tofu, until slightly browned,
   stirring often. Turn off fire.

4) Now puree the soybeans in their water by putting small
   batches in a blender or food processor. Add ground
   soybeans and their water to the soup pot with **1–2 qt.
   water.** Simmer uncovered 10–15 minutes.

5) Optional: soak ⅓ pkg. **Hiziki seaweed** in water 5 or
   10 minutes. Then drain and chop coarsely.

6) Cut the dried tofu into cubes or strips. Place **2 t.
   Chinese* sesame oil** in a frying pan. Fry tofu pieces,
   turning them till light brown. Add Hiziki, if you have it,
   and **1 clove garlic,** crushed. When Hiziki ceases to
   give up its sea-like smell, add a **few Tb. water,** and a
   dash tamari. Cover and simmer 5 minutes, then add
   to soup.

7) Put ⅔ **c. miso** (hatcho, or other kind) in a bowl and stir with enough **water** to make a thin puree. Add miso to soup but don't boil again. Heat portion by portion so that miso does not boil.

8) Stir into each serving a little **tamari,** a **splash rice wine vinegar, sesame oil,** and top with **sliced scallions.**

Serves 6–8

* Chinese sesame oil is very pungent. Neither middle eastern tahini nor American health-store sesame oil is a valid substitution for it.

The decision to feed the world
is the real decision. No revolution
has chosen it. For that choice requires
that women shall be free.

"Hunger"   (For Audre Lorde)
The Dream of a Common Language
Adrienne Rich; Norton

FRENCH CREAM OF MUSHROOM SOUP

1) Wipe clean (do not wash) and slice **1 lb. mushrooms.**
   Fry in soup kettle in **1 stick sweet butter** until
   mushrooms are well cooked, liquid is gone, and
   mushrooms are beginning to brown. Add **3** or **4 cloves
   garlic,** crushed, and stir until garlic is lightly cooked.
   Add **½ c. unbleached white flour** and cook, stirring,
   until flour is well blended.

2) Gradually add **1 qt. milk,** stirring with a wooden
   spoon. Then add **⅓ c. dry white wine, 1 t. salt,
   fresh ground pepper, grated nutmeg***. Bring to a
   boil and taste. Add about **1⅓ c. water, 2 Tb. Italian
   parsley,** chopped, and **2 Tb. fresh dill,** chopped .

* **Mace** is more expensive, but has a nicer, more delicate flavor.

Serves 4–6

*I would get a head of garlic out from the garlic bottle
in the icebox, and breaking off ten or twelve cloves
from the head, I would carefully peel away the tissue
lavender skin, slicing each stripped peg in half lengthwise.*

"My Mother's Mortar"
Audre Lorde
Sinister Wisdom, *Volume 8, Winter, 1979*

CASHEW CHILI

From *Wings of Life*, Julie Jordan, Crossing Press, and used with their permission.

1) Soak **1 c. dried red kidney beans** overnight. Rinse and cover again with water. Bring to a boil, turn heat down and simmer until done, about 45 minutes.

2) In a large soup pot, saute **4 medium onions, chopped,** in **4 Tb. oil.** Chop **2 green peppers** and **2 stalks** of **celery,** including the **leaves,** and add to pot together with **3 cloves garlic,** crushed, **1 bay leaf, 1 t. dried basil, 1 t. dried oregano, 1 t. ground cumin,** and **2 Tb. chili powder.** Stir the pot often with a wooden spoon.

3) When the vegetables have browned evenly and the beans have cooked, add beans to soup pot. Add **1 qt.** canned **tomatoes, ¼ c. red wine vinegar, ½ c. cashews, ¼ c. raisins, 1 t. salt,** and some **fresh ground pepper.** Bring to a boil, adding as much liquid from bean pot or water as seems necessary to make an appropriate soup consistency. Simmer for at least 1½ hours to develop flavor. This soup improves on reheating and long, slow cooking.

4) Before serving, adjust seasoning. Taste especially for salt and cumin, and add more chili powder if you like. Top each serving with extra **cashews** and serve with **cornbread** (see recipe index).

Serves 6–8

ENDIVE, AVOCADO, AND WATERCRESS SALAD

A sensuous salad that can be eaten with the fingers.

For each diner, use **1 small whole Belgian endive.**
Cut ¼″ off its base and separate the leaves, arranging them
on a dinner plate in a fan shape. Slice the smallest inside
leaves and heap at the base of the fan. Cut thin slices of
avocado to fit into each leaf. Depending on the size of the
avocado, you will need ¼ to ½ of the avocado for each
plate. Slice ⅓ **bunch watercress leaves** (discarding
stems) over endive hearts at base of fan. Cut a thin **slice** of
a **red Bermuda onion** and separate it into rings on top of
the cress. Drizzle **vinaigrette** (see recipe index) over the
salad and serve immediately.

*I firmly believed that if art speaks clearly about
something relevant to people's lives it can change
the way they perceive reality.*

The Dinner Party
Judy Chicago; Doubleday

SHREDDED ROOT VEGETABLE SALAD

1) Use a shredder to grate **6 carrots, 3 peeled white turnips,** and **2** or **3 small scraped beets.** Keep them in separate bowls. Chill.

2) When ready to serve, arrange the three vegetables in small mounds on beds of **Boston lettuce.** Top with **onion rings** and dress with **vinaigrette** (see recipe index).

Serves 6–8

*and when we speak we are afraid
our words will not be heard
nor welcomed
but when we are silent
we are still afraid.*

*So it is better to speak
remembering
we were never meant to survive.*

"A Litany For Survival"
The Black Unicorn
Audre Lorde; Norton

SPINACH SALAD WITH SHERRY DRESSING

From Liz Shanklin.

1) Make salad dressing: In a jar combine ⅓ **c. dry sherry,**
   ¼ c. salad oil, 3 Tb. wine vinegar, 1 t. lemon
   juice, ¾ t. tamari or soy, **¼ t. curry powder,** and a
   pinch of crushed dry **marjoram.**

2) Prepare croutons by drying cubes of leftover **homemade**
   bread at 300° until hard. You will need **¾ c. croutons.**

3) Clean, remove stems, and break up leaves from
   1–2 lbs. fresh leaf spinach. Place in salad bowl.
   Slice **½ lb. fresh mushrooms** into bowl and add
   croutons.

4) When ready to serve, shake salad dressing, pour over
   and toss. Top the salad with sprinkles of **gomahsio** (see
   recipe index).

                                          Serves 6–8

No more genocide in my name.

"No More Genocide"
Hang In There
Holly Near; Redwood Records

GNOCCHI

1) Peel and cut up **4 Idaho potatoes.** Cover with water
   and boil until done. (Always save potato cooking water
   to thin soups out or to make bread with.) Defrost frozen
   chopped **spinach** or cook and chop enough to yield
   ⅓ **c.** Puree the spinach in a food processor or blender.

2) In a mixer, mash potatoes while they are still hot.

3) In a pot, bring **1 c. water** to a boil with ¾ **stick
   unsalted butter, 1 t. salt, ¼ t. pepper** and a
   grating of **nutmeg.** When it boils, dump in **1 c. flour**
   and beat vigorously with wooden spoon. Turn off heat
   and beat in **2 eggs,** one at a time.

4) Turn mixture into mixer and continue beating. Add
   2 more **eggs,** one at a time. Add spinach puree and
   ½ **c. parmesan.** When mixture is smooth, turn out into
   covered container and refrigerate.

5) The gnocchi will be poached in boiling, salted water.
   Using a little **flour** and 2 spoons, roll them into ovals
   and coat lightly with flour. Simmer, covered, 15
   minutes. Drain, brush with **butter** and sprinkle with
   parmesan cheese.

Serves 6–8

TAMALE PIE

From *Wings of Life* by Julie Jordan, Crossing Press, and used with their permission.

1) Soak **1 c. dried kidney beans** overnight.* When ready to use, bring the beans to a boil in a pot with **3 c. water** and turn down to a simmer. Cook the beans until done (about 45 minutes) and set aside.

2) Prepare the filling: Chop **4 medium onions** and start to fry them on high heat in a soup pot with **4 Tb. vegetable oil.** Add **2 green peppers,** coarsely chopped, **2 stalks celery,** finely chopped, **3** or more **cloves garlic,** crushed, **1 bay leaf, 1 t. dried basil, 1 t. oregano, 1 t. ground cumin,** and **2 Tb. chili powder.** Stir the bottom of the soup pot frequently, making sure the vegetables don't burn but brown evenly.

3) When vegetables are browned, add the cooked beans to the soup pot, adding as much liquid as necessary for the chili to be thick but not dry.

4) Turn the heat on high and add **1 qt.** canned **tomatoes, ¼ c. red wine vinegar, ½ c. cashews, ¼ c. raisins, 1 t. salt,** and some freshly ground **black pepper.** Bring to a boil and let chili cook a half hour to develop flavor. Add more bean liquid if necessary.

5) Meanwhile, prepare cornbread topping: Mix **1 c.
    cornmeal, 3 c. water,** and **1 t. salt** in a pot.
    Bring the mixture slowly to a boil, stirring constantly
    with a spoon or whisk so it doesn't lump. Cook the
    mixture until it is thick, forming a cornmeal mush.
    Remove it from the heat.

6) Beat **2 large** or **3 small eggs** in a bowl with a fork.
    Spoon some of the hot mush into the eggs stirring
    constantly until eggs and mush are combined.

7) Pour chili into a lightly oiled baking pan. Spread the
    cornmeal mush evenly over the chili. (Optional: You
    can top the tamale pie with ½ c. of **grated Monteray
    Jack cheese** if you like.) Bake the pie at 350° for about
    40 minutes or until the crust is brown and firm.

8) Take the pie out of the oven and let rest at least 10
    minutes or more to allow the pie to set. Tamale pie is
    even better reheated the second day, when the layers
    have firmed up.

9) Serve with **guacamole salad** (see following recipe).

* If beans cannot be soaked overnight, they can be brought
   to a boil in water, removed from heat for 1 hour and then
   returned to stove and cooked until tender.

GUACAMOLE

1) Cut **2 large** ripe **avocados** in half lengthwise. Remove pit and any brown fibers clinging to flesh. Peel off skin. Mash avocados in mixing bowl with fork until some avocado is pureed but some is still in chunky pieces.

2) Add **1 Tb. onion,** finely chopped, **1 Tb.** canned **hot chili peppers,** chopped, (we use Jalapeno peppers), **1 Tb. fresh cilantro***, finely chopped. Add **salt** and **pepper** and mix well.

3) Finely dice **1 medium tomato** and fold in.

Yields 2–3 cups

*Available in Chinese and Puerto Rican markets and essential to authentic guacamole.

Even novice Furies are accused of thinking or saying that "men are the enemy." This is a subtly deceptive reversal, implying that women are the initiators of enmity, blaming the victims for The War.

Gyn/Ecology
Mary Daly; Beacon Press

KASHA PLATTER

This recipe has evolved from a mixed Russian-Jewish background to suit our vegetarian tastes. It is, we think, an excellent approximation of several side dishes never served together, since the kasha usually accompanied meat, as did the tzimmes, which usually had meat cooked with it. The cauliflower latkes was a separate "dairy" dish Fay Davidson created for family suppers. We like them served all together, with the miso gravy, our own invention. You can make a supper of the cauliflower latkes if you like. This would be most appropriate in October when they are least expensive. Note: **Miso gravy** should be made in advance (see recipe index).

1) Stir **1⅓ c. whole kasha** (buckwheat groats) into a pot of boiling water and cook till just puffed. Taste, and don't overcook. Drain in a small-holed colander or strainer and run cold water over kasha till cool. Turn into shallow ovenproof pan.

2) Boil **1 c. small bowtie pasta** in **salted water** until done. Drain and add to kasha in pan.

3) Chop **3 medium onions**. Slice **1½ c. mushrooms.**

4) Melt **½ stick sweet butter** in a fry pan and saute **1 c. cashew pieces** a few minutes. Add mushrooms and onions and cook until light brown. Add to kasha in pan and season with **salt, pepper,** dash **tamari,** and another **½ stick sweet butter.** Grate **1½ carrots** and add. Cover pan with aluminum foil and bake for 20 minutes. This is **"kasha varnitchkes."**

5) Steam **1 small head of cauliflower** divided into
flowerets in the least amount of water possible. Mash
together with the remaining water with potato masher
or fork. Add **3 beaten eggs, nutmeg, salt,** and
pepper to taste, and ½–¾ c. **unbleached white
flour.** This mixture will be used to make small pancakes
("latkes") and must rest ½ hour minimum in the
refrigerator before cooking. Be cautious with the flour, a
little more can be added later.

6) Peel and slice **1 bunch carrots.** Cook **2** or **3 medium
yams** in **boiling water.** Put carrots into fry pan with
**1 Tb. honey, 1 t. salt, ½ stick sweet butter, ¼ c.
water.** Cover and simmer. When almost done, remove
cover and brown slightly. Peel and slice cooked yams
and add to carrots. This carrot-yam mix is called
"Tzimmes."

7) Both kasha and tzimmes can be reheated in a 350°
oven, uncovered, until brown. Saute small cauliflower
latkes (4″ diameter pancakes) in butter. Pat out each
latke into hot butter in fry pan with a fork. When brown,
turn gently with spatula, and brown other side. Serve
with **sour cream.**

8) Top kasha and tzimmes with chopped **parsley** and
miso gravy (see recipe index).

Serves 6–8

COUS-COUS

A North African dish usually made with meat, but not here!
This recipe is very different from an authentic cous-cous,
but its flavor seems quite right to those who know the real
thing. This long recipe is easier to make than it seems.

1) Soak **1½ c. dried chickpeas** (garbanzos) overnight,
   or bring them to a boil in **water** to cover, turn off fire
   and leave 1 hour. In either case, simmer gently until
   cooked (2 or more hours).

2) Saute **2 c. millet** in **2 Tb. olive oil.** We use millet
   instead of the cous-cous grain, which is steamed
   semolina, because of its superior nutritional value and
   excellent flavor. When millet is toasted, add **4½ c.
   water, 2 t. salt, ½ t. cinnamon** and simmer till
   steamed. Do not overcook it. Fold in **¾ stick sweet
   butter.** Millet can be steamed in a couscousier, if you
   have one, while the vegetable stew cooks beneath in the
   couscousier base.

3) In couscousier base or in a large pot, saute **1 large
   onion,** coarsely chopped, in **2 Tb. olive oil.** Add
   2 cloves garlic, crushed, **¾ t. turmeric, 2 t. dried
   mint, 2 t. dried oregano, 1½ t. cumin seed,** dry-
   roasted and ground, **¾ t. ground ginger, ⅓ t.
   coriander.** Saute until medium brown. Cut **2 carrots**
   into ½" pieces and add to pot with **water** to cover.
   Simmer about 15 minutes. Meanwhile soak **1 c.
   raisins** in **hot water** to cover in a bowl. Peel
   2–3 white potatoes, cut into 1" chunks and add to
   carrots. Cook 10 minutes, adding water as necessary.

Peel and cut **2 sweet potatoes** into chunks and add
together with ½ **c. cabbage,** sliced, and the raisins.
Continue simmering vegetables adding water as
needed. Add **2 c.** canned **tomatoes** or tomato sauce,
and when chick peas are done, drain them of their water
and add. If you have **Chinese chili paste with
garlic,** add **1½ t.** If not, add **cayenne pepper** to make
a spicy gravy. Add up to **2 Tb. tamari** or good soy,
juice of **1 lemon,** and ¼ **c. hatcho** or **aka miso** (this
gives the meat-like flavor). Simmer 1–2 hours or till
vegetables are done and gravy tastes good. Adjust
seasoning. Be sure there's enough water as you go
along for there to be ample gravy.

4) Make **"hrisa"** or hot sauce: Remove about 1 c. gravy
from pot into a small bowl. Add **1 t. cayenne,**
½ **t. ground cumin,** ½**t. ground coriander,**
1 t. dried oregano and **1 Tb. tamari** to make a very
concentrated spicy sauce for individual seasoning.

5) When ready to serve, steam millet to reheat and reheat
stew. Just before serving, add **1 c. green peas,** fresh or
frozen. Don't overcook them. For each plate make a
ring of millet. Put several large serving spoons of
vegetables and gravy in the center. Top with **slivered
almonds.** Serve with **Radish Orange Escarole
Salad** (see following recipe) and hrisa on the side.

Note: Other vegetables may include **turnips, rutabaga,
zuccini** or **brussels sprouts.**

Serves 6–8

RADISH ORANGE ESCAROLE SALAD

1) Use a small sharp knife to peel **4 California oranges** removing white pith as well as rind. Slice thinly into a bowl. Also slice **10 large red radishes** into bowl.

2) Mix together **1 Tb. sugar, ⅛ t. salt, ⅓ c. lemon juice** and pour this dressing over the oranges and radishes.

3) Serve on bed of **escarole.** Drizzle a little **vinaigrette** (see recipe index) over the escarole.

Feminism is potentially the most threatening of movements to Black and other Third World people because it makes it absolutely essential that we examine the way we live, how we treat each other and what we believe.

Barbara Smith
"Notes For Yet Another Paper On Black Feminism, Or Will The Real Enemy Please Stand Up?"
Conditions: Five, The Black Women's Issue

INDONESIAN TEMPEH DINNER

Once you locate ready-made tempeh, you will find it easy
to prepare. The fussing (and expense) is involved in
preparing the coconut rice, sambal, and steamed vegetable
salad accompaniments. Tempeh can be frozen until you
want to cook it.

1) If you are planning on the sambal, rice and salad, start
   by soaking **6 c. dry coconut** (unsweetened) in **7 c.**
   hot tap water. Also, cover **2 c. brown rice** (we like
   short grain) with **warm water.** If you can get it, soak **2
   oz. tamarind pulp** in **1 c. boiling water.** Tamarind is
   usually available in Indian markets.

2) Make **Coconut Milk:** In about 6 batches, put coconut
   and water in a blender and puree. Pour into a strainer
   over a bowl or container. Squeeze the coconut dry with
   your hands and discard. Its flavor will be in the creamy
   milk that passes through the strainer.

3) Make **Sambal:** Preferably in a food processor, or by
   hand, chop about **2 inches fresh** peeled **ginger,** add
   2 dry bay leaves, the **peeled rind** of ½ **lemon, 1
   large garlic clove,** and ½ **c. onions.** Chop well till
   quite fine. Saute in **3 Tb. oil** till wilted but not brown.
   Add **1½ t. coriander,** ½ **t. turmeric, 1 t. cumin** (dry
   roasted in fry pan and ground with mortar and pestle).
   Now de-seed and cut into slivers **3 hot chili peppers**
   and add to pan and saute. Wash your hands thoroughly
   with soapy water after handling hot chilis. When chilis
   are slightly cooked, add **1½ c. coconut milk.** Use a

spoon to mash **tamarind pulp** and **water** and add
2 Tb. of this water. Discard tamarind seeds. Simmer
sambal 5 minutes; add **1 t. honey.** If you don't have
tamarind water, use lemon juice to make sambal as sour
as you like.

4) Prepare **Steamed Vegetable Salad:** See following
recipe for **Urab,** Indonesian steamed vegetable salad.

5) Make **Coconut Rice:** Chop **4 shallots** and **1 garlic
clove** with a heavy knife. In a fry pan saute shallots and
garlic in **1½ Tb. oil** together with **½ t. turmeric,
½ t. cumin, 1 t. coriander** and the drained rice. Stir
rice and spices together over high heat until rice
becomes slightly opaque. Add **1½ t. salt, 1 Tb. fresh**
(or 1 t. dried) **lemon grass,** if available,* and **2 bay
leaves.** Add **4 c. coconut milk,** and cover and
simmer until rice is tender. Leftover rice may be
reheated in a steamer.

6) About ½ hour before you're ready for dinner, puree in a
blender: **2 cloves garlic, 2 t.** ground **coriander,
1 t. salt,** and **½ c. water.** Cut **4 eight oz. pieces** of
tempeh into 8 squares each and pour marinating liquid
over tempeh pieces. Heat about **2 c. oil** in a wok and
deep fry tempeh pieces until brown and crisp, in 3 to 4
batches. Serve with rice and sambal on the side.
Lemon wedges, tamari and **gomahsio**** taste good
with tempeh also.

Serves 8

* Lemon grass is available in Chinese markets.
** See recipe index for gomahsio.

URAB: INDONESIAN STEAMED VEGETABLE SALAD

This salad can be chilled or served at room temperature.

1) Remove stems from **1 package** fresh **spinach** and steam leaves until barely done. Turn out on platter.

2) Shred ½ of a **small red cabbage** and steam so that it is still crispy. Turn out on platter next to spinach.

3) Steam **1 lb. mung bean sprouts** until they are barely done. Place them on the platter.

4) Cube **1 cake** of **tofu** and arrange on platter. Add **⅓ c. peanuts.**

5) Prepare dressing: Combine **5 Tb. tamarind water***, **4 t. sambal** (see recipe index), **½ t. powdered ginger, 1 Tb. tamari** or good soy. Add **3 Tb. Chinese sesame oil.** Pour over salad platter.

Serves 6–8

* The tamarind water is mildly sour so lemon juice diluted in water may be substituted.

"INDIAN" PUDDING

1) Preheat oven to 275°.

2) Bring **1 qt. milk** to a boil and using a whisk, gradually stir in **1 scant c. ground cornmeal**.* Cook, stirring, about 5 minutes or until cornmeal is slightly thickened. Set aside.

3) In a pyrex loaf pan or other baking dish, combine **1 c. milk, ½ c. molasses, ¾ t. cinnamon, ½ t. ginger, ½ t. nutmeg.** Add cornmeal and stir together well.

4) Bake 1 hour and then pour **1 c. milk** over the top. Don't mix it in. Bake 4 hours more.

5) Serve warm with **ice cream** or **heavy cream.**

Serves 6–8

* If you can get fresh ground cornmeal from a health food store, your pudding will taste much better.

*. . . any idea that you cannot comprehend
you'll put the handcuffs on and that will be the end
and anything that grows, you'll cover with cement.
They'll make a man of you, my son.*

"You'll Be A Man"
Malvina
© *1969 Malvina Reynolds, Schroder Music Co.*

LEMON TART

1) Preheat oven to 400°. Roll out **pie crust** (see recipe index) for 1 pie pan. Prick around bottom of crust with fork tines. Use foil and dried beans, lentils, etc., to weight down crust while it bakes. When edges start to brown (about 5 or 10 minutes), carefully remove beans and foil. Turn oven down to 375° and continue baking until crust is golden brown (about 10 minutes more). Remove from oven and let cool.

2) Cut **1½ sticks sweet butter** into small pieces. Set aside.

3) In stainless steel pot* combine **6 whole eggs, 5 yolks, ⅓ c. honey,** and grated **rind** and **juice** of **3 lemons**. Whisk together over medium-low heat until well mixed. Add the butter and continue whisking until mixture starts to thicken. Cook and whisk about another 30 seconds until mixture is creamy and slightly thick. Do not overcook.

4) Remove from heat and whisk for another minute. Set aside to cool about 10 minutes, then pour into baked pie shell. Place pie in refrigerator until set up (about 2 hours).

5) Before serving, top pie with **honey whipped cream:** Whip together until stiff **1 c. heavy cream, 1½ t. honey** and **¾ t. vanilla extract.**

* Aluminum pot will discolor mixture.

ORANGES ISABEL

Named for Isabel Brach who inspired this adaptation of Zabaglione.

1) In the top of a double boiler (or in a stainless steel bowl that will fit on the rim of a pot as a double boiler does) place **5 egg yolks,** and ¼ **c. honey.** The bowl or double boiler top must be enamel or stainless steel or the sauce will discolor. Put enough water in bottom pan to last 10–15 minutes without touching upper bowl.

2) Beat and/or stir constantly with whisk over low-medium heat until sauce becomes quite thick and sticks to sides of bowl. (About 10–15 minutes.)

3) Remove from heat and add a scant ½ **c. Grand Marnier liqueur,** whisking until sauce is smooth. Place in refrigerator until sauce is very cold.

4) Whip **1 c. heavy cream** stiff and fold into sauce until mixture is smooth and even. Fold, do not stir.

5) Use a small knife to peel **1 large California orange** for each serving, removing white part as well as rind. Slice thinly and top with 2 spoonfuls of the sauce.

Serves 6–8

Note: Always serve Sauce Isabel over the best fruit of the season: jet-fresh pineapples, local field-ripened June strawberries, peaches or mangoes in August, and Comice pears in November.

ORANGE COCONUT LAYER CAKE

A sugar and leavening-free cake.

1) Warm **6 eggs** (in their shells) in a bowl of hot water. Grease (butter) three 9" cake pans and line with wax paper. Preheat oven to 325°. Scrape **rind** and squeeze juice of **2 oranges.** You should have ½ **c. juice.**

2) If you have a food processor, separate eggs so that whites go into a mixer and yolks go into processor. Or just put yolks into a bowl. In another bowl, whisk or sift together **1⅓ c. unbleached white flour** and **¼ t. salt.** Then whisk yolks (or run machine) to beat them thick and light. Add ½ **c. honey,** orange juice and rind to yolks and mix well.

3) Add **1 t. cream of tartar** to whites and beat to soft peak stage. Add **2 Tb. honey** and beat to stiff peaks.

4) Fold yolk mix and flour together. Fold in whites. Divide into 3 pans and bake until cake shrinks from sides of pans. Cool 5 minutes on racks, then turn out and remove wax paper. Do not frost until cool.

5) **Frosting:** In mixer (no need to wash it) cream **5 sticks** soft **sweet butter** with ½–⅔ c. honey. Add **2 t. vanilla extract** and ½ **t. almond extract.** Slowly add **1½ c. non-instant dry milk powder.** Add grated

rind and **juice** of **2 oranges** (⅓–½ c.). Judge consistency of frosting. Add more milk powder if necessary. Frost cake, sprinkling layers and top generously with dried (unsweetened, of course) coconut. Best served at room temperature.

Note: For a lactose-free diet make lemon curd (from lemon tart recipe) and chill until it sets up. Use instead of frosting between layers and on top of cake.

Ma would be sore too. Ma would call that man all kinds of names and ask me questions in between. Ma would ask, "Why'd you take a ride?" Ma would say, "You had a five, why were you begging a ride?" Ma would say, "Why a man? Plenty women driving cars!" Ma would say, "Why'd you drink his Coke? Why'd you drink his beer?" Ma would say, "Why didn't you scream?" Ma would say, "I told you never trust a stranger. I told you not to go. I told you and told you and told you!"

The Pearl Bastard
Lillian Halegua; The Women's Press

CAROB ALMOND TORTE

A rich festive cake that is sugar, flour, and leavening free.

1) Grease rectangular pan 8" x 16" or two smaller pans each 8" x 8". Preheat oven to 375°.

2) Grate ⅔ **c. almonds** in food processor or blender. Measure **1 scant cup roasted carob** and be sure it is powdered. The processor or blender will guarantee this.

3) Separate **6 eggs,** yolks in small bowl, whites into clean mixer. Beat whites with **2 pinches salt** and **1½ t. vanilla** till foamy. Add **½ c. honey.** Scrape down. Beat till very stiff. Add carob powder and beat briefly on low speed. Don't overbeat or you will lose the air in the egg whites which is what makes the cake light. Remove bowl from machine.

4) Fork-stir yolks and add to whites. Use rubber scraper to fold in. Add almonds and fold all together gently but thoroughly. Turn into pan(s) and bake 10 minutes. Lower temperature to 350° and bake until edges pull away from pan(s). Cool cake in pan(s) on racks. Turn out onto racks and, if using one pan, divide cake in half to make 2 square layers.

5) In mixer (no need to wash it), cream **3⅓ sticks** soft
    sweet butter with scant ½ c. **honey.** Add **1¼ t.
    vanilla, ½ t. almond extract.** Gradually add **1–1½
    c. nonfat noninstant dry milk powder, ¼ c.
    powdered roasted carob** and **3–4 Tb. heavy
    cream.** Judge consistency and add more powdered
    milk or cream depending on need.

6) Frost cake when it is cool, and top with **slivered
    almonds.**

I do not know the rituals
the exhaltations
nor what name of the god
the survivors will worship
I only know she will be terrible
and very busy
and very old.

"When the Saints Come Marching in"
Coal
Audre Lorde; Norton

CAROB CHEESECAKE

Note: If you want a crust or a crumbled topping for this cake, you can make the following cookie a few days in advance, let it get stale, and then pulverize it. A crust, however, is not necessary.

Carob Almond Cookies: Grate **1 c. almonds** in food processor or blender. Cream together **1 stick sweet butter** and ½ **c. honey.** Add **2 eggs, 1 t. vanilla extract,** ⅓ **c.** pulverized **carob powder,** ⅔ **c. whole wheat flour** and ½ **t. baking powder.** Add **3 Tb. milk** and the grated almonds. Drop by spoonfuls on a greased cookie sheet and bake at 350° for 20 minutes. You will have 12 large cookies to eat or crumble and line bottom of cheesecake pan.

1) Soften **1½ lb. cream cheese.** Grease 12″ springform pan (or one that will hold 14 c. of volume, such as dried beans). Preheat oven to 325°.

2) Pulverize scant ¼ **c. dark roasted carob powder** in food processor or blender. Separate **5 eggs,** whites into a mixer and yolks to join the carob. Add ⅔ **c. honey,** ½ **t. cinnamon, 1½ t. vanilla, 1½ Tb. corn starch,** and, if you like, **1 Tb. coffee substitute** like Pero or Bambu to carob-yolk mixture. Mix well and, if using a food processor, add the cream cheese and blend thoroughly. If using a blender, wait till later to mix carob and cream cheese together.

3) Beat egg whites stiff, first adding **1 extra white** if available. Turn out into bowl.

4) Beat **1½ c. heavy cream** stiff and turn it out into
   another bowl. Now, if you have not yet combined carob
   and cheese, mix them thoroughly together in mixer.
   Fold whipped cream and carob-cream cheese together,
   then fold this mixture and egg whites together. Turn into
   prepared pan and bake 1½ hours. Turn off oven and
   leave cake inside with door shut 1 hour. Let cool, then
   chill in refrigerator.

5) Serve with carob whipped cream: Whip together until
   stiff **1½ c. heavy cream, 2 Tb. powdered carob,
   1 Tb. honey, ¼ t. almond extract.**

*I waz cold/ i waz burnin up/ a child
& endlessly weavin garments for the moon
wit my tears*

*i found god in myself
& i loved her/ i loved her fiercely*

**For Colored Girls Who Have Considered
Suicide/When The Rainbow is Enuf**
Ntozake Shange; Bantam

CHOCOLATE CHEESECAKE

1) Soften **1 ½ lb. cream cheese.** Grease 12″ spring form pan, (or one that will hold 14 c. of volume, such as dried beans). Preheat oven to 325°.

2) Bring **1 c. heavy cream** to a boil and add **2 ½ oz. bitter chocolate** (unsweetened). Cover pot and let stand a few minutes. If chocolate is not melted, simmer gently until it is. Stir chocolate and cream together thoroughly. Let stand at room temperature (or in refrigerator) until cool but not cold and stiff.

3) Separate **5 eggs,** whites into a mixer and yolks into a food processor if you have it. If not, put them into a small bowl. If you have **1 extra egg white,** add it with a **dash** of **salt** and beat whites stiff. Turn out into a large bowl.

4) Beat **1 ½ c. heavy cream** till stiff. Turn it out into another bowl.

5) Using food processor or mixer, beat yolks well. Add cooled chocolate and blend. Add **1 scant c. honey** and the softened cream cheese. Mix briefly. Add **½ t. almond extract, ¾ t. vanilla extract, ½ t. cinnamon, ¼ t. ground cardamom,** and, if you like, **1 Tb. instant expresso.** Add **3 Tb. cornstarch.** Mix, scrape sides, and mix again.

6) Fold whipped cream and chocolate-cheese mixture together, then fold in stiff beaten egg whites. Turn into pan and bake 1½ hours. Turn oven off, leave door closed and leave cake 1 hour more. Remove from oven and cool, then chill in refrigerator.

7) Serve with chocolate whipped cream: Whip together until stiff, **1½ c. heavy cream, 1 Tb.** good quality **unsweetened cocoa** such as Droste's, **1 Tb. honey, ¼ t. almond extract** and, if you like, **1 Tb. coffee liqueur.**

"I've been both a winner and a loser, but after I lose someone else wins, because this is a relay race."

"Pauli Murray" (an interview) by Casey Miller and Kate Swift **Ms.**, *March, 1980.*

REFRIGERATOR BRAN MUFFINS

This batter should be made up ahead and stored in a closed
container in the refrigerator where it will keep for 2–3
weeks. The recipe makes about 40–44 good sized muffins.
You bake only the number you want on a given day.

1) Pour **2 c. boiling water** on **2 c. bran flakes.** * Let
   stand until cool.

2) In a large bowl, stir together **2½ c. honey** and **1 c. oil.**
   Beat in **4 eggs, 1 qt. buttermilk** and the cooled bran.
   A whisk works well for this mixing.

3) Sift or whisk together **2½ c. unbleached white flour,
   2½ c. whole wheat flour, 5 t. baking soda** and **1½
   t. salt.**

4) Combine wet and dry mixtures.

5) Fold in **4 c.** more **bran** and **12 oz.** (3 c. loosely packed)
   raisins.

6) Store batter covered in the refrigerator. Do not stir.

7) When ready to bake, preheat oven to 425° and butter
   muffin tins or line them with papers.

8) Gently spoon batter into prepared tins. Don't stir! Fill
   the tins quite full since most of the rising has occurred in
   the refrigerator. Bake in 425° oven. Lower the heat to
   400° after the muffins have risen. Bake till brown on top
   (about 20–25 minutes altogether).

* Use bran flakes from a health food store.

*Coming out? I said it was a miracle. Each of us a
miracle. But it wasn't courage, I just never could
learn to stop believing in magic, in feeling, in
women, in myself. That I would have my wish come
true. That the first star of the evening would make
me happy.*

Susan Leigh Star
"How I Spent at Least One Summer Vacation"
the coming out stories
Ed. Julia Penelope Stanley and Susan J. Wolfe;
Persephone Press

Persephone

CHAPTER 4   EARLY SPRING
Spring Equinox, March 22, to May Eve, April 30.

FASSOULADA

A wonderful Greek soup that is quick to make and which reheats beautifully, from Hope Zachariades, a neighbor of many years ago, a wonderful and generous cook.

1) Soak **1 c. dried cannelini beans** in **water** overnight.*

2) Cook beans in their liquid until tender.

3) Dice by hand **1½ carrots, 2 stalks** of **celery** and their **leaves, 1 medium onion.** Vegetables should be chopped neatly and evenly. Heat ¼ **c. olive oil** in soup kettle and begin frying carrots first. After 5 minutes add onions, then celery. When all vegetables are medium brown, add **1 t. salt, pepper,** and **1 small can** (8 oz.) **Italian plum tomatoes.** Simmer, covered, 10 minutes.

4) Add **1–2 c. water** and cook another 10 minutes or until vegetables are tender. Add the cooked cannelini beans. More water may be added for best consistency. Chop a small bunch Italian **parsley** and add.

Serves 6

* If beans cannot be soaked overnight, they can be brought to a boil in water, removed from heat for 1 hour and then returned to stove and cooked until tender. Or you may use canned cannelini beans.

CHEESE SOUP

We do this with leftover cheese. Obviously, the cheeses selected will determine the final taste of the soup.

1) Finely chop **1 medium onion, ¼ c. shallots, 1½ carrots, 1 stalk celery** and its **leaves.** Saute vegetables in **½ stick sweet butter** together with **1 t. celery seed.** Cook until light brown. Add **¼ c. unbleached white flour** and cook together, stirring, about 3 minutes.

2) Add **1½ qt. milk, ⅓ c. dry white wine** and **1 c. water** (potato water—water in which potatoes were boiled—is best if you have it). Add **nutmeg, Tabasco** and **tamari** to taste. Now begin to add cheeses. You will need about **3 cups.** We have used *cheshire, raclette, havarti;* firm cheeses are recommended. Simmer gently until cheeses melt, but do not boil or they may become stringy.

3) Taste for seasoning. If soup seems too sweet, add a little **wine vinegar.** Use **tamari** if it seems to need salt.

4) To serve, garnish with chopped **parsley** and **garlic croutons.** To make croutons, bake slices of stale homemade **bread** (or slices of purchased French bread) in a 300° oven until dry and crisp but not brown. Rub these crouts lightly with a peeled **garlic clove.**

Serves about 10

CREAMED SPINACH SOUP

From Diane Kerner.

1) Wash **2 lbs.** fresh **spinach.** Cook in the **water** that clings to the leaves in a stainless steel pot. Don't overcook. Remove from heat and puree. Set aside.

2) Meanwhile peel and slice **2 medium onions.** Saute in **3 Tb. sweet butter.** Add **3 Tb. unbleached white flour** and cook together for a couple of minutes. Add **2 c. milk** and bring to a boil whisking constantly. Remove from heat and puree.

3) Combine the pureed spinach and white sauce in pot; add **2 c. milk, ½ t. salt, fresh ground pepper, grated nutmeg** and **½ Tb. chopped** fresh **dill,** if available. Bring to a boil. This soup is best fresh and not overcooked. If you must reheat it, do not do it more than once and be as brief as possible. Be sure to use a stainless steel pot. Good chilled, too.

Serves 4–6

I live to watch the seasons change
And I listen to the whisper of the rain

"Feather In The Wind"
Oregon Mountains
Woody Simmons; Waffle Pub.

ASPARAGUS SOUP

1) Break off top three to four inches of **6 lb. asparagus** and reserve. Wash stalk bases and put into soup kettle. Add **1½ qt. water** and **1 Tb. salt.** Bring to a boil and simmer until stalks are very soft.

2) Use a food processor or blender to puree stalks and liquid in several batches. Each batch will also have to be turned into a colander or sturdy strainer over a bowl. Press down hard on the pulp to extract the liquid and discard the stringy fiber that remains.

3) In soup pot, melt **1½ sticks unsalted butter.** Add **2 cloves garlic,** crushed, and saute a few minutes. Add **¾ c. flour** and cook flour and butter mixture until well blended. Add **¾ c. heavy cream** and the stock from the asparagus stalks. Bring to a boil and season with grated **nutmeg, dash Tabasco, 1 Tb. lemon juice, pinch dried marjoram, 1 Tb. tamari.** Taste and add **salt** and **pepper** as needed.

4) Cut reserved asparagus tips into ½ inch pieces. When soup is seasoned and has simmered a few minutes, add asparagus tips and cook 2–3 minutes only. Serve immediately. To reheat, gently warm only as much as will be eaten at once.

Serves 8–10

ARTICHOKE MUSHROOM SOUP

It is most practical to make this soup after you have been
cooking artichokes and have some cooked ones left over.
We save the cooking water and boil it down to concentrate
it. If we are serving poached eggs on artichoke bottoms, we
have cooked leaves left over which we save and strip. Or, if
we are serving artichokes stuffed with scallops, the central
leaves which are removed are saved for this soup.

1) Use a serrated knife to scrape flesh off the leaves of
   2 leftover **artichokes** and set aside. You also need at
   least **3 artichoke bottoms,** diced.

2) Boil **1½ qt. artichoke water** with the **stems** of
   ½ lb. mushrooms. Slice the tops of the mushrooms
   and set aside.

3) Melt ½ **stick sweet butter** in a soup kettle. Add
   1 clove garlic, crushed, and the sliced mushrooms
   and saute till light brown. Add **nutmeg, salt,** and
   pepper. Add ⅓ **c. flour** and stir together thoroughly.

4) Add ⅔ **c. heavy cream, 2 t. lemon juice, 1 Tb.
   tamari** or good soy, and add strained artichoke broth.
   Taste for seasoning. Now add scraped artichoke leaves
   and diced bottoms. If you have a little leftover
   hollandaise sauce, 1 Tb. can be stirred into this
   soup.

Serves 6–8

ORANGE ASPARAGUS SALAD

1) Select **6 fat asparagus stalks** for each salad you wish
    to serve. Break off the base as low as it will snap. Using a
    small sharp knife, thinly peel each asparagus stalk. The
    peelings and asparagus bases may be used to add flavor
    to asparagus soup (see recipe index).

2) Use a steamer to cook asparagus stalks briefly. Three to
    four minutes should be enough. Turn into container
    and spoon **vinaigrette** (see recipe index) over
    asparagus while it is still hot.

3) Use a sharp knife to peel **California oranges** of their
    skin and pith simultaneously. One orange will make two
    salads. Slice oranges thinly and add to asparagus
    container. Spoon **vinaigrette** over oranges. Chop
    about **1 Tb. onion** per salad and sprinkle on top of
    asparagus and oranges. Chill until ready to serve.

4) Arrange **Boston** or **Red Tip lettuce** on a plate. For
    each salad, arrange three overlapping orange slices in
    the center and three asparagus spears on each side.
    Drizzle vinaigrette over and add **onion rings** if desired.

NEW POTATO, CARROT AND BROCCOLI SALAD WITH GARLIC MAYONNAISE

This salad is made with waxy white new potatoes when they are available in the Spring. It is served with a garlic mayonnaise made with fresh herbs. If you do not have the herbs called for, use those that are accessible. For example, parsley, scallions, and ½ clove crushed garlic would work just as well.

1) Prepare the vegetable marinade as follows: Combine **¼ c. red wine vinegar** with **¾ c. oil**. We use a blend of 25% olive oil and 75% vegetable oil. Add **salt** and fresh ground **pepper**. Set aside ¾ c. of this for the potatoes, and add **2 t.** good quality **prepared mustard** to it. The remaining dressing is for the carrots and broccoli.

2) Wash and quarter but do not peel, **4 lbs. new potatoes.** Boil in water to cover and be sure they do not overcook. When a small sharp knife can pierce them easily, drain immediately and toss in a bowl with the dressing. Add **3 Tb. straight leaf parsley,** chopped, and **salt** and **pepper** to taste. When cool, refrigerate.

3) Peel **1 package carrots** and cut into sticks. Steam until just done. Add some dressing and chopped **burnet** or **comfrey** if you have it. Refrigerate.

4) Cut **1 small head broccoli** into flowerets. Steam for a few minutes only. Add dressing and refrigerate.

5) Prepare **Garlic Mayonnaise.** Choose herbs such as **garlic leaves, burnet, chives,** or **parsley** and chop fine. Use an electric mixer or food processor to beat **2 egg yolks.** Add **1 Tb. wine vinegar, ½ t. salt, ½ t. prepared mustard,** and **1 c. oil,** adding the latter drop by drop while beating. When most of the oil is in, the remainder may be added in a stream. When mayonnaise has thickened, turn machine off and taste for seasoning. Mix in the chopped herbs. Refrigerate until ready to serve.

6) Make a bed of **lettuce** and place 2 large spoonfuls of potatoes in the center. Arrange broccoli and carrots around the plate. Top with thin slices of **onion** and a dollop of mayonnaise.

Serves 6–8

Rape is the only crime where the victim is treated as the accused, because it is a crime which society prefers to deny rather than punish . . . . The fact of being alive is in itself proof of consent.

Crimes Against Women: Proceedings of the International Tribunal
Diana E. H. Russell and Nicole Van de Ven; Les Femmes

SHREDDED CARROT AND SUNFLOWER SEED SALAD

For each diner, shred or grate **1½ carrots.** Arrange on a bed of **Boston lettuce.** Slice **2–3 raw mushrooms** over the salad, top with **2 Tb. sunflower seeds,** a **slice** of **Bermuda onion, 1 t. gomahsio** and **vinaigrette** (see recipe index).

MY MOTHER SAYS WE'RE HEALTH NUTS

You're happy if you're healthy, she keeps saying, so we eat sunflower seeds and do push-ups and headstands together . . . You should taste our salads. We can't grow much in our apartment, but we have onions and radishes and cilantro in our window boxes and on the fire escape.

MI MAMÁ DICE QUE ESTAMOS CHIFLADAS POR LA SALUD

Estás contenta si estás sana, dice muchas veces, así que comemos pepitas de girasol y juntas hacemos planchas y paradas de cabeza . . . Deberías probar nuestras ensaladas. No podemos cultivar mucho en nuestro apartamento, pero tenemos cebollas y rabanitos y cilantro en nuestros maceteros y en la escalera de salvamento.

My Mother and I Are Growing Strong
Mi mamá y yo nos hacemos fuertes
Inez Maury; New Seed Press

DANDELION SALAD

This salad is only for the first couple of weeks in April (in the Northeast) when **dandelions** make beautiful bouquets of leaves but there are no signs at all of flower buds. Don't bother with the few in your lawn that are trying to compete with the grass. Find a waste space that dandelions are making their own. Use a sharp knife to collect the cleaner central leaves. Wash thoroughly and dry well in a towel. Crisp in refrigerator and serve with **vinaigrette** (see recipe index) and **onion slices.** This first salad of Spring is most welcome and not at all bitter if dandelion leaves are picked early enough.

Perhaps that flowering of women, that gathering of women in our time who choose not to conceive literally, those who choose at a young age to be (paradoxically) past the Age of Childbearing, are those to whom the burden of a cultural labor has fallen.

Mothers and Daughters
Nor Hall; Rusoff Books

PARSNIP PIE

An English rite of Spring. The old English parsnip pies were
much sweeter than this and had no peanuts and probably
no ginger, either. They were more like American pumpkin
pie, i.e. a dessert. This recipe is a nice supper when served
with salad. If you want to be traditional, you can put
primroses on your table. Old recipes call for them on top of
the pie. Adapted from *Wings of Life* by Julie Jordan,
Crossing Press.

1) Peel **7 bunches** (or bags) **parsnips** and **2 very large
   onions.** Slice thinly. In 2 large frying pans, fry parsnips
   and onions in **oil** with **3–3½ c. peanuts.** When nicely
   brown, turn out into bowl and sprinkle with **2½ c.
   golden** or **cocktail sherry.**

2) Make sauce: Peel, quarter, and slice **2 very large
   onions** and saute in fry pan in **⅓ c. oil** till light brown.
   Add **3 Tb.** shredded **fresh ginger** (or 1 Tb. dry ginger).
   Cook another minute. Add **⅓ c. unbleached white
   flour.** Cook till well blended. Add **1½ c. heavy
   cream, juice** of **2–2½ lemons, ⅔ c. tamari, 12 oz.
   peanut butter, 1½ Tb. dry ginger, ⅓ c. sherry,
   2 Tb. honey,** and **1 qt. milk.** Taste. Sauce should
   taste strongly salty and gingery and be sweet-pungent.

3) Add sauce to parsnips using just enough to make a
   liason with the parsnips. Too much will be soggy.

4) Prepare pie crust (*see* recipe index) using **9 c. flour, 2¼ t. salt, 1 lb.** plus **½ stick sweet butter, ⅔ c. vegetable shortening** and **1½ c. ice water.** These amounts will yield ample to fit a pan 11″ x 17″.

5) Preheat oven to 375°. Roll out crust and line a pan 11″ x 17″ with it. Add sauced parsnips. Roll out top crust. Crimp edges and slash top. Bake at 375° till browned. Leftover portions can be reheated in oven.

Serves about 12

Considering the hatred the Hebrews felt toward the asherim, a major symbol of the female religion, it would not be too surprising if the symbolism of the tree of forbidden fruit, said to offer the knowledge of good and evil, yet clearly represented in the myth as the provider of sexual consciousness, was included in the creation story to warn that eating the fruit of this tree had caused the downfall of all humanity. Eating of the tree of the Goddess, which stood by each altar, was as dangerously "pagan" as were Her sexual customs and Her oracular serpents.

When God Was A Woman
Merlin Stone; Dial Press

MANICOTTI

You will need 1 box manicotti pasta. If not available, use jumbo shell pasta instead. Sauce recipe from Ann Bottone.

1) The sauce should be made first. In a 3 qt. pot fry **2 medium onions,** coarsely chopped, **3 cloves garlic,** coarsely chopped, **1 t. dried oregano, 1 t. dried basil** in **¼ c. olive oil.** Let onions saute about 10 minutes, then add a **6 oz.** can **tomato paste.** Cook the sauce a few minutes and add **6 oz.** of **water** using the tomato paste can. A **splash** of **red wine** may also be added. Cook the sauce till it thickens and then add a **2 lb. 3 oz. can** of **tomatoes in puree.** Bring the sauce to a boil adding **1 Tb. salt, 1 t. pepper,** and **3 Tb. pesto,** if you have it (see recipe index). Turn down to a simmer and let the sauce cook a good 3 hours to develop its full flavor.

2) The cheese and spinach filling should be made next. In a bowl, combine **2 lbs.** whole milk **ricotta cheese, 1 lb. mozarella,** diced, **¾ c.** freshly **grated parmesan cheese, 4 Tb. Italian parsley,** chopped, **½ lb.** defrosted frozen chopped **spinach** (drained of its liquid), **2 eggs, 1 t. salt, ½ t. pepper** and a **grating** of **nutmeg.** Mix the ingredients thoroughly and taste for seasoning. Refrigerate until ready to stuff manicotti.

3) When the sauce has finished cooking, the pasta can be cooked. Fill a 6 qt. pot with water and bring to a boil. Carefully drop **1 box** unbroken **manicotti** into the boiling water. Stir gently with a wooden spoon to

separate any that might be sticking together. Do not cook more than 5 to 6 minutes and drain the shells in a strainer or carefully take them out of the water with a slotted spoon. Immediately pour cold water on pasta to keep them from cooking further and splitting apart.

4) The manicotti shells should be filled immediately. Hold the manicotti carefully, and with a butter knife gently stuff each tube with the cheese spinach filling. Line them up close together in a pan and spread some of the tomato sauce on top. Refrigerate.

5) When ready to serve, bake in a 350° oven for 20 minutes or until the manicotti are puffed and the cheese has melted. Remove from the oven, spoon more hot tomato sauce on top and sprinkle each serving, 2 manicotti per person, with freshly grated **parmesan.** Serve immediately.

Serves 7

Wise woman, wise woman, what do you know of life?

"Wise Woman"
Mooncircles
Kay Gardner; Wise Women Enterprises

ASPARAGUS PLATTER

1) You will need ½ lb. asparagus for each diner, so buy (or pick) **3–4 lb. asparagus.** Snap off the smallest amount of base possible and discard. Then, using a small sharp knife, carefully peel off the skin up to the bottom of the tip. We don't think potato peelers do this job as well as paring knives. This is a laborious job, but worth it for the tender result.

2) Simmer **2 c. white rice** in **3½ c. water** with **1½ t. salt** until done, about 15 minutes. Taste rice and if it doesn't seem done and liquid is all gone, add a little more water. When rice is done, add **3 Tb. sweet butter** and keep covered.

3) Prepare **Sauce Maltaise:** Melt **1½ sticks sweet butter** in a small pot and set aside. In a stainless steel pot place **6 egg yolks, ½ c.** fresh squeezed **orange juice, 2 Tb. lemon juice.** Whisk over low heat until sauce thickens slightly, then add melted butter slowly while whisking. This sauce is a variation of hollandaise. Remove from heat when sauce is thickened and season to taste with **salt** and freshly ground **pepper.** If you like, add some **grated orange rind.** Set sauce aside, covered.

4) Now place the asparagus in a large fry pan (or two, if they don't all fit in one) and add **½ c. water** to each pan. Cover and steam until asparagus are barely done, no more than 5 minutes. They cook quickly when they are peeled.

5) Arrange rice on two sides of each dinner plate with asparagus in the middle. Pour the asparagus cooking liquid over the rice and serve the sauce maltaise over the asparagus, with the remainder in a sauce boat.

Serves 6–8

Wasn't there something in each of us calling out to someone, "Do as I do. Stamp me approved. Follow me and prove that I was valid." I could do it, find a man, cast myself as his wife and get on with my part. I knew the right lines, had the smile down pat. Mom would be pleased. But would she? . . . Regardless, I wouldn't . . . I was not going to do what she wanted me to do with my life. That meant I owed her the first move. The daughter who breaks the chain becomes the mother.

Give Me Your Good Ear
Maureen Brady; Spinsters, Ink

NOODLE SOUFFLE

A good dinner with salad or soup. Though this dish is reminiscent of Jewish lokchen kugel or noodle pudding it is quite different, almost like a non-sweet cheesecake with noodles, meant as a main dish.

1) Boil **1 lb. wide egg noodles** in boiling salted water till just done. Drain. Meanwhile grease a 3 qt. pyrex or other baking dish.

2) In mixer, cream **2 sticks sweet butter,** add ½ **lb. cream cheese.** Mix well. Add **8 eggs,** one at a time, beating well. Add **4 c. sour cream, juice** of **2 lemons** (¼ c.), **2 t. salt,** and ½ **c.** plus **2 Tb. sugar.** Taste for sour, sweet and salt. All flavors should be strong.

3) Turn noodles into greased pan; pour cream cheese batter over noodles. Stir lightly.

4) About an hour before serving, preheat oven to 325° and bake noodle souffle until puffed and browned. Leftover portions may be reheated, uncovered in oven or toaster oven.

Serves 12

MATZAH BRIE

A breakfast dish from Fay Davidson.

1) Break up **6 large squares** of **matzah** in a large bowl and cover with water.

2) Beat **6 eggs** thoroughly and add **2 t. salt.** Stir well.

3) When matzah is uniformly soft, turn into a colander, then squeeze out the water, doing one handful at a time. Put each dry handful into egg mixture. When all the matzah is in the egg mix, stir together with a fork.

4) Melt **butter** in a large frying pan and when quite hot, pat out small thin cakes in the hot fat using the fork. When browned and crispy, turn each cake over and brown the other side. The matzah brie can be turned over several times until properly crisp and brown. Serve immediately, telling diners to add **salt** to taste. Repeat, making more cakes. Matzah brie requires a lot of butter. For this quantity you will probably need ½–¾ **lb.** of **butter.** Some people (not us) like it served with **jam** or **sour cream.**

Serves 6

Note: Obviously the cook doesn't eat until all the matzah brie is cooked. You can trade off cooking or keep matzah brie hot in the oven (it won't be as good) or only make it for yourself! One matzah and 1 egg serves 1 person.

JAPANESE SOBA NOODLES

Soba noodles are made of buckwheat flour. Some kinds
also contain jimenju, wild mountain sweet potato. We find
them delicious. To make a complete dinner, serve with sea
vegetable salad and makizushi (see recipe index).

1) Prepare side dishes before cooking soba. Bake **1 sheet**
   of **nori** in a 325° oven until crisp. Cut into small squares.
   Slice **2 bunches scallions** into rounds. Shred **1 large
   daikon** (Japanese radish) if available, or shred
   1 bunch icicle radishes. You will need **wasabi,** dried
   horseradish which is mixed to a soft paste with cold
   water just before eating in the same fashion as dry
   mustard. It is equally sharp, so each diner needs a very
   small dab of it. If you are serving the sea vegeable salad
   and the makizushi with the soba, prepare them also.
   The makizushi takes time and patience to do.

2) Make **Soba Tsuyu,** the sauce: Flame **½ c. dry sherry**
   by heating it and then tipping the pot so the wine
   catches flame. Add **¾ c. tamari** or soy and **3 c. water.**
   Add a **1 inch square kombu** and bring to a boil,
   covered. Once it has boiled, set the sauce aside and
   remove the kombu and discard.

3) When ready to serve, bring a large pot of **water** to a
   boil. Add **3 eight oz. packages soba noodles** and
   boil no more than 5 minutes, or till just done. Drain and
   serve immediately, or drain and run cold water over
   soba and reheat in a steamer.

4) Serve soba in shallow bowls. Add the soba tsuyu sauce
   to each bowl and serve extra pitchers of sauce on the
   table. Top each serving with scallions and nori squares.
   Side dishes of wasabi, daikon, makizushi, and sea
   vegetable salad are served with the soba. Stir daikon
   and wasabi in your soba dish as you eat.

Serves 9

*The products of necrophilic Apollonian male
mating are of course the technological "offspring"
which pollute the heavens and the earth . . . .
Nuclear reactors and the poisons they produce,
stockpiles of atomic bombs, ozone-destroying
aerosol spray propellants, oil tankers "designed"
to self-destruct in the ocean, iatrogenic
medications and carcinogenic food additives,
refined sugar, mind pollutants of all kinds—these
are the multiple fetuses/feces of stale male-mates
in love with a dead world that is ultimately co-
equal and consubstantial with themselves.*

Gyn/Ecology
Mary Daly; Beacon Press

SEA VEGETABLE SALAD

1) Soak ½ **package** of **arame** seaweed and ½ **package wakame** seaweed separately in **cold water** for about 5 minutes or until freshened. Don't let seaweed soak too long. Remove from water, squeezing slightly. Cut off tough stems from wakame and cut into smaller squares. Arame will probably not need cutting. Arrange the seaweeds in rows on a large platter. (Use the soaking water as food for your plants.)

2) Shred or grate **6 carrots** and **4 medium white turnips.** Arrange them on the platter with the seaweed.

3) In a cup, mix together ¼ **c. rice wine vinegar, 4 t. honey** and ¼ to ⅓ **c. tamari.** Pour this dressing over the sea vegetables and over the carrots and turnips. Sprinkle **gomahsio** (see recipe index) over the salad. Cover and refrigerate until ready to serve.

4) Simmer **1 square tofu** in water for 5 minutes. Place tofu in a blender. Add **2 Tb.** of the **water** it simmered in, **1 Tb. rice wine vinegar,** ½ **t. honey, dash cayenne pepper,** and **2 Tb. gomahsio.** Puree the tofu until smooth. Add more water if necessary. It should have the consistency of thin mayonnaise. Add more rice wine vinegar if you think it should be more sour.

5) Serve each diner small portions of carrot, turnip, and
   each sea vegetable. Sprinkle this salad with chopped
   scallions and place a tablespoon of the tofu sauce in
   the middle of each small salad plate. More **gomahsio**
   can be sprinkled on top.

                                              Serves 9

But remember to bury
all old quarrels
behind the garage for compost.
Forgive who insulted you.
Forgive yourself for being wrong.
You will do it again

"The spring offensive of the snail"
To Be Of Use
Marge Piercy; Doubleday

MAKIZUSHI

A vinegared rice appetizer rolled in seaweed.

1) Soak **5 large Japanese mushrooms** (*shiitake*) in just enough **water** to cover for ½ hour. Remove from liquid, cut off and discard tough stems and slice mushrooms. Put mushroom slices and their soaking liquid in a small pot. Add **2 Tb. tamari** and **1 Tb. honey.** Simmer until liquid has reduced to less than a tablespoon.

2) Wash **2 c. rice,** preferably Japanese, under running water and drain. Place in a pot with **2½ c. water** and a **1 inch square** of **kombu** (kelp). Let soak 20 minutes. Bring to a boil and simmer 10–15 minutes. Let rest off heat 5 minutes, covered.

3) In a pot, mix **¼ c. rice wine vinegar, 2 Tb. honey, 1¼ t. salt,** and **2 Tb. dry sherry.** Bring to a boil and then cool. Use fork or chopsticks to mix rice and vinegar dressing together in a bowl. *

4) Prepare **8** or **9 leaves** of **fresh spinach** by steaming them until barely done. Grate **2 carrots.** Peel **1 cucumber,** cut into quarters lengthwise, remove seeds and cut each quarter into 3 long strips. If available, cut very thin strips of **beni shoga** (Japanese pickled ginger). It will also help if you have a placemat made of reeds to roll the makizushi.

5) You will need **6 sheets** of **nori** (a kind of seaweed).
Pass 1 sheet at a time over a flame on one side only to
enhance its flavor and place it on your placemat or on a
dish towel. Place a thin layer of vinegared rice over the
nori, leaving 1 inch bare at the edge facing you and
½ inch bare at the other end. In the center place a
cucumber strip, a couple of spinach leaves, a thin line of
grated carrot, a row of shiitake mushrooms, and beni
shoga strips. Carefully roll up the nori in the mat and
squeeze gently to firm up the makizushi roll. Remove
from mat or towel, let rest a few minutes, and then use a
very sharp knife to cut into 9 rounds. Chill, covered,
until ready to serve. Repeat with remaining nori.

* Be sure to use freshly made rice which will be sticky and
will hold together when makizushi is rolled and cut. Using
Japanese rice, known as **kokuho,** will make the job easier.

*It should be clear that a fact is a function of the
system it purports to validate. The psychiatric
system, for instance, can produce volumes of
"objective" facts, all of which validate the
assumptions of that system but which have often
invalidated our own individual and collective
experience, emotions, thoughts, motives and acts.*

I Dream In Female
Barbara Starrett; Cassandra

COCONUT CAROB CUSTARD

This recipe is an adaptation of Caribbean recipes that call for sweetened condensed milk. The carob will separate somewhat from the custard, but it will taste fine.

1) In a large heavy pot, bring **2⅔ c. milk** and **1⅓ c. heavy cream** to a boil with **1 stick** of **cinnamon.** Simmer until it reduces to 2⅔ cups. Be careful it doesn't boil over. Preheat oven to 325°.

2) You will need **2 Tb.** plus **2 t. roasted carob powder.** If not already roasted, toast gently in toaster oven. Then use food processor or blender to be sure carob is powdered. Add **1 egg** and mix with carob.

3) In mixer, or using a bowl and whisk, combine **3 eggs, ⅔ c. heavy cream, ½ c. honey, dash salt, ¼ t. cinnamon** and **1 t. vanilla.** Don't overbeat.

4) Slowly add reduced milk and cream to carob mix in food processor or blender while machine is on. You should now have a thin carob syrup. Slowly add carob syrup to egg mix, stirring well to prevent eggs from curdling. Add **½ c. dried unsweetened coconut.** Fill 9–10 custard cups and place in pan. Fill pan with enough water to come ½ way up the sides of the custard cups. Bake 40–50 minutes, or until just set. Remove from water bath and chill. Serve with **heavy cream.**

TOPFENKUCHEN

Almond Cheese Torte with no flour or leavening. This is a
light cake, a nut torte with cheese, very different from heavy
cheesecakes to which we're accustomed. From Esta Kramer.

1) Butter a 10" springform pan and sprinkle with **bread
   crumbs.** Preheat oven to 350°. Soften **3 sticks
   unsalted butter.**

2) Push ⅔ **lb. farmer cheese** through sieve. Set aside.

3) Use a food processor or cheese grater to finely grate
   5 c. almonds. A blender does not work since it tends
   to make nut-butter instead of a dry grated product.

4) Separate **10 eggs,** yolks into a small bowl and whites
   into mixer. Add the **grated rind** of **2 lemons** to the
   yolks and set aside. Beat whites until stiff but not dry.
   Turn out into another large bowl. In mixer, cream the
   softened butter with **1½ c. sugar.** When light and
   fluffy, add egg yolks and lemon rind and mix well. Now
   add sieved farmer cheese, **1½ t. vanilla, ½ t. almond
   extract,** and the grated almonds. When all is well
   blended, fold in the stiffly beaten egg whites.

5) Turn into prepared springform pan and bake about 1
   hour or until a cake tester comes out dry and cake is
   slightly shrunk from sides of pan. Cool on a rack and
   chill. Serve with **whipped cream.**

CARROT CAKE
WITH CREAM CHEESE "HARD SAUCE"

This cake is lighter in texture than most carrot cakes because the whites are beaten stiff and folded in at the end. It is also a recipe in which the whole wheat flour is present for its good flavor.

1) Butter and flour a 10″ tube pan. Preheat oven to 350°. Grate or shred enough **carrots** to measure **6 c.**

2) In a bowl mix together **5 c. whole wheat flour** (pastry preferred, but bread flour works fine, also), **4 t. cinnamon, 1 t. cardamom, 1½ t. salt, 4 t. baking powder, 2 t. baking soda.** Use a whisk to mix dry ingredients together thoroughly.

3) Separate **8 eggs,** whites into a mixer and yolks into a food processor or bowl. Beat yolks well and add **2½ c. vegetable oil** and the grated carrots. If using a food processor, keep this mixing brief.

4) If you have extra **egg whites,** add **2** to the 8 in the mixer. Beat until rounded peaks form, add **1¼ c. honey** and beat until stiff.

5) First stir dry ingredients and egg yolk mixture together and then stir in ¼ to ⅓ of the stiff beaten whites. Gently fold in remaining whites. Turn into pan, filling to within ½" of the rim. If there is too much batter, use remainder for a few cupcakes. Bake until cake shrinks slightly from its sides, 1 to 1½ hours. Place pan on rack to cool and turn out only after cake has cooled.

6) Cream together **½ c. honey** and **2 sticks sweet butter.** When well mixed, add **1 lb.** softened **cream cheese** and mix briefly. Finally add **⅓ c.** fresh squeezed **orange juice** and **½ t. vanilla extract.** A food processor mixes these together well. Turn this mock hard sauce into a bowl and refrigerate. Instead of frosting cake, serve each cut piece with a dollop of the sauce. For a lactose intolerant diet, you can make an **orange glaze** for this cake by boiling together **1 c. fresh** squeezed **orange juice** with **⅓ c. honey** for 5 minutes. Add **2 Tb. Grand Marnier Liqueur,** if you like, and pour over the turned out cake.

For you are the sister of each one living there,
Of the beasts in the forest, of the birds in the air.
May you love and defend them, womanchild,
    womanchild. . .

"Womanchild"
Womanriver Flowing On
Carole Etzler; Sisters Unlimited

BANANA CAKE

From Fay Davidson.

1) Preheat oven to 300°. Grease an 8" x 8" pan or a loaf pan.

2) Mash enough ripe (or overripe) **bananas** to yield **1 c.**

3) In mixer cream **1 stick sweet butter.** Add ½ **c.** plus **2 Tb. sugar** and beat well.

4) Meanwhile, whisk or sift together **1½ c. unbleached white flour, ¼ t. salt,** and **1 t. baking soda.**

5) Add **2 eggs** to butter and sugar and mix on low speed. Then add ¼ **c. sour cream, 1 t. vanilla,** and mashed banana.

6) Fold in dry ingredients together with ½ **c. chopped walnuts.** Turn into pan and bake 1 hour, or until cake pulls away slightly from sides of pan. Needs no frosting.

"Everybody gets married. It's something you have to do, like dying."
"I ain't doin' it."

Rubyfruit Jungle
Rita Mae Brown; Daughters

BANANA CREAM PIE

1) Preheat oven to 375°. Make **pie crust** to line one pie pan (*see recipe index for pie crust*). Prick bottom rim, line with foil and weight with dried beans. Bake until edges are light brown. Remove foil and beans and finish baking.

2) Force **½ small jar apricot preserves** through a sieve into a small pot and bring to a boil. Simmer 5 minutes. Use a brush to coat bottom of baked pie shell with the apricot glaze. This is a waterproofing measure. Line crust with **3** sliced **bananas.**

3) Scald **1¾ c. milk.** In a bowl, beat **7 yolks** until light yellow. Add ⅓ **c. sugar** and continue beating. Add **¼ c. unbleached white flour** and a **pinch salt.** Gradually add milk to egg mixture, stirring constantly. Return to pot and cook very slowly until mixture thickens, stirring with whisk carefully in the corners of the pot. Add **1¼ t. vanilla extract.** Let cool slightly. Pour over bananas. Refrigerate pie until it sets up.

4) Before serving, whip **2 c. heavy cream** stiff with **2 Tb. Kirsch** and **1 Tb. sugar.** Top pie with whipped cream and **banana slices.**

HAZELNUT TORTE WITH
MOCHA BUTTER CREAM FROSTING

This cake is very easy to make once nuts are roasted,
rubbed, and grated. With patience, the frosting is easy too.
The result is rich and wonderful considering the cake has no
flour, sugar, or chocolate. The biggest drawback is the price
of the nuts. Of course, walnuts or almonds may be
substituted.

1) Roast **3 c. hazelnuts** (filberts) in a 400° oven stirring
    often. When browned, turn out onto a dish towel or
    tablecloth and use cloth to rub nuts together to loosen
    their skins. All the skins will not come off, but separate
    nuts from the skins as much as possible and grate the
    nuts in a cheese grater or food processor, being careful
    not to grind them into a nut butter.

2) Butter three 9" cake pans or 1 large 11" x 17" pan and
    line with waxed paper. Preheat oven to 325°.

3) Separate **6 eggs,** placing yolks in a stainless steel pot to
    make frosting later. You will need another **6 whites** for
    the cake totaling 12, or 1½ c. (Remaining yolks can
    enrich scrambled eggs or be used for Hollandaise,
    Sauce Isabel, etc.) Put the 1½ c. whites into mixer with
    ¼ **t. salt** and beat until rounded peaks form. Add **1⅓ c.
    honey, 1½ t. vanilla extract, ¾ t. almond extract.**
    Beat until stiff but not dry. Fold in grated nuts, turn into
    prepared pan(s) and bake cake 1-1½ hours or until
    sides look slightly brown and top is no longer sticky.

4) Remove pan(s) to racks and let cool 5 minutes. Turn
   cake out and peel off wax paper. Let cool thoroughly. If
   using rectangular pan, halve cake to make two layers.

5) To make **Mocha Butter Cream Frosting:** Soften **3
   sticks unsalted butter.** Add the following to the 6
   reserved yolks in stainless steel pot: **¾ c. milk***,
   **2 Tb. roasted carob powder, 1 Tb. coffee
   substitute** (Bambu, Pero, Pioneer) or powdered
   coffee, **½ c. honey.**

6) Whisk over medium-low heat until mixture thickens to a
   creamy consistency. This takes between 15 and 20
   minutes and will happen suddenly.

7) Turn this mocha cream into a mixer (no need to wash it
   from the cake) and beat until the cream is tepid to your
   touch. Now add the butter, one tablespoon at a time
   and continue beating. The frosting will be thin at first,
   then grainy, and finally silky smooth. Add **1 t. vanilla.**

8) Frost cooled cake with this mocha butter cream. Top
   with a **few whole hazelnuts** if desired.

9) Other possible frostings include: a) honey sweetened
   whipped cream (see Lemon Tart recipe); b) honey
   and carob flavored whipped cream (see Carob
   Cheesecake recipe); c) apricot or raspberry preserves
   (honey sweetened); or dried apricots simmered in water
   and pureed, then sweetened to taste with honey. Use
   the fruit puree or jam between layers and either
   whipped cream or butter cream on top.

* For a lactose intolerant diet, use water for the liquid.

BROWN RICE PUDDING

1) In a large shallow baking pan, combine **⅓ c. brown rice** (we use short grain), **2½ Tb. honey, dash salt,** grated **rind** of **1 lemon, ½ c. raisins, 1 t. vanilla,** and **1 qt. milk.***

2) Bake at 325° for 1½ to 2 hours, stirring occasionally. The pudding will repeatedly get a brown skin which should be stirred in. About 20 minutes before it is done, stir in a **splash** of **brandy.**

3) Remove from oven when it still seems soft and loose. It will thicken up as it cools. Serve with **heavy cream.**

Serves 6–8

* If you like a richer pudding, substitute **1 c. heavy cream** and **3 c. milk** for the 1 qt. milk.

There are many connections between a carnivorous race and a sexist society. The rape of the land by meat-eaters (it requires 6 to 10 times as much land to feed meat-eaters) is taken for granted just as the rape of women is condoned.

"The Oedible Complex: Feminism and Vegetarianism"
The Lesbian Reader
Carol Adams; Ed: Gina Covina and Laurel Galana; Amazon Press

APRICOT WHOLE WHEAT MUFFINS

1) Preheat oven to 425°. Butter muffin tins or line them with papers.

2) Snip with scissors or chop with a large French chef's knife enough **dried apricots** to make **1 cup.**

3) Melt **½ stick sweet butter.**

4) Use whisk to stir together **1 c. whole wheat flour, 1 c. unbleached white flour, 1½ t. baking powder, ½ t. baking soda, ½ t. salt.**

5) Whisk **1 egg.** Add **scant ½ c. honey** and beat well so that honey is in solution. Stir in **1¼ c. buttermilk** and the melted butter.

6) Quickly stir together liquid and dry mixtures adding the apricots and **½ c. chopped walnuts.** Don't overmix. Spoon into prepared muffin tins and bake at 425° until lightly browned (20–25 minutes). These muffins freeze well. Reheat at 350°.

*As the whale goes and the dolphin
and the ocean and the forest
so will we.*

"The Whale"
Malvina Held Over
© 1974 Malvina Reynolds, Schroder Music Co.

The door itself makes no promises . . . Adrienne Rich

~~~~~~~~~~~~~~~~~~~~~~~~~~~~~~~~~

CHAPTER 5   LATE SPRING
May Eve, April 30, to Summer Solstice, June 22.

OKRA GUMBO

In the northeast, tender baby okra can be found in the
Spring in Puerto Rican and Black markets. Only small sized
okra, no more than 3 inches long should be used;
otherwise, they are tough and stringy. In other parts of the
country small okra pods will be available at other times of
the year.

1) With a small sharp knife scrape the skins of **1½ lbs.
   baby okra** lightly to remove surface fuzz. Unless the
   okra is really dirty, do not wash it as it will become
   soggy. Cut off the stems of each okra and slice each pod
   into rounds. Set aside.

2) In a soup pot melt **3 Tb. sweet butter** and add
   1½ c. finely chopped **onions.** Cook until soft but not
   brown. Stir in **2 t. fresh hot peppers,** finely chopped,
   6 cloves garlic, crushed, **2 Tb. green peppers,**
   chopped, and **2½ c.** canned **tomatoes.** Cook for 10
   minutes.

3) Add **1½ qts. water,** bring to a boil and add **½ c.
   brown rice.** Cook the soup at a simmer for 15 minutes
   and then add the okra, **1 Tb. salt,** and some fresh
   grated **pepper.** Let the okra and rice cook another 15
   minutes or until the rice is done and okra is tender. You
   may need to add another cup of **water** at this time if the
   soup is too thick. Serve at once. This soup reheats well.

Serves 6–8

WATERCRESS VICHYSSOISE

1) Coarsely chop **onions** to measure **1 c.** Lengthwise slice **4 leeks** and thoroughly wash them. Slice thinly. Melt ½ **stick butter** in a pot. Add **1 clove garlic,** crushed, and the onions and leeks. Saute over low heat until very tender.

2) Add **4 c. potatoes,** peeled and sliced, **1 Tb. salt** and **2½ c. water.** Cover and simmer until potatoes are almost done.

3) Remove thickest stems from **1 bunch watercress,** reserving a few sprigs, and add to soup pot together with **1½ c. milk** and **1½ c. water.** Cook another ten minutes. Puree in food processor or blender.

4) Mix **2 egg yolks** and ½ **c. cream** in soup pot. Gradually add pureed soup, stirring constantly so yolks don't curdle. Heat soup but do not let it boil.

5) Serve hot or cold, garnished with reserved cress sprigs and snipped **scallions** or **chives.**

Serves 6–8

LEEK AND SORREL SOUP

French sorrel can be purchased in early Spring in some
markets. It is a perennial plant which is also easy to grow.
There is a wild sorrel which is equally good; however, the
leaves are so small it would be hard to collect enough for
this soup.

1) Slit **4 leeks** lengthwise and wash thoroughly,
   discarding dried or brown tops. Slice the leeks into small
   pieces and saute in a 4 qt. pot with **2 Tb. sweet butter**
   for 10 minutes. Add **1 qt. sorrel,** washed, and **1 ½ qts.
   water.** Let cook for a half hour.

2) Pour the leeks and sorrel through a strainer, saving the
   broth in a bowl. Set aside until ready to puree.

3) Using the same pot, melt **3 Tb. sweet butter** and add
   3 Tb. unbleached white flour. Cook together a few
   minutes. Add **2 c. heavy cream** and cook until a thick
   white sauce has formed.

4) Using a food processor or blender, puree the leeks and
   sorrel with enough reserved broth for the machine to
   work adequately. Add this puree to the soup pot. Bring
   to a boil, stirring well. Add as much reserved broth as
   you deem necessary. Season the soup with **2 Tb.
   tamari, 1 t. salt,** and some freshly **grated pepper.**
   Soup should be somewhat thick and quite sour.

5) Chill the soup and serve with **chives** or **scallions,** or serve hot, garnished the same way.

Serves 6

The experts' rise to power over the lives of women was neither swift nor easy. The old networks through which women had learned from each other had to be destroyed, or discredited. . . . The experts were "scientific" and it seemed that only science could vanquish ignorance and injustice. Had not science opposed the patriarchal authorities of the Old Order, and, by implication, the entire web of constraints which had bound women for centuries? This was the basis of the "romance" between women and the new experts: science had been on the side of progress and freedom. . . . It would take another two generations for the "romance" to unravel itself, and for women to discover that the experts had, in fact, betrayed science, and betrayed them.

For Her Own Good
150 Years Of The Experts' Advice to Women
Barbara Ehrenreich and Deirdre English; Doubleday

FRESH PEA SOUP
WITH HERB DUMPLINGS

1) Prepare herb dumplings first. Put **⅔ c. water, ½ stick sweet butter,** and **½ t. salt** into a pot. Bring to a boil. Add **⅔ c. flour** and beat with a wooden spoon until mixture is smooth and thick. Remove from heat and add **2 large** or **3 small eggs,** one at a time, beating vigorously until each one is mixed into the batter. A mixer does this easiest, but it can be done by hand. Season dumpling batter with **fresh grated nutmeg** and **pepper** and **2 Tb.** chopped **fresh herbs** such as **garlic leaves, chives, savory,** or **thyme.** Taste to be sure seasoning is adequate.

2) Bring a pot of **salted water** to a boil. Dip a spoon into the boiling water and then scoop out an oval of dumpling batter. Place spoon in the boiling water until dumpling slips off. Repeat, but don't crowd dumplings. Cover pot and turn to lowest simmer. Cook about 5 minutes or until somewhat puffed. Drain on absorbent paper while preparing soup. You should get 16 small dumplings.

3) Bring **1½ qt. water** to a boil and add **3 lb. freshly shelled** or **frozen peas,** reserving ½ c. of peas to garnish the soup. Barely cook; 1–2 minutes of boiling is plenty. Add **2 c. cold water** to stop cooking.

4) Puree soup in a food processor or blender.

5) Melt **1 stick sweet butter** in a pot and add ½ **c. flour.**
    Stir well together a few minutes to cook flour and
    gradually add pea puree. Finish seasoning by adding
    1 c. dry white wine, 2 t. salt, fresh ground pepper,
    and a **dash** of **Tabasco.**

6) Add dumplings to soup and bring to a boil just once
    before serving. Overcooking will make this fresh and
    simple soup taste and look like a split pea soup. It should
    stay a fresh and minty green. Top each serving with
    fresh ground pepper and the reserved peas.

Serves 8

*. . . because I know I am made from this earth, as my
mother's hands were made from this earth, as her dreams
came from this earth and all that I know, I know in
this earth . . .*

Woman and Nature
Susan Griffin; Harper & Row

ESCAROLE SOUP

1) Pull apart and wash thoroughly **1 large head** of **escarole.** Break large leaves in half and place in soup pot. Barely cover with **water** and simmer until cooked, about 15 minutes after liquid comes to a boil.

2) In a small frying pan, gently saute **1 clove garlic,** crushed, in **2 Tb. olive oil** until lightly cooked. Add oil and garlic to soup pot. Add **1 Tb. tamari** and taste for saltiness. Add **salt** if necessary and fresh ground **pepper** to taste. Be sure the broth-escarole relationship is satisfactory to you. If soup seems to need it, add more water and readjust seasoning.

3) When ready to serve, beat **2 eggs** in a bowl and slowly add hot soup to eggs, stirring constantly to prevent curdling. Return to pot and heat gently, not allowing soup to come to a boil. Serve soup with fresh grated **parmesan cheese.**

Serves 6–8

When you open up your life to the living, all things come spilling in on you.
And you're flowing like a river, the Changer and the Changed
You got to spill some over . . .

"Waterfall"
The Changer and the Changed
© 1975 Cris Williamson; Olivia

MADZOON SOUP

This Armenian soup can be served hot or cold. Cold seems best to us and fresh mint a prerequisite.

1) Cook **1 c. oatmeal** in **4 c. water** with **2 t. salt** about 5 minutes. In a large bowl put **4 c. yoghurt** and add the cooked oatmeal mixture gradually so the yoghurt won't curdle. Set aside.

2) Finely chop **2 small onions** and saute in **2 Tb. sweet butter** until slightly brown. Add this to the madzoon with **1 Tb. fresh mint,** chopped. Refrigerate and serve cold, adding water to thin the soup if it is too thick. Garnish with a **sprig** of **mint** in each bowl.

Serves 6–8

It is the thirtieth of May,
rain pours on ancient bushes, runs
down the youngest blade of grass.
I am trying to hold in one steady glance
all the parts of my life.

"Toward The Solstice"
The Dream of a Common Language
Adrienne Rich; Norton

CHICK PEA SALAD

1) Soak **2 c. dried chick peas** overnight in water. Rinse
   and cook chick peas in fresh water until soft. Drain and
   cool. Cover with water in bowl and rub chick peas
   lightly between your palms to release their skins. Skim
   skins from surface of water. You won't be able to
   remove all of them. Drain chick peas and turn into bowl.

2) Shred **1½ carrots.** Finely chop **1½ stalks** of **celery**
   (hearts of celery are best), **1 pepper, ½ small onion**
   and **2 leaves** of **comfrey.** (Comfrey is an easy to grow
   plant whose long hairy green leaves are high in vitamin
   B12 for those who are interested. It adds a wonderful
   cucumber-like taste to the salad. The leaves of borage
   or burnet can be substituted or, if none of these are
   available, some diced cucumber can be added to the
   finished salad. However, many believe comfrey has
   healing properties.)

3) Make **vinaigrette:** In a small bowl combine **1 Tb.
   tamari** or soy, **1 t. lemon juice, 1 small clove
   garlic,** crushed, **1 t. chili paste with garlic** (can be
   purchased by the jar in Chinese food outlet, or
   substitute cayenne pepper or Tabasco), **salt** and
   pepper to taste. The vinaigrette should be fairly
   concentrated in taste.

4) Add vinaigrette to chick peas. Toss and refrigerate.
   Serve cold on center of a bed of **Boston lettuce** with
   avocado slices, slivers of **red onion,** and **alfalfa
   sprouts.** Sprinkle with **gomahsio** (see recipe index).

Serves 8–10

CHINESE CABBAGE SALAD WITH YOGHURT DRESSING

1) Prepare **Yoghurt Mayonnaise:** In a food processor or in an electric mixer, beat **2 egg yolks** for a minute. With the machine still on, add **1 Tb. lemon juice, ½ t. salt, fresh ground pepper.** Add **1 c. vegetable oil** with the machine still on, drop by drop at first and then more quickly as mayonnaise thickens. When oil is well incorporated and mayonnaise is quite thick, turn machine off. Add **½ c. plain yoghurt** and mix again. Taste for lemon juice, salt and pepper.

2) Using a large heavy French chef's knife, shred **1 large head Chinese cabbage** and arrange on 6–8 plates. Cut off and discard tough stems from **1–2 bunches watercress** and scatter over cabbage. Slice **2 bunches** of **radishes** over the salads and dribble a little **vinaigrette** (see recipe index) over each. Serve with a dollop of the yoghurt dressing on each salad with the rest in a sauceboat.

Serves 6–8

Takes a war to keep them perking,
And they have to bleed the world
To keep their bloody system working . . .

"World In Their Pocket"
Malvina Held Over
© 1975 Malvina Reynolds, Schroder Music Co.

POKEWEED GREENS

It is worth learning how to identify **Pokeweed.** This
succulent weed of waste places (it can be found in your
garden, too), comes up the first few weeks in May in
Connecticut. Called the poor person's asparagus, the stalks
taste much like asparagus and the new leaves like spinach.
Poke is delicious. Don't eat flowers or fruit which appear
later in the season. They are reputedly poisonous.

1) Use a knife to cut shoots under 12″ high. Larger stalks
    are bitter. Poke requires minimum washing. Simmer in
    a little water for about 5 minutes or until tender.

2) Serve with **salt** and **butter.**

*"Men and women aren't different species, Ruth.
Women do everything men do."*
*"Do they?" Our eyes meet, but she seems to be
seeing ghosts between us in the rain. She mutters
something that could be "My Lai" and looks away.*
"All the endless wars . . . ." Her voice is a whisper.
*"All the huge authoritarian organizations for doing
unreal things. Men live to struggle against each
other; we're just part of the battlefields. It'll never
change unless you change the whole world . . ."*

"The Women Men Don't See"
Warm Worlds and Otherwise
James Tiptree, Jr.; Ballantine

GINGERED BROCCOLI STEM SALAD

We save the stems from broccoli used in the Raclette dinner, broccoli omelet, and on the potato salad with garlic mayonnaise. The stems will keep at least a week in the refrigerator.

1) Whisk together in a large bowl **¼ c. vinegar, ¼ c. Chinese sesame oil, 2 Tb. honey, 3 Tb. tamari, ½ t. fresh ginger,** grated, **1 clove garlic** cut in half. Set aside.

2) Peel **2 bunches broccoli stems.** Discard the hard bottom of each stem. Slice the stems crosswise into thin rounds. (A food processor slicer works well for this.) Steam the sliced stems briefly so they remain crisp.

3) Put broccoli into bowl with dressing. Toss and discard garlic pieces. Add **½ c.** sliced **mushrooms** and **½ c.** slivered **almonds.** Mix again and chill.

4) Serve on a bed of **lettuce** (we prefer Boston). A little shredded **carrot** on top adds color and sweetness.

Serves 6

ARUGALA SALAD

Arugala or rocquette (rocket) is an easily grown herb in the
cress family. If sown early in the spring with radishes, both
will mature in about 25–30 days. As soon as flower buds
show it becomes too bitter to eat. Lacking a garden, you
may find arugala for sale in Italian markets.

1) You will need a small bunch of **arugala** for each diner.
   Wash it well and combine with **other greens** or not, as
   you prefer, on each plate. Slice **radishes** over.

2) Make a garlic dressing by combining in a screw cap jar,
   1 c. olive oil, ¼ c. wine vinegar, 1 clove crushed
   garlic, 1 Tb. prepared mustard. Add **1 t. salt** and
   pepper to taste. Pour over salads and serve at once.

Yields enough dressing for 6–8 salads

And so we've got to fight back!
In large numbers
Fight back!
I can't make it alone
Together we can make a safe home.

"Fight Back"
Imagine My Surprise!
Holly Near; Redwood Records

NEW POTATOES WITH RACLETTE

You will have to locate raclette cheese. It is a strong flavored hard cheese from Switzerland and should be available at a well-stocked cheese store. Raclette is traditionally done by placing a wheel of cheese next to an open fire and scraping off melting portions onto potatoes as an appetizer. In recent years an expensive machine has been merchandised to melt the raclette at the table. However, the broiler in your stove works just as well, and we like raclette enough to want to make a dinner of it.

1) For each diner, scrub **4–5 new potatoes** (red bliss or golden), peel and cut into sticks **1 carrot,** and separate **broccoli flowerets** to provide **3 small** ones for each person. Steam the vegetables until barely done. We use a tiered steamer purchased in a Chinese hardware store. Set vegetables aside.

2) Use a cheese plane to cut thin slices from a **½ lb. piece** of **raclette cheese.** Preheat broiler. Arrange the vegetables in a shallow pan, top with raclette and grill until cheese melts and turns light brown. Serve at once, with **cornichons** or other small sweet pickles.

*Those who lie in the arms of the "individual solution,"
the "private odyssey," the "personal growth,"
are the most conformist of all. . .*

"Monster"
Monster
Robin Morgan; Vintage

ARTICHOKES
STUFFED WITH SCALLOPS

A rich and delicious combination; this dish is definitely fingerfood.

1) Gently cook **1¼ lb. sea scallops** in **⅓ c. dry white wine** with **1 bay leaf.** Don't overcook. When barely done, turn off heat and remove from burner. Let the scallops finish cooking in the hot wine another minute or two. Then remove lid.

2) Clean **¼ lb. mushrooms.** Quarter and stew, covered, in **½ c. water.**

3) Melt **3 Tb. butter.** Add **¼ c. flour** and stir together until well blended. Add **¼ c. milk** and scallop liquid, reserving the scallops separately. Use whisk to stir mixture until it comes to a simmer. Add **⅓ t. dried tarragon,** crumbled, and a **pinch thyme.** Add **salt** and **pepper** to taste and **1–1½ t. lemon juice.** Stir and taste for seasoning.

4) In a small bowl, whisk together **2 egg yolks** and **¼ c. heavy cream.** Slowly add hot sauce to yolks, stirring carefully so that yolks do not curdle. Now add mushrooms with their liquid. If scallops are large, cut them into pieces and combine with sauce. If sauce seems too thick, thin with a little cream. Let cool.

5) Cut off the stems and the top inch from **8 large artichokes.** Snip pointed tips from remaining leaves. Cook artichokes in boiling water to cover until they are just done (you can tell by pulling out a leaf and tasting it to see if it is tender). Remove from water with tongs and let cool until you can handle the artichokes. You may want to boil down the liquid and save it for Artichoke Mushroom Soup (see recipe index).

6) Pull out some of the central leaves of each artichoke and use a pointed tea spoon to scoop out the choke. Discard the choke. When artichokes are quite cool, they can be carefully filled with several tablespoons of scallops and sauce and refrigerated. There should be some scallops and sauce remaining.

7) Cook **2½ c. long grain white rice** in **4 c. water** until barely done, about 15 minutes. Taste to be sure and add more water if necessary. Add **2 t. salt** and **3 Tb. butter.**

8) To reheat artichokes, place in a steamer (or a colander in a pot big enough to hold it) over boiling water and simmer about 15 minutes. The remaining scallops and sauce can be heated gently in a small pot and served over the rice.

Serves 8

SPINACH AND MUSHROOM CREPES WITH BEARNAISE SAUCE

Crepes are green, mushrooms are brown and sauce is golden.

1) It is easiest using **frozen chopped spinach** for this recipe. Defrost **4 lb.** of it.

2) Make crepe batter: In a blender, combine **1 c. flour, ½ c. milk, ½ c. water, 2 eggs, 2 egg yolks, ½ stick butter,** melted, and **¾ t. salt.** Puree thoroughly. Add about ½ lb. of the defrosted spinach, or enough to color the batter quite green. Puree again. Chill batter in the refrigerator for at least one hour before making crepes.

3) Make spinach and mushroom filling: Finely chop **3 c. mushrooms,** with their stems, and **1 medium onion.** (Both can be chopped most efficiently in a food processor). Use a large frying pan to saute mushrooms and onions in **6 Tb. butter** until they have dried out and are beginning to brown. Add **2 Tb. lemon juice, 12 oz. light beer** and **⅓ c. heavy cream.** Simmer 5 minutes. Drain remaining spinach of excess liquid (reserving it) and add to pan. Add **1½ c.** grated **gruyere or Swiss cheese** and stir well together. Dissolve **1½ Tb. cornstarch** in **¼ c. spinach juice** and add to pan. Bring to a simmer, stirring constantly. Turn off heat and season mixture with **salt, pepper, nutmeg,** and a **dash Tabasco.** Add more **lemon juice** if needed. Cool. Add **2** beaten **eggs.**

4) It is necessary to use a crepe pan (preferably three of them) to make crepes. See blintze recipe. Wipe out a heated crepe pan with an oiled piece of absorbent paper and make a sample crepe. If it is too thick, add equal amounts of milk and water to batter and mix thoroughly, so that crepes come out thin and delicate. This recipe should produce about 20 crepes, so you will have extra batter for mistakes.

5) Using a butter knife, smear filling over each crepe and roll up loosely. There will be filling enough for about 18 crepes. Arrange in a baking dish, cover and refrigerate until ready to serve.

6) Make **Bearnaise Sauce:** Combine in a small pot **½ c. white wine vinegar, ½ c. dry white wine, ¼ c. shallots,** chopped, **4 small cloves garlic,** unpeeled, **1 bay leaf,** a **pinch** each **dried thyme** and **tarragon.** Bring to a boil and simmer until liquid is reduced to ¼ c. Strain into a measuring cup when you think it is about right, and boil down again if necessary. In a separate small pan, melt **2 sticks butter.** In a stainless steel pot place **6 egg yolks.** Whisk in the reduced and strained wine mixture. Whisk over gentle heat until foamy and slightly thickened. Turn off heat and add melted butter slowly until sauce thickens like a hollandaise. Season to taste with **salt** and **2 Tb.** chopped fresh **tarragon.** Cover to keep warm. Don't try to reheat sauce.

7) Slice ½ **lb. large mushrooms.** Chop **1 small onion.**
   Fry both in **2 Tb. butter** over high heat until the
   mushrooms give up their liquid and brown nicely. **Salt**
   them, and add **3 Tb. port wine.** Turn out into a bowl
   and cover.

8) To serve, preheat oven to 400° and heat crepes for
   10–15 minutes or till light brown. Top with port
   flavored mushrooms for the last few minutes of heating.
   Spoon bearnaise over the top and bring casserole dish
   to the table with the rest of the bearnaise in a sauceboat.
   This makes an elegant dinner. Serve with a salad.

Serves 6–8

As you know from your own experience . . .the
daughters . . . have always done their thinking from
hand to mouth; not under green lamps at study
tables in the cloisters of secluded colleges. They
have thought while they stirred the pot, while they
rocked the cradle . . . Let us never cease from
thinking—what is this 'civilization' in which we find
ourselves? What are these ceremonies and why
should we take part in them? What are these
professions and why should we make money out of
them? Where in short is it leading us, the procession
of the sons of educated men?

Three Guineas
Virginia Woolf; Harcourt, Brace, & World

GRILLED MA-PO TOFU AND RICE

1) Soak **5 dried Chinese mushrooms** in hot water to cover. Separately soak **1 Tb. fermented black beans** in **water** for a few minutes. Drain and chop. Cut **1 large green pepper** in thin slivers. Also cut up **4 scallions** into halves and then into ¾" pieces. Peel **3 cloves garlic.** Drain mushrooms, reserving liquid, discard tough stems and slice.

2) Use **1 Tb. peanut oil** and **1 t. sesame oil** to stir fry mushrooms, peppers, and crushed garlic. When light brown, turn off heat and add fermented black beans, **2½ Tb. tamari, 1 Tb. miso, 1 Tb. hoisin sauce, 2 t. chili paste with garlic, 2 Tb. dry sherry, 1½ Tb. tomato paste** and the reserved mushroom liquid. (Be careful not to add any grit from the bottom of the bowl.) Simmer until slightly thickened and then add **1½ Tb. rice wine vinegar** and enough **water** until consistency seems right.

3) Prepare brown rice: Simmer **2½ c. brown rice** (we prefer short grain) in **4½ c. water** for about one hour or until tender. Add more water if necessary if rice seems too hard and liquid is all gone; add **salt** to taste.

4) Split **4 large pieces** of **tofu** in half diagonally, making
   a large triangle; then cut each triangle in half horizontally
   making a thinner triangle. Put **1 Tb. sesame oil** in a
   pan and turn tofu pieces in the oil to coat. Slice **4
   scallions** thinly. Set aside.

5) Preheat broiler. Grill tofu pieces until bubbly on one
   side only. Make a ring of brown rice on a dish. Lift out 2
   pieces of grilled tofu and place at center of dish, point to
   point, resembling a butterfly in shape. Spoon some
   sauce over the top, sprinkle with scallions and
   gomahsio (see recipe index), if desired.

Serves 8

eat rice have faith in women
what I dont know now
I can still learn
if I am alone now
I will be with them later
if I am weak now
I can become strong
slowly slowly
if I learn I can teach others
if others learn first
I must believe
they will come back and teach me
they will not go away
to the country with their knowledge
and send me a letter sometime
we must study all our lives

women coming from women going to women
trying to do all we can with words
then trying to work with tools
or with our bodies
trying to stand the time it takes
reading books when there are no teachers
or they are too far away
teaching ourselves
imagining others struggling
I must believe we will be together
and build enough concern
so when I have to fight alone
there will be sisters who
would help if they knew
sisters who will come
to support me later
giving back what was taken away
our right to the control of our bodies
knowledge of how to fight and build
food that nourishes
medicine that heals
songs that remind us of ourselves
and make us want to keep on with
what matters to us
lets come out again
joining women coming out
for the first time
knowing this love makes
a good difference in us
affirming a continuing life with women
we must be lovers doctors soldiers
artists mechanics farmers
all our lives
waves of women
trembling with love and anger

singing we must rage
kissing, turn and
break the old society
without becoming the names it praises
the minds it pays

eat rice have faith in women
what I dont know now
I can still learn
slowly slowly
if I learn I can teach others
if others learn first
I must believe
they will come back and teach me

"Eat Rice Have Faith In Women"
Dyke Jacket
Fran Winant; Violet Press

COTTAGE CHEESE BLINTZES

This recipe from Fay Davidson make a lot, but if you like them, you will want them for breakfast as well as for dinner.

1) Make **Crepe Batter:** In blender or mixer, beat together thoroughly; **4 eggs, ½ t. salt, 1 c. milk** and **1 c.** plus **2 Tb. unbleached white flour.** (You will also need **1 c. water,** but if you are using a blender you may not have room to add it and still mix batter thoroughly. Scrape sides down and be sure batter is smooth; then add water.) Chill batter at least one hour.

2) Meanwhile, combine in bowl **2½ lb. farmer cheese** with **1½ lb. creamed cottage cheese, 5 eggs** (unbeaten), **⅓–½ c. sugar, grated rind** of **2 lemons** and **salt.** Mix well and taste for salt and sugar.

3) You must have a crepe pan to make the blintze crepes; preferably you should have 3 pans to make 3 at a time. (These pans are like omelet pans in that they require seasoning: heat slowly over low heat for 15 minutes with a tablespoon of oil. Then use absorbent paper to wipe out oil. Never use the pans for anything but crepes or omelets.) When ready to make the crepes, heat the pans till a drop of water dances on the pan. Wipe pan lightly with a little oil on absorbent paper. Try out one crepe by pouring batter into pan and immediately returning excess to pitcher. Crepe should be thin. If it is not thin enough, add equal parts **milk** and **water.** It takes practice to make good crepes. Once crepe has

started to curl away from the pan, use a spatula to loosen it and then your fingers to turn it over to cook lightly on the other side. Don't overcook or crepes will be brittle. Turn crepe out and repeat. No need to add any oil or fat of any kind. Stack crepes as they are completed.

4) Fill each crepe with a large spoonful of filling. Make rectangular packages by folding 2 sides over, then 2 ends. Store on tray (covered) in refrigerator until ready to serve.

5) To serve, heat **2 Tb. sweet butter** in a large fry pan until hot. Place 4 blintzes at a time in hot butter and fry till brown on one side. Carefully turn over to brown other side. Serve immediately. Allow 4 blintzes per person. Serve with **sour cream** and a bowl of fresh sliced **strawberries.**

Serves 8–10

Fathers at the beginning of consciousness were only brothers. Just as they still are until the child reaches an age of acculturation and is "taught" who her "real father" is. In reality there is no "real father." There is only a real mother. The fiction of fatherhood is a giant religion called christianity.

Lesbian Nation
Jill Johnston; Simon and Schuster

RHUBARB CUSTARD PIE

From Beatrice Beaven.

1) Preheat oven to 400.° Prepare **pie crust** (see recipe index) and roll out enough to line 1 pie pan with enough left over to cut into lattice strips for the top. Line pan with pastry, prick at juncture of rim and bottom. Top with foil and dried beans to weight the crust, and bake 5 minutes. Remove from oven and remove foil and beans. Turn oven heat to 450.°

2) Slice **7 large stalks** of **rhubarb** (3 c.) thinly. Set aside.

3) In a bowl, beat **4 eggs** until foamy with a whisk. Add **¼ c. flour, 1⅓ c. sugar, ¼ t. salt, 1 t. vanilla extract,** and beat thoroughly.

4) Turn rhubarb into prebaked pie shell, top with custard, and arrange lattice strips on top. Bake at 450° for 15 to 20 minutes, then at 350° until pie seems "set" when jiggled (about 30 minutes). Best served warm.

as if the moon and you and I were slivers
of one mirror, gazing on herself at last.

"A Ceremony"
Lady of the Beasts
Robin Morgan; Random House

COEUR A LA CREME

1) Optional: Make **Creme Fraiche** by heating **1½ c. heavy cream** with **2 Tb. buttermilk** until just warm. Turn into a screw cap jar and leave in the sun or a warm place for 8–12 hours or until thickened. Sometimes this won't happen until overnight. Chill.

2) Soften **8 oz. cream cheese.** Push **6 oz. pot cheese** through a strainer into a mixer. Add softened cream cheese, **½ t. vanilla extract, pinch salt, 6 Tb. confectioner's sugar** (or 3 Tb. honey) and beat well together. Turn out into bowl.

3) Whip **1½ c. heavy cream** until stiff. Fold into cheese mixture. Rinse out **cheese cloth** and line small ceramic heart shaped molds, small baskets, or a large oval basket with a double layer of the cheesecloth. Add the cheese-whipped cream mixture to the mold(s) and refrigerate on a tray. Excess moisture will drip out.

4) Strain ¾ **c. honey sweetened raspberry preserves** into a small pot. Add ¼ **c. dry sherry** and cook for about 5 minutes until blended and slightly thickened. Cool. Slice **1 pt. fresh strawberries** and pour jam-sherry mix over them. Chill.

5) Turn out cheese mixture from molds onto individual plates or onto a large serving dish. Spoon strawberry sauce over the "hearts of cream" and serve Creme Fraiche in a sauceboat.

Serves 8

STRAWBERRIES ISABEL

1) In the top of a double boiler or in a stainless steel bowl that will fit on a pot snugly, place **5 egg yolks** and **¼ c. honey.** Put enough water in bottom pot to last 10–15 minutes without touching upper bowl.

2) Beat or stir constantly with whisk over low-medium heat until sauce becomes quite thick and sticks to the side of the bowl. This takes about 10 minutes.

3) Remove from heat and add a **scant ½ c. Grand Marnier liqueur,** whisking until well blended. Refrigerate until sauce is very cold.

4) Whip **1 c. heavy cream** stiff and fold into sauce.

5) Hull and slice **strawberries** into glass dessert dishes. Top each serving with two spoonfuls of sauce.

Yields enough sauce to serve 6–8

Ma, can I be a feminist and still like men?
Sure . . . . Just like you can
be a vegetarian,
and like fried
chicken.

Nicole Hollander; St. Martin's Press

STRAWBERRIES ROMANOFF

1) Mix together ½ **c.** fresh squeezed **orange juice,** ⅓ **c. Grand Marnier liqueur** and **1 Tb. honey** in a bowl. Slice **2 pt.** fresh local **strawberries** into this mixture and refrigerate until ready to serve.

2) Beat **2 c. heavy cream** until stiff. Fold strawberries and liquids into whipped cream. Serve at once.

Serves 6–8

But feminism is a political term and it must be recognized as such: it is political in women's terms. What are these terms? Essentially it means making connections: between personal power and economic power, between domestic oppression and labor exploitation, between plants and chemicals, feelings and theories; it means making connections between our inside worlds and the outside world.

Feminism As Therapy
Anica Vesel Mander and Anne Kent Rush; Random House

FRESH STRAWBERRY SUNDAE

1) Fill blender ⅔ full of decapped **strawberries,** about **1½ pints.** Add good **fruit juice** (we use L & A apple-boysenberry) to come half way up the height of the berries. Puree. Add **2 Tb. Kirsch** (a liqueur) and puree again. Add **sugar** or **honey** only if needed. Turn out into a container and slice **1 c.** fresh **strawberries** into the sauce. Refrigerate.

2) Beat **1½ c. heavy cream** stiff with **1 Tb. honey** and ½ **t. vanilla extract.**

3) Serve bowls of **ice cream** with strawberry sauce and whipped cream over each one.

Serves 6–8

When I started my search for the women who've made it within the corporation system, I found that hen's teeth weren't scarce at all. Women were. And it's not merely that women are scarce. It's that women in a position of power are practically nonexistent.

Jane Trahey on Women & Power
Jane Trahey; Avon

STRAWBERRY WHIP CREAM ROLL

1) Preheat oven to 375°. Place **4 eggs,** in their shells, in a bowl and cover with hot tap water. This is to warm them so that when beaten, they will achieve a high volume.

2) Break eggs into mixer. Add ¼ **t. salt, 1 t. baking powder** and begin beating at top speed. Slowly add ¾ **c. sugar** and **1 t. vanilla extract** and beat until eggs are tripled in bulk, around 10 minutes.

3) Meanwhile butter a jelly roll pan and line it with waxed paper.

4) Remove mixer bowl from machine. Sift ¾ **c. flour** (unbleached white) over eggs and carefully fold flour and egg mix together. Turn into pan, smoothing top gently with spatula, and bake 10–15 minutes or until light brown.

5) Prepare a dish towel the size of the pan by sifting **confectioner's sugar** over it. Turn cake out onto towel and peel off waxed paper in strips. Roll up cake in towel and lift onto racks to cool.

6) Slice **2 c. strawberries.** Set aside. In mixer beat **1½ c. heavy cream,** scant ¼ **c. sugar** and ½ **t. vanilla extract** until stiff.

7) Unroll cooled cake. Use a rubber spatula to spread
   whipped cream over cake. Distribute strawberries over
   the whipped cream. Reroll cake and chill until serving
   time. Slice and serve.

Serves 8–10

*By the mid-twentieth century the experts were
grimly acknowledging that despite their constant
vigilance the American mother was failing at her job.
There was only one person to turn to now, and that
was the long-neglected father. . . . But as the experts
made abundantly clear, Dad was not being called
home just to "help out." He was needed to protect
the children, especially the sons.*

For Her Own Good
150 Years Of The Experts' Advice to Women
Barbara Ehrenreich and Deirdre English; Doubleday

BANANA OATMEAL MUFFINS

1) Preheat oven to 425°.

2) Butter muffin tins or line with papers.

3) In a large bowl mix together (whisk works well)
   **1 c. oatmeal flakes, 1½ c. unbleached white
   flour, 1½ t. baking powder, ¾ t. baking soda,
   ½ t. salt.**

4) Cream together thoroughly ¾ **stick sweet butter** and
   ½ **c. sugar.** Break into chunks **2 small ripe bananas**
   and add them to the creamed mixture. Beat well. Then
   beat in **2 eggs,** one at a time, and **1 t. vanilla.**

5) Quickly stir together dry ingredients, creamed mixture,
   scant 1 c. buttermilk, and **1 c. walnuts,** chopped.
   Don't overmix.

6) Spoon into muffin tins and bake at 425° until the
   muffins have risen (about 10 min.). Turn the oven
   down to 400° and continue baking until light brown.

Yields 12 muffins

ONION CHEESE BREAD

From Pat Croner.

1) Preheat oven to 400°. Butter a square baking pan
   8" x 8". Melt **2 Tb. sweet butter.** Set aside.

2) Chop **1½ c. onion** and saute gently in **2 Tb. butter.**
   Grate **1–1½ c. cheddar cheese.**

3) Beat **1 egg** in a bowl, add **1½ c. milk** and mix
   together. In a separate bowl, mix together **2 c. flour,
   2 t. sugar, 1½ t. salt, 2½ t. baking powder.** A dry
   whisk works well.

4) Stir together onions, milk and egg, flour mix and ½ c. of
   the grated cheese. Turn into prepared pan and top with
   remaining cheese. Sprinkle top with **¼ c. grated
   parmesan.** Drizzle melted butter over top and sprinkle
   with **2 Tb. poppy seed.**

5) Bake 20 minutes, until puffed and browned. Serve hot
   with soup and salad. This quick bread is also good party
   food.

Serves 9

MAY WINE

From Nancy Gilchrist.

1) To make May Wine, you will need **sweet woodruff,**
   asperula odorata. It is a perennial herb easy to grow in
   semi-shade and in rich humusy soil. It is difficult in full
   sun and in dry or windy places. If you find a good spot
   for it, you will find it a lovely ground cover.

2) In May, cut the new growth (including the flowers).
   Open a bottle of **California Rhine Wine** and push in
   as much woodruff as you can. Close the bottle and chill
   overnight.

3) Strain wine into glasses and add a **strawberry slice** to
   each glass. You can keep May Wine in the refrigerator
   for up to a week. It is thought that woodruff has the
   effect of releasing the alcohol more rapidly into the
   bloodstream, so be careful how much you drink!

We don't have time for centuries of slow evolution.
The specter of computer-rule is all too near. And
women have waited long enough.

I Dream In Female
Barbara Starrett; Cassandra

STRAWBERRY YOGHURT SHAKE

1) Fill blender half full with decapped **strawberries,**
   about **2 c.** Add **1 c. fruit juice,** such as L & A
   apple-boysenberry. Add ½ **t. almond extract** and
   ½ **t. vanilla extract.** Puree.

2) Pour fruit and juice puree into a serving pitcher and stir
   in **2 pt. plain yoghurt.** Add **honey** to taste.

Serves 6–8

*She walked home. Though her face was angry and
defiant, she understood that her new
independence had left her vulnerable. Before, she
would always turn to the nearest man for
protection. Now she knew that she could turn to
them no longer. With the slightest twist in situation
or character or mood, she was not a damsel in
distress, but just another piece of ass.*

Seed Of A Woman
Ruth Geller; Imp Press

CHAPTER 6   **EARLY SUMMER**
Summer Solstice, June 22, to August 2.

HOT AND SOUR SOUP WITH WILD DAYLILY BUDS

1) Collect **1 qt. wild daylily buds.** Be sure you know what they are. Snap off buds without the stems.

2) Soak **½ c. dried "tree ears"** (a dried mushroom available in Chinese markets) in boiling water.

3) Shred **¼ red cabbage** and quarter and slice **1 summer squash.** Stir fry these vegetables in **2 Tb. sesame oil*** in fry pan.

4) Meanwhile, in large soup pot, bring **2½ qt. water** to a boil. Add **⅓ c. tamari** or well aged soy sauce and **¼ c. rice wine vinegar** (or 2 Tb. cider vinegar). Add fried vegetables and oil to broth with the daylily buds. Rinse tree ears, squeeze and tear apart. Pull off wood and dirt. When clean, add to soup pot. Simmer till vegetables taste done. Don't overcook.

5) Stir together **¼ c. cornstarch** and **½ c. water.** Add to simmering soup. Dice **1 large cake** of **tofu** and add it. Taste for seasoning. Soup will need dilution with water if it tastes too strong or sour, and it may need more tamari or salt. To make it spicy, add **1 t. chili paste with garlic** (can be gotten in Chinese markets) and add **2 Tb. Chinese sesame oil.**

6) If you can get them, roast **2 Tb. Szechuan pepper corns** in a hot dry skillet and then grind with mortar and pestle or in blender. Garnish each serving with **1 t. sesame oil, 2 Tb. chopped scallions,** and a sprinkle of Szechuan pepper.

* Sesame oil from health food stores is not an appropriate substitution for Chinese sesame oil.

"Once upon a time," began Bessie, "there was one rape too many . . ."
"The earth finally said 'no.' There was no storm, no earthquake, no tidal wave or volcanic eruption, no specific moment to mark its happening. It only became apparent that it had happened, and that it had happened everywhere."

The Wanderground
Sally Miller Gearhart; Persephone Press

CHILLED CUCUMBER SOUP

1) Peel and cut large seeds out of **12 cucumbers.** If cucumbers are not waxed because you have grown them yourself or they are sold for pickling, you need not peel them. Squeeze **juice** from **3 lemons.** Combine cut up cucumbers and lemon juice in a blender or food processor and puree coarsely. Pour into container.

2) Finely chop **2 c. fresh tomatoes** using a large heavy knife. Chop **1 Tb. fresh basil leaves** and **2 Tb. fresh garlic leaves** (or **1 small clove garlic,** crushed, or if you have **pesto,** you may use **2 Tb.** of it) and add to the container. Chop enough **scallions** to make **1 c.** and add. Chop **3 green peppers.** Add to the container together with **2 c. plain yoghurt.** Stir all together. If soup seems too thick, add more yoghurt. Add **salt** and fresh ground **pepper** to taste and chill thoroughly.

Serves 8

The moon is the ruler of the Sybil and the Sybil is the sister of the moon. All plants relating to waterbearing such as the melons, gourds, squashes, and cucumbers are the province of this card, as are the lettuces, the lotus, cresses, willows, mallows, and plants that alter mind states and consciousness: the opium poppy, the mescal cactus. Vervain, the "tears of Isis" is also called forth by this card.

A New Women's Tarot
Billie Potts; Elf and Dragons Press

CURRIED ZUCCINI SOUP

From Elaine Raskin.

1) Wash and trim **5 medium zuccini.** Cut up coarsely into pot. Add **1 large Spanish onion** and **1 seeded green pepper,** both coarsely chopped. Add **3 c. water, 1½ t. curry powder** and bring to a boil.

2) When vegetables are soft, puree in food processor or blender. Add **1 c. heavy cream, ½ c. milk, 2 c. plain yoghurt, 3 Tb. tamari** or soy, **¼ t. ground coriander, ½ t. turmeric,** and a **small bunch** of **straight leafed parsley,** chopped by hand. Taste for seasoning. Chill. Serve cold garnished with matchstick strips of **zuccini** and a dollop of **yoghurt,** if desired.

Serves about 8

The sun is three-quarters, I have become hungry . . . I head for the garden and prowl through it, then squat, wrapped in my blanket. I eat the green peas out of their shells and the raw yellow beans, I scrape the carrots from the earth with my fingers, . . . There is one late strawberry, I find it among the matted weeds and suckers. Red foods, heart color, they are the best kind, they are sacred; then yellow, then blue; green foods are mixed from blue and yellow.

Surfacing
Margaret Atwood; Popular Library

CARROT SOUP

From Sonja Bay.

1) Peel and chop **1 bunch carrots** and **1 large Spanish onion** by hand or in food processor. Saute in soup pot in **1¼ sticks sweet butter.** When vegetables start to stick to bottom of pot it will be necessary to stir and scrape often. Brown well (this is the secret to this soup), but do not burn.

2) When vegetables are quite brown, barely cover with **water,** add ¼ t. **ground cloves** and simmer, covered, until very tender.

3) Remove from heat and puree mixture in blender or food processor, with ¼ **c. flour** and ⅔ **c. heavy cream.**

4) Return to pot. Add **1⅓ c. buttermilk** and **2⅔ c. milk.** If soup seems too thick, add water. Add **fresh ground pepper, 1 t. salt** and simmer, covered, for 10 minutes.

5) Add the **juice** of ½ **lemon,** ½ t. fresh **rosemary,** chopped (optional) and **1 Tb.** fresh **dill,** chopped. Herbs must be fresh.

6) Taste and judge whether more salt and/or lemon is desired.

Serves 8

CHILLED AVOCADO SOUP

1) Peel **2 small avocados,** discard seeds and place in a blender. Add **½ c. heavy cream** and puree. Turn out into a tall narrow container.

2) Make a cold "broth" by mixing **3 c. cold water** with **1 Tb. tamari.** Add to avocado puree and taste for **salt.** Chill at least 2 hours.

3) Dice **2 medium fresh tomatoes** and finely chop **5 scallions.**

4) Stir soup to disperse any discoloration on top. Stir in tomatoes and scallions. Serve immediately.

Serves 6

FRUIT SALAD & CREAMY DRESSING

1) Prepare dressing first. In a food processor or mixer combine **2 egg yolks, 1 Tb. lemon juice, ½ t. salt.** Turn machine on and add **1 c. vegetable oil,** drop by drop at first and, as mayonnaise thickens, in a slow dribble. When oil is entirely incorporated, let machine run another 15 seconds and turn off. Add **⅓ c. sour cream** and **1 Tb. honey.** Turn machine on briefly to mix again and then taste for sweet, sour and salt. Refrigerate until ready to use.

2) For each diner, place a **single leaf** of **Boston** or **red tip lettuce** on a dinner plate. Cut a **wedge** of **Cranshaw melon** into bite sized pieces on the lettuce. Cut **½ dozen red grapes** in half lengthwise and remove seeds with knife tip. Cut a **small wedge** of **pineapple,** remove skin and core and cut into pieces on the salad.

3) Serve each salad with a dollop of dressing and pass extra in a bowl.

Yields about 1½ cups dressing

We have lost our wings.
A glass dome has closed around us.
We have traded our eyes for mirrors.

The Return Of The Great Mother
Roberta Kosse and Jenny Malmquist;
Ars Pro Femina

LENTIL SALAD

1) Prepare lentil sprouts 3 days in advance.*

2) Finely chop **1 c. carrots** and **1 small onion.** Bring to a boil **2½ c. water** and add the carrots, onion, **1 c. lentils, ½ t. dry thyme, 1 t. salt.** Simmer ½ hour until tender. Drain if any liquid remains.

3) Spread out in a bowl and add ¼ **c. olive oil** and **1½ t. lemon juice.** Toss and let cool.

4) When cool, mix in **1** or **2** small **tomatoes,** diced. Taste for **salt** and **pepper.**

5) To serve, pile lentil salad on bed of **lettuce** and sprinkle generously with **lentil sprouts, red onion rings** and **avocado slices,** if desired.

* **Lentil sprouts:** (this procedure can be applied to any sprouts). Put 2 to 3 Tb. lentils in a good sprouting jar. Canning jars are ideal; however, any jar which can be covered with plastic screening and turned upside down is okay. Cover with water. Let soak an hour or more and then drain. Find suitable dark spot which will allow air, and place jar upside down. Sprouts should be rinsed with water twice a day and returned to their dark spot to drain and grow. When sprouted (after 3 days), they should be refrigerated.

SNOW PEA SALAD WITH TOFU SAUCE

Tofu Sauce recipe from Betty Ann Patsenka.

1) Heat **1 Tb. sesame oil** and **1 Tb. cooking oil** in a large frying pan. Add **2–3 c. sugar snap** or other **snow peas** to the pan and stir and turn peas for no more than 30 seconds over very high heat. Turn out into a bowl. Add **¼ c. tamari, ¼ c. rice wine vinegar** (or 3 Tb. regular vinegar), **1 t. salt, 2 Tb.** chopped **garlic leaves** (or a small clove garlic, crushed), and **½ t. Szechuan peppercorns,** crushed, if available. Chill.

2) Put **2 tofu cakes** in a blender. Add **3 Tb. lemon juice, ¼ c. tamari** and a few sprigs of fresh herbs. We use **1–2 small leaves** of **lovage, 8 stalks burnet** and **1 medium comfrey leaf.** Puree, and taste. Add lemon juice and tamari as needed to make sauce sour and salty.

3) Arrange **lettuce** on dinner plates. Top with marinated snow peas and spoon some marinade over the salad. Also add a little **vinaigrette** to the lettuce. Top with the tofu sauce and, if you grow it, a leaf of **mitsuba** (Japanese parsley). A sprinkle of **gomahsio** (see recipe index) finishes the salad.

Serves 6–8

GREEK SALAD

This salad requires access to a market which sells Greek products.

1) For each diner arrange on a bed of **lettuce** (Boston preferred) **2–3 slices** of **fresh tomato,** a few **calamata olives, 2 salonika peppers,** a few slices **celery hearts, feta cheese** cut into thin slices and some thin slices of **red onion.**

2) Drizzle on a vinaigrette of **3½ parts oil** to **1 part fresh lemon juice, salt, pepper** and some **dried oregano.**

> *. . . I am the one allowed in*
>
> *to the royal chambers, whose small foot conveniently fills the slipper of glass. The woman writer, the lady umpire, the madam chairman, anyone's wife.*
>
> *"Cinderella"*
> ***Beginning With O***
> *Olga Broumas; Yale University Press*

STROZZAPRETI

Italian Swiss chard dumplings so tasty that the priest choked on them—strozzapreti means priestchokers! You will need some good homemade tomato sauce for this.

1) Wash **1 large** bunch **Swiss chard.** You will need about **2 lb.** or a little less than **3 c.** once it is cooked. Cook it in the **water** that clings to the leaves. Drain, cool, and squeeze dry. It is easiest to use a food processor here, however a blender or even chopping by hand with a heavy knife will do. Puree the chard adding **3 eggs** (if using a machine) or beat the eggs by hand and add to finely chopped chard. Melt **⅔ stick butter** and add with **1 c. parmesan** and **1–1½ c. bread crumbs.** Add **salt** and **pepper** to taste. Chill.

2) Make **Tomato Sauce:** In a large pot heat **¼ c. olive oil.** Finely chop **2 medium onions** and saute together with **½ t. red pepper flakes** (optional). Saute slowly; don't let it burn. Add **2 cloves garlic,** crushed, and **1 small can tomato paste** and cook, stirring with a wooden spoon, until the paste is dry and thick. Using tomato paste can, add **1 can water** and cook again slowly, stirring often, until sauce thickens. Now add a **3 lb. can Italian plum tomatoes.** Break up the tomatoes somewhat with your wooden spoon. Add several leaves of fresh **basil,** or **2 t.** dried. Simmer partly covered for at least one hour. Taste for salt. Some canned tomatoes are very salty. Add **salt** if necessary, **pepper** to taste. Leftover tomato sauce can be frozen.

3) When ready to serve, fill a large pot ⅓ full of **water;** add
   1 Tb. salt and bring to a boil. Turn heat down to a
   simmer. Test one dumpling to see if it holds together in
   the poaching liquid. If not, stir in more **bread crumbs.**
   The point is, of course, to keep them as light as possible
   and not have them fall apart. When batter is perfect,
   poach about 5 dumplings per serving using 2 spoons to
   shape ovals. Drain on paper towel before placing in
   shallow soup bowl. Sprinkle with fresh grated
   parmesan and serve tomato sauce on the side.

Serves 8–10

*The men have made quite an industry of pictures,
moving and still, that depict the torture of women
. . . . And I hate it that everywhere I turn, people
seem to accept without question this false notion of
freedom. Freedom to do what to whom? Freedom
to torture me? That's not freedom for me . . . . And
that leads to a terrible recognition: if pornography is
part of male freedom, then that freedom is not
reconcilable with my freedom. If his freedom is to
torture, then in those terms my freedom must be to
be tortured. That's insane.*

"Nervous Interview"
Andrea Dworkin
Chyrsalis: a magazine of women's culture
No. 10, 1980

SZECHUAN NOODLES

A trip to a Chinese market is necessary to make this dish.
You will need to buy the fresh noodles, Chinese sesame oil,
chili paste with garlic and sesame paste in small jars, a small
can of hot pickled turnip, and rice wine vinegar. You will
also need fermented black beans if you are doing the
eggplant accompaniment.

1) Purchase fresh noodles in a Chinese market. Store in
   refrigerator for a few days, or freeze for longer periods of
   time. To cook, use a large pot and a lot of water. When it
   boils, add **3 lb. fresh Chinese noodles.** Watch very
   carefully to be sure noodles don't overcook. Turn out
   and rinse with cold water. Shake well, and turn into
   large tray or bowl. Add ½ **c. sesame oil** and mix
   noodles and oil together thoroughly.

2) Make spicy sauce. Open a **small can hot pickled
   turnip** and very finely chop ½ of it. Place in a small
   bowl. Add **6–7 scallions,** chopped, **3 cloves garlic,**
   crushed, **4 Tb. chili paste with garlic,** and ⅓ **c.
   tamari** or soy sauce. Add **3 Tb. rice wine vinegar**
   and ¾ **Tb. honey.** Stir well together. Don't taste;
   this sauce is very hot!

3) Make **Sesame Sauce:** Make a **cup** of **tea** and let it
   cool. Turn out **1 jar** of **Chinese sesame paste** into a
   bowl and thin with cooled tea until syrupy. Add
   1–2 Tb. sesame oil. Add **soy sauce** to taste. This
   sauce should be thin.

4) Add about half the spicy sauce and half the cooling sesame sauce to the noodles and mix well together. Taste. Add **soy sauce** if necessary. Cover and chill.

5) Put chilled noodles on dinner plates. Top with chopped **scallions** and offer remaining spicy sauce and sesame sauce separately for each diner to add. Serve with dishes of **Eggplant in Black Bean Sauce** (following recipe).

Serves 8

EGGPLANT IN BLACK BEAN SAUCE

1) Peel and slice **1 eggplant** and cut into strips 4″ long by ½″ thick and ½″ wide. In large fry pan, fry the strips in **3 Tb. oil** over high heat until tender and cooked. Turn out into bowl.

2) Cut **3 scallions** in half lengthwise and then into strips 3″ long. Place **1 Tb. fermented black beans** (available in Chinese markets) in a bowl, cover with cold water and let soak 5 minutes. Drain, squeeze, and chop finely with a heavy knife. Peel **3 cloves garlic**. Use same fry pan and another **2 Tb. oil** to saute scallions, the crushed cloves of garlic, and the fermented black beans. Add **1 t. Chinese sesame oil** and **1 Tb. chili paste with garlic** (available in Chinese markets). Stir into cooked eggplant and add **tamari** or soy to taste. Can be served at room temperature or hot.

SPANOKOPITES

This recipe produces individual triangular spinach pastries
instead of a large spinach "pie." From Hope Zachariades.

1) Defrost **1½ lb. frozen chopped spinach.**

2) Chop **1 medium onion** or **5–6 scallions** and saute
   in **2 Tb. olive oil** until softened. Squeeze defrosted
   spinach dry and add to onions. Cook until all moisture is
   evaporated. Remove from heat and add **⅓–½ lb.**
   crumbled **Feta cheese, ⅓ c.** chopped **fresh dill,
   ½ lb. potcheese** (the driest possible cottage cheese),
   fresh ground pepper, nutmeg to taste, and **1–2
   eggs.** Start with 1 egg, mix well together, and add the
   second egg if mixture seems dry enough to incorporate
   it. A mixture that is too moist will break through the filo.

3) You will need about **½ lb.** good quality **filo pastry**
   (available at Greek markets). Once the pastry is opened
   you must work quickly before it dries out and becomes
   useless. To give yourself more time, enclose it in two
   sheets of waxed paper and cover with a damp towel.

4) Melt **¼ lb. sweet butter** and use a pastry brush to
   butter a cookie sheet. Cut filo pastry in half lengthwise,
   using a sharp knife, and return to waxed paper
   enclosure. Remove one piece at a time and place

lengthwise in front of you. Brush lightly with melted
butter and place 1–2 Tb. of spinach filling at the narrow
end nearest you. Fold filo over spinach in thirds, making
an even more narrow lengthwise strip. It helps to not
fold evenly but to let filo flare slightly open at far end.
Butter lightly along top of strip and begin folding right-
angled triangles until you get to the end of the strip. It
takes practice to produce neat spanokopites.

5) As you complete each piece, place on cookie sheet. The
spanokopites can touch each other as they are laid in
the pan. Brush each completed triangle with melted
butter. When pan is full, it can be refrigerated or frozen.

6) Bake at 375° until puffed and browned, about 30
minutes. Serve with a **Greek Salad** (see recipe index).

Serves 6–8

Note: The amount of filling indicated uses half the package
of filo. To not waste the remainder, you can double the
amount of filling and freeze the spanokopites on a cookie
sheet covered with plastic wrap. Don't defrost; simply
remove plastic and place frozen spanokopites in preheated
oven. Or you can make **Tiropetes** by omitting the spinach
and using feta, pot cheese, eggs, and the remaining
seasonings in a combination to suit your taste. Or, to make
a version of **Baclava,** you may grind walnuts and almonds
together, mix to a paste with honey and flavor with
cinnamon and nutmeg. Thin rolls of this may be placed on

buttered strips of filo which are then rolled up into thin cigar
shapes, buttered and baked. Later they will need a syrup of
1 part honey and 1 part water boiled together for five
minutes and flavored with lemon and orange rind or rose
water. The syrup is then poured over the baclava.
Spanokopites, Tiropetes, and Baclava may alternatively be
made by buttering whole sheets of filo and placing them in a
large casserole. When half are in, add the filling of your
choice and top with remaining buttered filo sheets. Cut
diagonally through finished casserole to yield diamond
shapes and bake. In working with filo, remember
to have your filling ready before opening the package, and
to constantly butter sheets before folding or adding more
sheets. Also remember Baclava in any version needs some
syrup to finish it.

*The way we stand, you can see we have grown up
this way together, out of the same soil, with the same
rains, leaning in the same way toward the sun . . . .
And we are various, and amazing in our variety, and
our differences multiply, so that edge after edge of
the endlessness of possibility is exposed . . . . you
can see, in the way we stand, each alone, yet none
of us separable . . .*

"Forest"
Woman and Nature
Susan Griffin; Harper & Row

HOW TO BROIL FISH

1) Place 1–2 servings of **fish filet** or fish steak(s) in a
baking dish. We use 9" cake pans. Add **3 Tb. dry white
wine** and **1 Tb. shallots,** peeled and chopped, to the
pan. Brush fish with melted **butter** and sprinkle with
salt, fresh ground pepper and **paprika.**

2) We serve fish with rice and fried zuccini strips. To
prepare the **zuccini,** cut it into sticks about ½" by ½" by
4". Roll in **flour** seasoned with **salt** and **pepper.** Fry in
a little **oil** over high heat while fish is broiling, turning as
each side browns. Turn out onto plate and sprinkle
lightly with **tamari** and **gomahsio** (see recipe index).

3) Broil fish on one side only. Test with a knife to be sure
fish is cooked through. Remove fish to a serving plate
and place pan on top of stove. Reduce wine to 1 Tb.
If wine is all gone, add a little more and reduce it. Add
1½ Tb. butter to pan and pour this sauce over fish.

Serves 1–2

It's a woman's dream this autonomy
Where the lines connect
And the points stay free

"Our Purpose Here"
Testimony
Ferron; Lucy Records

FELAFEL DINNER

1) Rinse **3 c. dried chick peas** and look them over for stones. Soak in **water** to cover overnight.

2) The next day, drain and rinse chick peas well. Let sit in a colander half an hour, then grind in a meat grinder or food processor, in small batches if using processor. Use processor or hand chop **2 small onions** and **2 bunches straight leaf parsley** very fine. Mix into ground chick peas.

3) In a small bowl, mix together **2 Tb. ground cumin seed, 1 Tb. ground coriander, 1 T.** plus **2 t. salt, ¾ Tb. ground black pepper, ⅛ t. cayenne pepper** and **1 Tb. Spanish paprika.** Mixture should be dark red-brown color and should smell predominantly of cumin. Add to chick peas with **3 cloves garlic,** crushed, and mix thoroughly, using your hands. Taste and add salt, cumin or parsley as you like. Pat mixture down firmly and let rest at least 1 hour before cooking. Store mixture in refrigerator.

4) Prepare **Tahini Sauce:** Open a **small can (15 oz.)** of **tahini** (available in Greek or Arabic markets. Do not use health food store sesame butter; it is not the same). Turn out into a bowl and gradually add **1 can cold water,** stirring tahini thoroughly to make a creamy mixture. Add **2 t. salt** and the **juice** of **2–3 lemons.** Refrigerate.

5) Make **Yoghurt Sauce:** Peel and seed **1 small cucumber** and chop it. Mix with **16 oz. plain yoghurt** and add **1 small clove garlic,** crushed, **salt,** and **fresh ground pepper** to taste, **1 Tb. straight leaf parsley,** chopped, and **1 Tb. cilantro,** chopped, if available. Refrigerate.

6) When ready to serve, moisten hands and use a spoon to shape and roll felafel balls. Heat **3 c. oil** in a wok or pot and deep fry the balls until nicely browned. Drain.

7) Serve 6 felafel per diner on beds of shredded **lettuce** with the yoghurt and tahini sauces. Warmed **pita bread,** canned **hot peppers** such as **jalapeno** or **salonika,** and chopped **fresh tomatoes** are good accompaniments.

Serves 6–8

Yes, for some time we might contemplate
not the tiger, not the eagle or grizzly
but the snail who always remembers
that wherever you find yourself eating
is home, the center
where you must make your love,
and wherever you wake up
is here, the right place to be
where we start again.

"The spring offensive of the snail"
To Be Of Use
Marge Piercy; Doubleday

STIR FRIED VEGETABLES

A consideration of color, texture, and flavor are essential to any good stir fry. Vegetables should be prepared in advance, cut thinly and uniformly to cook quickly. They are added to the pan with reference to the time they take to cook; obviously, those vegetables requiring the most time go in first. Vegetables may be chosen according to preference in taste and availability. Eggplant, broccoli, zuccini, peppers, mushrooms, scallions, snow peas, and mung bean sprouts are just some of the possibilities. It's impossible to prepare stir fried vegetables for more than three people without it all becoming rather soggy.

1) Cook brown rice. In a suitable pot with a tight fitting lid, combine **1 c. brown rice** (we prefer short grain) and **2 c. water.** Bring to a boil and turn heat down to the barest simmer. Cook until done, about 45 minutes. This amount of rice serves three.

2) Prepare vegetables. Cut the following into slices no more than ¼" thick and 2" long, making them as uniform in size as possible: **1 small zuccini, 1 small green pepper, 5 scallions,** and **1 baby eggplant.** Quarter or slice **12 medium mushrooms** and chop **½ small head** of **bok choy** or use **2 c. fresh spinach leaves.** Arrange all the vegetables on a platter in the order in which they will be cooked with the crisper ones such as peppers, eggplant, and scallions to be used first. Set out a **handful** of **mung bean sprouts** and **¼ lb. snow peas,** also. Mince **2 t. fresh ginger** and finely chop **3 cloves garlic** and set aside.

3) Prepare seasoning. Combine **3 Tb. tamari** with **1 Tb. dry sherry, 2 Tb. water, 2 t. cornstarch** and stir well. Or see Charlotte's Sauce in *Wings of Life*, p. 216.

4) A wok is, of course, ideal for stir-frying, but if you are cooking on an electric stove, a large cast iron skillet is the better choice. Heat **3 Tb. oil** in the pan until quite hot and add firmer vegetables in appropriate order. Turn with spatula and, after about three minutes, add ginger and garlic and the more tender vegetables. Fry one or two minutes more, constantly stirring. Remix tamari cornstarch and add. Bring to a boil and serve with the rice. Real **Chinese plum sauce** makes a nice accompaniment.

Serves 2–3

But women writers can—as Black writers, male and female, have also done—make a virtue of necessity. If we are considered separately, do not be surprised when we become separatists: found our own presses and periodicals; demand audience and appraisal of our peers.

"Whose Myths, Whose Voices"
Marilyn Hacker
Chrysalis: a magazine of women's culture
No. 10, 1980

FRUIT CHEESE TART

1) Roll out **pie crust** (see recipe index) to fit pie pan and chill in refrigerator. Soften **6 oz. cream cheese.**

2) In a pot combine **3 c.** peeled sliced **peaches, ½ c. blueberries, ⅓ c. sugar, 1 Tb. flour, ⅛ t. cinnamon,** and grated **rind** of ½ **lemon.** Stir together well, cover and simmer about 5 minutes or till fruit is tender. Uncover pot to cool fruit. Preheat oven to 375°.

3) Separate **3 eggs,** whites into mixer and yolks into a bowl or food processor. Beat whites until stiff but not dry. If you have a food processor, yolks and remaining ingredients can be mixed in it. If not, turn whites out into another bowl and beat yolks in mixer, combining them with **2 Tb. lemon juice,** the softened cream cheese, **1 Tb. flour, ¼ c. sugar, 1 t. grated lemon rind, ½ t. salt,** and lastly, add ½ **c. heavy cream.** Scrape mixer bowl or food processor sides and beat again. Fold egg whites and cheese-yolk mixture together carefully but thoroughly.

4) Turn cooked fruit into chilled pie shell. Top with cheese mixture and place in oven. Bake for 30–40 minutes or until cheese topping is light brown. Serve tart at room temperature.

BLUEBERRY PIE

1) Roll out **pie crust** (see recipe index) to fit a pie pan.
   Prick at edge of bottom and sides and line with foil.
   Weight with beans or rice and bake at 400° for 5
   minutes. Remove foil and beans, turn oven down to
   375° and continue baking pie crust until it is done.
   Remove from oven and cool.

2) Combine in a pot **1 c. sugar, 3 Tb. cornstarch,
   ⅛ t. salt, 1 c. water, 1 c. blueberries, ½ t.
   cinnamon,** and the grated **rind** and **juice** of
   ½ lemon. Pick over enough **blueberries** to yield
   3 c. and set aside. Cook the mixture in the pot, stirring,
   until it comes to a simmer and thickens. Stir over heat
   for another 30 seconds and remove from heat.
   Immediately add reserved blueberries and **1 Tb.
   butter.** Let cool. Turn into pie shell and chill.

3) Serve with **whipped cream:** Beat **2 c. heavy cream**
   until stiff with **1½ t. vanilla extract** and **2 Tb. sugar.**

*I will not live a life
Forever on my knees
You tell me: why not change
To make you more at ease*

"I've Got a Fury"
Margie Adam. Songwriter.
Margie Adam; Pleiades Records

BLUEBERRY PEACH SUNDAE

1) Peel and slice enough fresh **peaches** to yield **3 c.** Place in a pot with **½ c. blueberries, ⅓ c. sugar** and a **dash cinnamon.** Add ⅓ **c.** good **fruit juice** (we prefer L&A apple-boysenberry), cover the pot and simmer 5 minutes or until fruit is tender. Cool and chill.

2) Serve blueberry peach sauce over **vanilla ice cream** and top with whipped cream (**1 c. heavy cream** beaten stiff with **1 Tb. sugar** and ½ **t. vanilla extract**).

Serves 6

I think: what is my responsibility to my roots—both white and brown, Spanish-speaking and English? I am a woman with a foot in both worlds; and I refuse the split. . . . it is in looking to the nightmare that the dream is found. There, the survivor emerges to insist on a future, a vision, yes, born out of what is dark and female. The feminist movement must be a movement of such survivors, a movement with a future.

"La Güera"
Cherríe Moraga Lawrence
the coming out stories
Ed. Julia Penelope Stanley and Susan J. Wolfe;
Persephone Press

BLUEBERRY WHIP CREAM ROLL

1) Put **4 eggs** in their shells in a bowl and cover them with hot tap water. Meanwhile preheat oven to 375° and butter and then line a jelly roll pan with waxed paper.

2) Break warmed eggs into mixer bowl, add ¼ **t. salt, 1 t. baking powder** and begin beating at high speed. Add ¾ **c. sugar** gradually and beat until eggs are tripled in volume. Add **1 t. vanilla extract,** mix it in well, and remove bowl from machine. Sift ¾ **c. unbleached white flour** over bowl and fold it in, gently but thoroughly. Turn into pan and bake 10–15 minutes until light brown. Be careful, this cake burns easily.

3) Have ready a dish towel covered with sifted **confectioner's sugar.** Turn cake out onto towel and peel off waxed paper carefully in strips (it won't come off in one piece). Roll up the cake in the towel and place on racks to cool.

4) Combine in a pot ½ **c. sugar, 1½ Tb. cornstarch,** ½ **c. water,** ½ **c. blueberries,** ¼ **t. cinnamon** and **1½ t. lemon juice.** Simmer mixture stirring well. As it begins to thicken, add **1½ c. blueberries** and immediately remove from stove. Let cool.

5) Beat **1 c. heavy cream** and ½ **t. vanilla extract** until stiff. Unroll cooled cake and spread with whipped cream. Top with cooled blueberry mixture. Reroll cake and store in refrigerator until time to serve.

BLUEBERRY MUFFINS

1) Preheat oven to 400°. Melt **1 stick sweet butter.**

2) Pick over **2½ c. blueberries** removing stems, leaves, etc., and puree ½ c. of them in a food processor or blender.* In a small bowl, dust the remaining 2 c. with a little flour to separate them.

3) Line muffin tins with papers.

4) Stir together, using a whisk: **⅔ c. sugar, 2 c. white unbleached flour, 2 t. baking powder, ½ t. salt, ⅓ t. cinnamon,** and a **grating** of **fresh nutmeg.**

5) Beat **2 eggs.** Stir in **½ c. milk,** the melted butter and the pureed berries.

6) Quickly mix together the liquid and dry ingredients along with the whole berries. Don't overmix.

7) Spoon into prepared muffin tins and bake at 400° until lightly brown on top, (about 20–25 minutes). These muffins can be frozen and reheated in a 350° oven.

Yields 12 muffins

* If you are using a blender to puree you may want to add some of the milk from step #5 to make the berries wet enough to puree efficiently.

BLUEBERRY PEACH YOGHURT SHAKE

Fill blender ⅔ full of peeled and stoned **fresh peaches.**
Add **⅔ c. blueberries, ½ t. almond extract, ½ t.
vanilla extract,** and just enough good **fruit juice** to
puree mixture. **Papaya juice** or **apple-boysenberry**
will do. Mix with **2 pt. plain yoghurt** and taste for
sweetness. Add **honey** if it seems necessary and chill until
ready to serve.

Serves 6

ICED TEA

Bring **1 qt. water** to a boil. Add ⅓ **c. loose tea.** Let steep
4 minutes. Place a strainer over a pitcher containing **1 qt.
cold water** and ¼ **c. sugar** or **2 Tb. honey.** Pour steeped
tea through strainer. Stir tea mixture well. ½ **orange** and ¼
lemon may be squeezed and added to iced tea pitcher. Let
come to room temperature and pour over ice. Garnish with
fresh mint sprigs. Refrigerating tea makes it cloudy.

CHAPTER 7   LATE SUMMER
August 2 to Autumn Equinox, September 22.

GAZPACHO

An excellent soup to be made only when local tomatoes are in season. It's not worth eating otherwise.

1) Using a sharp knife, finely chop **4 medium tomatoes, 1 small cucumber, 1 small green pepper, 3 scallions, 4 Tb. straight leaf parsley,** and **4 small stalks celery hearts.** Put these vegetables into a container which can be refrigerated later.

2) Add to the container **1⅓ c. canned tomato juice, ¼ c. olive oil,** and **2 Tb. lemon juice.** Season to taste with **salt** and **pepper** and a **dash** of **Tabasco.** Stir and chill thoroughly.

3) Rub soup bowls, preferably glass, with a cut **clove** of **garlic.** Add gazpacho to bowls and place an ice cube in each bowl before serving.

Serves 6

"We must make immediate plans to recover the Grail and restore it to the Goddess," said Christabel. "Her flight after the atomic war was the final nail in the coffin of this generation. If the planet is to survive . . . she must be induced to return . . . "

The Hearing Trumpet
Leonora Carrington; Pocket

CHLODNIK

A Russian soup that is an improbable combination of
ingredients. From Nancy Gilchrist.

1) Bring lightly salted water to a boil and add **1½ lb.
   shrimp** in their shells. Cover, remove from heat and
   leave till pink (cooked). Remove from liquid and peel,
   clean, and coarsely chop shrimp.*

2) Peel, seed, and dice **2 thin cucumbers.**

3) Combine **1½ qt. buttermilk, 1 Tb. prepared
   mustard, 1 t. salt, 1 t. sugar,** chopped cucumbers
   and shrimp, and **2 Tb. chopped fresh dill.** Chill and
   serve.

* If you like, save liquid and shrimp shells. Chop together in
  a food processor, then boil up. Strain liquid and save for
  Champagne Shrimp Bisque (see following recipe).
  This liquid can be frozen; however, it's not worth doing
  this unless shrimp are very fresh.

                                                   Serves 6

CHAMPAGNE SHRIMP BISQUE

1) Gently cook **1 lb. shrimp** in their shells in **water** to cover. Remove shrimp and peel, clean and chop. Set aside. Reserve cooking water and shells. Chop **shells** together with the **cooking water** in food processor or blender. Boil together 5 minutes, then strain liquid and reserve.

2) Chop ¼ c. **shallots** and slice ¼ **lb. mushrooms.** Saute in ½ **stick sweet butter** until mushrooms begin to brown slightly. Add **1 small clove garlic,** crushed, and cook another minute. Add ¼ c. **unbleached white flour** and stir together until well blended over low heat.

3) Add **1 c.** leftover **champagne** (or white wine), liquid from shrimp shells, **1 Tb. tomato paste, 1 c. heavy cream, 1 Tb. lemon juice, ½ Tb. dried tarragon** and simmer together 5 minutes. Season with **salt, pepper** and a **dash** fresh grated **nutmeg.** Taste for salt, pepper, lemon, and adjust seasoning. A **dash** of **golden sherry** or **port** may be added.

4) Beat **1 egg yolk** in a bowl. Gradually add soup to yolk, stirring carefully so that egg does not curdle. Return to pot and add the reserved shrimp.

5) To reheat, carefully stir soup over low heat; do not boil.

Serves 6

CREAM OF CORN SOUP

1) Use fresh local August corn. Scrape kernels from cobs of **1 dozen ears** of **corn** using a curved blade knife, if available. Boil **cobs** in **water** to cover about ½ hour. Set kernels aside.

2) Chop ½ **small onion,** ½ **green pepper** and **1 stalk** and **leaves** of **celery,** and saute in **2 Tb. butter.** Add **2 Tb. unbleached white flour** and cook, stirring, for two minutes. Add **1 c. half and half** and bring to a boil.

3) Remove cobs from their broth and discard. Add **cob liquid** to vegetables and bring to a simmer. Don't boil or soup will curdle. Add **salt, pepper** and **nutmeg** to taste. Now add corn kernels. If soup seems too thick, add **milk** until consistency is right. You may add **1 t. sugar** to intensify the sweet corn taste.

Serves 6–8

At harvest time she worked in the fields with the men. When we brought her water she straightened from the earth to loom above us, curving against the sky; a strong odour would come from her, like the odour of the earth when it is just turned; her yellow hair would glisten round her face and we thought it grew from her head exactly as the wheat grew from the earth.

"Persephone"
Meridel Le Sueur
Lady-Unique-Inclination-of-the-Night
Cycle 2, Autumn, 1977.

BOURRIDE

A fish soup for garlic lovers.

1) Prepare **Aioli** (garlic mayonnaise): Place **3 egg yolks**
   in a food processor or bowl. Add **salt** and **pepper,**
   1 Tb. good quality **prepared mustard, 1 Tb.** crushed
   garlic, and **1 Tb. vinegar.** Turn processor on or begin
   whisking while you add **2 c. olive oil,** drop by drop. As
   mixture begins to thicken, oil may be added a little
   faster. Taste for salt, pepper, vinegar and garlic. Aioli
   should taste strongly of garlic. Add a **dash** of **Tabasco**
   and mix again. Refrigerate until ready to serve.

2) Chop **1 medium onion, 2 stalks celery, 2 leeks**
   and saute in **2 Tb. olive oil** in a soup pot until softened.
   Add **1 clove garlic,** crushed, **1 bay leaf, 1 t. saffron**
   threads if you have them, and **1 c. dry white wine**
   and bring to a simmer. Peel and dice **2 c. potatoes** and
   add with **2½ c. water.** Add **salt** and **pepper** to taste
   and a **dash Tabasco.** Simmer until potatoes are nearly
   done.

3) If you like, prepare "crouts" of **French bread** by drying
   out slices of it in a 300° oven. Rub these toasts with a
   peeled **clove** of **garlic.**

4) Cut into large bite sized pieces **fish filets** from a
   delicate non-oily fish such as cod, halibut, flounder,
   etc., and add to soup. Don't cook any longer than
   3–5 minutes. Place 2 Tb. aioli in each soup bowl.
   Gradually add a little broth to each while stirring. Dip
   out more soup for each bowl, top with crouts, and serve
   with remaining aioli in a bowl.

Serves 8

In Rhode Island, near my house, was a lake. In a
secluded spot lived a tree that I found out was my
mother. I don't know how I knew. I was ten, twelve.
It had a long limb that stretched out towards the
water, but low enough so I could climb onto it with
ease. Each week I went there to kiss her. I rubbed
my cheek against her bark and knew that it was her
skin and she could feel me rubbing her. The crook in
her arm would hold me for a long time. It was a
secret from everyone but my sister. She had her
own tree.

"How I Spent at Least One Summer Vacation"
Susan Leigh Star
the coming out stories
Ed. Julia Penelope Stanley and Susan J. Wofle;
Persephone Press

BEACH PLUM OR ELDERBERRY SOUP

Rose hips and wild chokecherries make a good soup, too.
Be sure to adjust sugar, lemon juice and water dilution to
the particular fruit you are using.

1) First find your wild fruit. This soup recipe is insipid made
   with cultivated fruits. You will need a little less than
   1 qt. wild fruit. Wash and place in a pot with
   1 qt. water. Simmer until very soft, about ½ hour.

2) Turn into a sieve or food mill to separate seeds and pits
   from fruit. Discard seeds or pits.

3) Return the fruit juice to the pot and add **½ t. salt** and
   ½ c. sugar. Bring to a simmer again. Mix together
   2 t. cornstarch and **2 Tb. water.** Add to simmering
   soup, stirring a minute until cornstarch thickens and
   clears. Remove from heat and taste. Add more **sugar** or
   up to **1 Tb. lemon juice** as you think necessary. If
   soup seems too strong or "foxy" in flavor, it may need
   more water dilution.

4) Serve at once or chill and serve cold. Garnish with
   sour cream.

Serves 6

am I not   elder
berry
brandy

are you not wine before you find me
in your own beaker?

"a plainsong from an older woman to a younger
woman"
The Work of A Common Woman
Judy Grahn; St. Martin's Press

"Change of life by definition refers to the future;
one life is finishing therefore another life must be
beginning. The menopausal armies mass on the
brink of every city and suburb; everything that was
is over and there is nothing left there to keep our
sights lowered. See the rifles raised? This army
doesn't travel on its uterus anymore . . . . There is
no more beautiful word in the language than
withered."

Sister Gin
June Arnold; Daughters, Inc

CHILLED SIMPLE BORSCHT

From Fay Davidson.

1) Use a knife to scrape **2 bunches baby beets.** Don't wash beets, but knife may be rinsed. Cut off at stem and root. Put into pot with **6 c. water** and **1 Tb. salt.** Simmer for 20 minutes.

2) Add the juice of **2 lemons** and either ⅓ **c. sugar** or **3 Tb. honey.** Cook another 5 minutes and taste for sweetness, sourness and salt. Borscht should taste strongly of all three, and once it is chilled, will need more salt than when hot. Adjust seasoning accordingly.

3) In a large bowl, beat **4 eggs** thoroughly. Add borscht slowly to eggs, mixing well to prevent curdling. Remove beets from borscht and slice thinly. Refrigerate both beets and borscht.

4) Stir **2 Tb.** of **sour cream** in each soup bowl with a few tablespoons of the borscht. Slowly add more borscht to each bowl so sour cream and borscht are thoroughly mixed. Some will like a garnish of cooked beets; others like the soup plain.

Serves 6

TABOOLI PLATTER

A delicious Arabic salad to be made only when local
tomatoes are in season.

1) Soak **1 c. fine cracked wheat** (bulgur) in **2 c. water**
   for ½ hour. (Cracked wheat can be purchased at stores
   which sell Middle Eastern products.) Drain the wheat,
   squeeze it dry one handful at a time, and put it into a
   bowl.

2) With a sharp knife finely chop **4 large tomatoes,
   ½ cucumber, 1 bunch scallions, 1 bunch straight
   leaf parsley,** and **½ bunch fresh mint.**

3) Put these into the bowl of wheat and add the juice of
   2–4 small lemons, ½ c. olive oil, salt, and **pepper**
   to taste. The dressing should be absorbed by the
   cracked wheat. Chill in refrigerator until ready to serve.

4) Serve this salad on leaves of **Romaine lettuce** on a
   platter with wedges of **Syrian bread, calamata
   olives,** thin slices of **feta** and shreds of **Arabic
   braided string cheese, Baba Ghanouj,** and
   Humus Bi Tahini (see following recipes).

                                              Serves 6

BABA GHANOUJ

While you can make baba ghanouj in the oven by baking
the eggplant, the best way to do it is on an open flame. We
do this on a gas range. An electric stove can be used if the
burner is preheated till red hot.

1) Prop **1 eggplant** directly on your burner over high heat
   so it is vertical, stem up, for a few minutes. Then lay it on
   its side, turning every few minutes or so until the outside
   of the eggplant is charred and black and the inside soft.

2) Immediately remove the eggplant from the stove. Slit it
   open and scoop out the white soft flesh with spoon and
   put it into a bowl being careful to keep charred pieces
   out. You should know that cooking the eggplant this
   way makes a mess of the stove and you may choose to
   bake it in the oven; however the smokey smell and taste
   will be absent.

3) Before the eggplant turns black, add **2 cloves** crushed
   garlic, 2 Tb. fresh chopped **Italian parsley,** the
   juice of **1 lemon, 3 Tb. tahini** (tahini is a ground
   sesame seed paste which comes in a jar or can, and can
   be purchased at stores which sell Middle Eastern
   products), **salt** and **pepper** to taste.

4) Refrigerate and serve a small portion with **pita bread.**

HUMUS BI TAHINI

1) Soak **1 c. dried chick peas** overnight. Drain off the water and put the chick peas in a pot. To cook, add new water to cover chick peas. Cook till soft; about 1 hour.

2) Drain the chick peas when done and put them in a food processor or blender with **1 Tb. olive oil, ½ t. salt, 2 small cloves garlic, 2 Tb. fresh mint leaves,** the **juice** of **1 lemon,** and ½ c. tahini. (Tahini is a ground sesame seed paste which comes in a jar and can be purchased at stores which sell Middle Eastern products.)

3) Puree the mixture together till smooth. It should not be too stiff. Traditionally it is spread flat in a shallow dish and topped with a drizzle of olive oil. If the mixture is too thick, add water to thin. It may also require more tahini and lemon juice to suit taste. Refrigerate and serve with **Syrian flat bread.**

. . . Despite all the evils they wished to crush me
with/I remain as steady as the three legged cauldron.

Les Guérillères
Monique Wittig; Avon

SALAD NICOISE

A substantial salad which makes a good supper for summer nights. Salad Nicoise may be served at room temperature or prepared in advance and chilled. Our instructions assume the latter.

1) Wash, peel and slice into quarters **10** to **12** small **potatoes.** Cook in boiling water until a small sharp knife can pierce them easily. Drain and toss immediately with ¼ **c. white wine.** In small bowl make a vinaigrette of ¼ **c. vinegar,** ¾ **c. oil,** and **2 t. prepared mustard.** We use a blend of 25% olive oil and 75% vegetable oil. Add over half the vinaigrette to the potatoes and reserve the rest. Add **salt** and grate fresh **pepper** on the potatoes. Add chopped **scallions** and toss again lightly. Chill.

2) Steam ¾ **lb. green beans.** When cooked, toss with some of the reserved vinaigrette and chill.

3) Simmer **4 eggs** in water to cover for 10 minutes until they are hard cooked. Drain in cold water and tap shells gently all around to peel them. Chill.

4) Prepare **Garlic Mayonnaise** (see recipe index).

5) For each salad, prepare a bed of **lettuce** (Boston preferred) and place two large spoonfuls of potato salad in the center. Arrange **tuna fish,** marinated green beans, **tomato slices,** a few **salt cured olives,** hard boiled egg slices, and top with **onion rings.** Drizzle reserved vinaigrette around the lettuce and add a dollop of garlic mayonnaise to the top of each salad.

Serves 6–8

TOMATO SALAD

At last. We serve tomatoes only when they are vine ripened and locally grown, so as much as we love them, they appear in salads only in August, September, and October. Slice **tomatoes** thickly and place on a bed of **lettuce** (Boston or Salad Bowl preferred) with sliced **onions** and **vinaigrette** (see recipe index) on top. Or, alternate **tomato** slices, home grown **cucumber** slices (which, of course, don't have to be peeled or seeded) and very thin slices of sweet **onion.** Chop fresh **basil** and **oregano** or **thyme** leaves and sprinkle over the top. In a jar shake together a dressing of **2 parts olive oil** and **1 part wine vinegar.** Pour over salad, **salt** lightly and grind fresh **pepper** over. Refrigerate an hour or so before serving.

STUFFED VEGETABLE PLATTER

Consisting of green peppers stuffed with chick peas, tomatoes stuffed with eggplant mousse, and zuccini stuffed with rice, any one makes a nice summer dinner. The combination is a feast.

1) Soak ¾ **c. dried chick peas** overnight in **water to cover.** Drain, cover with new water, bring to a boil and simmer 2–3 hours until tender.

2) Bake **1 large eggplant** in a 400° oven ½ hour or until soft (check with a small knife). Scoop out flesh into mixer and add **1 clove garlic,** crushed, ¼ **c.** finely chopped **straight leaf parsley, 1 Tb. olive oil, 3 Tb. parmesan cheese** and ⅓–⅔ **c. bread crumbs.** Add **2 eggs** and **salt** and **pepper** to taste. Mixture should be soft but not sloppy. Cut off stem end of **6 firm** local **tomatoes** and scoop out flesh (reserve it). Fill tomatoes with eggplant mixture. Don't mound it too high. Dribble **olive oil** on top and sprinkle with **parmesan.** Refrigerate until ready to serve.

3) Choose **5 medium sized zuccini.** Cut in half crosswise and use an apple corer to make hollow tubes by first working from one side and then the other. Chop **1 medium onion.** Saute it in **2 Tb. olive oil** until soft. Remove pan from heat and add to it ½ **c. raw white rice, 2 Tb.** chopped **straight leaf parsley, 1½ Tb.** chopped **fresh dill,** ¼ **c. dried currants,** and **2 Tb. squash corings,** chopped fine. Also add **salt,**

pepper and ¼ **c. pignoli nuts.** Make a "broth" by mixing **1 t. tamari** in **1 c. water** and moisten the uncooked rice mixture with a few tablespoons of this. Taste for salt and pepper. Use your fingers to stuff zuccini tubes. Place in a pan and add the "broth" to ½" deep in the pan. Cover with foil and refrigerate until ready to serve.

4) Cut off stem ends from **6 small green peppers** and remove seeds and white pith. Discard. Chop **1½ c. onions** and saute in **2 Tb. butter.** Add **2 small cloves garlic,** crushed, **1 t. dried oregano, dash dried ginger, ⅓ t. ground cumin, ⅓ t. ground coriander, dash cinnamon** and a **dash ground cloves.** Add **1½ Tb.** chopped **fresh mint, 1 t. salt,** and **1½ c. reserved tomato pulp,** coarsely chopped. Add **fresh ground pepper** and **1½ t. lemon juice.** Chop remaining **zuccini cores** and add them also. Bring all to a simmer. Drain cooked chick peas and rub off their skins in cool water. All skins need not be removed. Combine cooked chick peas and sauce and add **1 Tb. tamari.** Taste. Chick peas are very bland and should be well seasoned. Stuff peppers with chick pea mixture, place in pan and add ½" water. Cover with foil and refrigerate until ready to serve.

5) Half an hour before serving time, bake all three stuffed vegetables in a preheated 400° oven. The zuccini and peppers are baked covered but the tomatoes are not. Serve **yoghurt** or **Avgolemono Sauce** (see next recipe) over zuccini. All 3 stuffed vegetables reheat (uncovered) very satisfactorily.

Serves 6

AVGOLEMONO SAUCE

In a small pot, mix together **1 Tb. cornstarch, 1 Tb. cold water** and the **juice** of **2 lemons.** Add **2 eggs** and beat over moderate heat until thickened. Thin out with ⅓–⅔ **c. water** and season with ½ **t. tamari.** Serve over stuffed zuccini.

. . . a great deal of white feminist thinking and writing, where it has attempted to address black women's experience, has done so laboring under a massive burden of guilt feelings and false consciousness, the products of deeply inculcated female self-blame, and of a history we have insufficiently explored. (There is a profound difference between actual guilt—or accountability—and guilt feelings.) We have also been laboring under feelings of ignorance of, and therefore inadequacy toward, the real lives of black women.

"Disloyal to Civilization"
On Lies, Secrets, and Silence
Adrienne Rich; Norton

ZUCCINI FLAN

This savory dish is a quiche without a pie crust shell.

1) Preheat oven to 475°. Thinly slice **6 medium** to **small zuccini** and **2 medium onions.**

2) Mix onions and zuccini together in 11" x 14" pan with **1 t. dried basil, 1 t. oregano,** and **salt** and **pepper** to taste. Add **1 large clove garlic,** crushed, and moisten vegetables with **oil.** Bake in preheated oven turning often until brown.

3) Slice **3 c. Swiss cheese** or a mixture of **2 c. Swiss** and **1 c. Raclette.** (Raclette is a kind of strong smelling Swiss cheese which is hard to locate but makes the flan tasty.)

4) Beat together in a bowl **5 eggs** and **1 qt. heavy cream.** Add a little **nutmeg, salt** and **pepper.** Pour this mixture over the browned squash. Top with cheese. Turn down oven to 350° and bake until puffed and brown. To reheat, bake at 350° for 10 minutes or until quite hot.

Serves 8–10

RATATOUILLE NICOISE

1) Choose **4 small** to **medium eggplants.** Slice in half lengthwise. Each half will be a serving casserole for one person, so consider how each eggplant will be cut to make it sit on the plate as level as possible.

2) Peel **4 large onions** and slice by hand. Using a large sharp edged spoon, scoop out the eggplant flesh. Chop it coarsely. Put eggplant halves together while mixture cooks.

3) Heat **3 Tb. olive oil** in large heavy frypan. You may be more comfortable using 2 fry pans, if you have them. If you are using 2 pans, 3 Tb. oil will be necessary in the second one as well. Add **1 t. dried oregano** to pan with sliced onions. Saute a few minutes. Add eggplant and turn heat high. Eggplant should brown and stick and be scraped up with a spatula. Scrape often.

4) Meanwhile, wash **8 small zuccini** (or 4–6 medium). Slice in half lengthwise, then slice in half circles. When eggplant is browned, add the zuccini and continue turning the vegetables in the hot pan often.

5) Core and slice **12 small Italian frying peppers** and add to pan. If pan is too full, dump vegetables into a pot, for they now need to simmer covered 45 minutes to one hour. Season generously first with **salt** and **pepper.**

6) Meanwhile, peel (optional) **10 small fresh tomatoes**
   by quickly dipping in a pot of boiling water and then
   running them under cold water. Chop the tomatoes
   coarsely and turn into a large bowl with their juice. Mix
   cooked ratatouille with tomatoes in the bowl and taste
   for salt and pepper. Set reserved eggplant halves in
   shallow baking pan and fill each one with ratatouille
   mix. There will probably be some mix left over. Save it
   for omelet fillings (see recipe index) or serve cold on
   toast like paté.

7) Bake eggplants at 375° for ½ hour uncovered. Serve
   with **brown rice.**

Serves 8

*Imagine, being so easy and happy with a grown
woman who had suckled you and with whom your
relations stretched back through your entire life! It
was wonderful to bask on the edge of the ease the
women had with each other, the rich
connectedness.*

Motherlines
Suzy McKee Charnas; Berkley

QUESADILLA DINNER

Another example of adapting recipes so that the essential
ethnic flavor remains even without the meat. We had a
wonderful Molé Sauce recipe, and we didn't want to serve it
with turkey, so we do it with quesadillas (cheese turnovers)
instead.

1) Prepare the beans: Rinse **1 lb. pinto** or **red kidney
   beans.** Slice **1 small onion** and put in a pot. Cover
   with **water** and simmer for 1½ hours, checking to see if
   more water is needed. When cooked, add **1 Tb. salt**
   and simmer another 10 minutes. Set aside.

2) Prepare **Molé Sauce:** You will need **2 ancho** and **1**
   each **mulato** and **pasilla chilis** (or 4 anchos). These
   are essential to the flavor of the sauce. They are
   available only at Mexican groceries. Remove stems and
   seeds from the chilis and cover with **boiling water.**
   Wash your hands in soapy water after handling chilis. In
   a food processor or blender combine **½ c. almonds,
   ¼ c. peanuts, ¼ c. raisins, 1 Tb. sesame seeds,
   ¼ t. coriander seeds, ¼ t. anise seeds, 1 whole
   clove, ½" piece stick cinnamon.** Grate fine. Add
   chilis and their water, **1 cut up onion, 2 garlic cloves,**
   and **2 whole tomatoes** (canned are okay). Puree
   thoroughly. Put **2 Tb. oil** in a large pot, heat and add
   sauce. Cook for about 5 minutes, stirring. Add **1 c.
   water, 1 t. tamari, ½ oz. unsweetened chocolate,**
   and **salt** and **pepper** to taste. Simmer, stirring, until
   it tastes just right.

3) Make **Quesadillas:** You will need a tortilla press. Mix
   together **2 c. masa harina** (from a Mexican grocer),
   1 Tb. flour, 1 Tb. gluten flour if you have it,
   ½ t. baking powder, ½ t. baking soda, ½ t. salt.
   Melt **½ stick butter,** beat **1 egg,** and add to dry
   ingredients with about **½ c. buttermilk.** Add only
   enough buttermilk to yield a fairly stiff dough. Mix well
   together. Tortilla dough cannot be overmixed. Divide
   dough into 15 balls and use 2 plastic baggies in the
   tortilla press to shape the tortillas. Don't make them too
   thin. Have ready strips of **jalapeno peppers** (available
   canned) and strips of **Muenster** or **Monteray Jack
   cheese.** Any firm cheese which melts well may be
   used. Pull off the top baggie but leave the tortilla on the
   bottom one. Center cheese and pepper strips and use
   the bottom baggie to fold the tortilla in half and press its
   edges together. If you find your tortilla mix to be too wet
   and sticky, add more masa harina. However, you will
   have to mix all the dough together thoroughly and
   divide again into individual balls. Line up the filled
   quesadillas in a container that can be tightly covered
   until ready to serve, and refrigerate. Alternatively, you
   can buy frozen tortillas, fill with cheese and pepper
   strips, roll them enchilada style, and bake them, topping
   with the molé sauce.

4) Prepare rice: In a pot combine **2 c. white rice** and **3 c.
   water.** Bring to a boil, cover, and simmer until tender,
   about 15 minutes. Meanwhile, saute **1 medium
   onion,** chopped fine and **2 cloves garlic,** crushed, in
   2 Tb. olive oil. When wilted and lightly browned, add
   ½ c. coarsely chopped **tomatoes,** (canned or fresh)
   and fry until liquid is almost all gone. Add cooked rice
   and **1½ Tb. tamari.** Simmer all together, stirring well.
   Cover and set aside.

5) Make **Guacamole Salad** (see recipe index) if you
   want to serve it with the quesadillas, as we do.

6) When ready to serve, be sure molé, beans and rice are
   heated. Use a frying pan and **2 Tb. oil** to fry 4–6
   quesadillas at a time. Be careful with them since they
   break easily. Medium heat works best. Carefully turn
   them when browned to brown the other side. Cut thin
   lengthwise slices from **2 ripe plantains** and fry in the
   oil next to the quesadillas.

7) Serve 2 quesadillas per diner with rice and beans and
   molé sauce. Guacamole salad and the plantains
   complete the dinner. Mexican beer makes a lovely drink
   with this food. Serve extra jalapenos for those who want
   them.

Serves 7

*. . . But this evening deep in summer
the deer are still alive and free,
nibbling apples from early-laden boughs
so weighted, so englobed
with already yellowing fruit
they seem eternal, Hesperidean
in the clear-tuned, cricket-throbbing air.*

"Transcendental Etude" (For Michelle Cliff)
The Dream of a Common Language
Adrienne Rich; Norton

HONEY ALMOND ICE CREAM

Hymettus honey is necessary for the special flavor of this ice cream.

1) Bring **1 qt. heavy cream** to a simmer. Meanwhile beat **6 egg yolks** in a large bowl with ¼ **c. Hymettus honey** (available in Greek markets) and ¼ **t. almond extract.** Carefully add hot cream to yolks, stirring constantly so that yolks don't curdle. Return to pot and cook gently, stirring, until mixture thickens slightly. Cool and then chill.

2) Roast ½ **c. sliced almonds** in a 300° oven 15 minutes or until browned.

3) Use an ice cream maker to freeze the chilled cream and yolk mixture. When cream is ready to be placed in freezer, stir in toasted almonds. If you don't have an ice cream maker, you can gently cook yolks, honey, and extract together with 1 c. of the heavy cream until slightly thickened. Chill. Then whip the remaining 3 c. of cream stiff and fold together with almonds. Freeze.

Yields over 1 qt.

BLUEBERRY PEACH FLUMMERY

A New England version of Russian kissl.

1) In a blender, in 2 or 3 batches, puree **5** unpeeled **peaches, 1 c. blueberries, 2¼ Tb. lemon** or **lime juice, ¼ t. salt, ¼ c. honey, 6 Tb. cornstarch** or arrowroot, and **¾ c. fruit juice** (without sugar or additives such as L & A apple-boysenberry). Turn each batch into a pot. Rinse blender with ¾ **c. water** and add to pot with **2 c. fruit juice.**

2) Bring to a rolling boil, stirring well. Let cool about 10 minutes. Turn into custard cups or glass serving dishes and chill.

3) Serve with **heavy cream** and **slivered almonds.**

Serves 12

*if we start loving women
we'll have to start worrying about
what women expect from us*

"Talking With Women"
Dyke Jacket
Fran Winant; Violet Press

BLUEBERRY PEACH PIE

1) Prepare enough pie crust for a two crust pie (see recipe index).

2) Preheat oven to 450°. Pick over **3 c. blueberries** and combine with **2 Tb. cornstarch,** a **dash** of **salt,** **½ t.** fresh grated **nutmeg, ⅔ c. sugar, 1 Tb. flour.** Toss together.

3) Peel and slice **4 small peaches** and squeeze **1 t. lemon juice** over them.

4) Roll out pie crust and fit into shell. Add blueberry mixture evenly. Top with peach mixture. Dot with **1½ Tb. butter.** Roll out top crust and place over the fruit. Trim pastry, crimp edges and slash top.

5) Bake at 450° 10 minutes and at 350° for about 30 minutes more. Best served warm, with **vanilla ice cream.**

PEACH PUDDING

From Anne Raulerson.

1) Preheat oven to 400°. In mixer combine **3 c. unbleached white flour, ¾ t. baking powder, ¾ t. salt.** While mixing, add **½ lb. sweet butter** cut into small pieces. Do not worry about overbeating. Remove from mixer and press into 9" x 12" baking dish.

2) Peel about **5 peaches** and cut into slices. Press peach slices into the dry mix. Pour **¾ c. honey** over slices and sprinkle lightly with **cinnamon.** Bake 10 minutes.

3) Meanwhile, in mixing bowl combine **3 c. sour cream, 3 egg yolks,** and **⅓ c. honey.** Whisk thoroughly. If too thick for pouring, add up to **¼ c. buttermilk.** Open oven and pour sour cream mixture over the peaches. Spread evenly. Sprinkle lightly with **cinnamon** and continue baking about ½ hour more. Pudding is done when top is golden brown and there is minimum of movement when pan is jiggled.

4) Serve warm with **heavy cream.**

MANGOES ISABEL

1) In the top of a double boiler or in a stainless steel bowl that will fit on a pot snugly, place **5 egg yolks** and ¼ **c. honey.** Put enough water in bottom pot to last 10–15 minutes without touching upper bowl.

2) Beat or stir constantly with whisk over low-medium heat until sauce becomes quite thick and sticks to the side of the bowl. This takes about 10 minutes.

3) Remove from heat and add a **scant ½ c. Grand Marnier liqueur,** whisking until well blended. Refrigerate until sauce is very cold.

4) Whip **1 c. heavy cream** stiff and fold into the sauce thoroughly.

5) **Mangoes** do not separate from their pits easily. The large pit is shaped like an oval and you will have to find the flatter side to cut the mango flesh from the pit without crushing it. Once large slabs are cut from the pit, slice the fruit off the tough skin and into pieces into a large serving bowl or into individual dessert bowls. Top each serving with Sauce Isabel, or serve separately. You will find the mangoes and Sauce Isabel an exquisite combination. **Peaches** are also good with this sauce.

Yields enough sauce to serve 6–8

BEACH PLUM SUNDAE

1) Simmer **2 c. beach plums** in **1 c. water** until beach plums are very soft. Use a food mill or spoon and sieve to separate fruit puree from the pits.

2) Return fruit juice to pot and add a **pinch** of **salt** and **sugar** to taste. Start with ¼ **c.** Simmer and taste. If sauce tastes slightly bitter, add water. Add more sugar as needed. When it tastes right, remove from stove and let cool. Chill.

3) Beat **1 c. heavy cream** stiff with **1 Tb. honey** and **1 t. vanilla.** Serve beach plum sauce over **vanilla ice cream** and top with the whipped cream.

Serves 6–8

If she were not to pick fruit from her own trees, there were common herbs and berries in plenty for her, growing wherever she chose to wander. It is best as one grows older to strip oneself of possessions, to shed oneself downward like a tree, to be almost wholly earth before one dies.

Lolly Willowes
Sylvia Townsend Warner; The Women's Press Ltd.

BEACH PLUM FLUMMERY

Since we are on Long Island Sound, we planted Beach Plums and we harvest the fruit for soup, flummery and ice cream sundaes. If you are near the ocean, you can hunt wild beach plums.

1) Simmer about **4 c. beach plums** in **2 c. water.** Use a food mill or a spoon and sieve to get the fruit pulp and pits separated. Discard pits.

2) Return juice to pot. Add **1 c. water,** a pinch **salt** and **sugar** to taste. Start with **½ c.** The amounts of water and sugar depend on how ripe your beach plums are. If the liquid tastes slightly bitter, you need more water. When flavor is right, stir together **¼ c. potato starch** and **½ c. cold water.** Add to simmering juice, stirring constantly. The flummery should thicken and clear immediately. Cool about 10 minutes, then pour into dessert bowls and chill.

3) Serve with **heavy cream** and **slivered almonds.**

Serves 8

All trees are sacredly possessed by an unseen life, but above all fruit trees are sacred. Earth sends up fruits, with the help of the moon.

Moon, Moon
Anne Kent Rush; Random House/Moon Books

CORN RYE MUFFINS

1) Preheat oven to 400°. Butter muffin tins or line with papers.

2) Melt ½ **stick sweet butter** together with ¼ **c. honey.**

3) Use a whisk to stir together: **1 c. whole wheat flour, ¾ c. corn meal, ¼ c. rye flour, 1 t. baking powder, ¾ t. baking soda, ½ t. salt.**

4) In a small bowl beat **1 egg.** Add **1½ c. buttermilk** and the melted butter. Stir well.

5) Combine liquid with dry mixture and then add **¾ c. currants.** Stir briefly, do not overmix.

6) Spoon into muffin tins and bake until lightly browned, about 30–45 minutes.

Yields 10–12 muffins

I left my mother in her frameless cage
But never could I shake her rage.

"White Wing Mercy"
Backed Up
Ferron; Lucy Records

WHITE WINE COOLER

Fill each wine glass ⅔ full with a good quality chilled
Chenin Blanc wine. Add **ice,** a **wedge of lime,** and
enough chilled **L & A apple-boysenberry juice** to color
the wine and flavor it nicely.

"*You think I don't know what your life is like just
because I ain't living it? I know what every colored
woman in this country is doing.*"

"*What's that?*"

"*Dying. Just like me. But the difference is they
dying like a stump. Me, I'm going down like one of
those redwoods. I sure did live in this world.*"

"*Really? What have you got to show for it?*"

"*Show? To who? Girl, I got my mind. And what
goes on in it. Which is to say, I got me.*"

"*Lonely, ain't it?*"

"*Yes. But my lonely is mine. Now your lonely is
somebody else's. Made by somebody else and handed
to you. Ain't that something? A secondhand lonely.*"

Sula
Toni Morrison; Bantam

Moonflower, Calonyction aculeatum

CHAPTER 8   EARLY AUTUMN
Autumn Equinox, September 22, to Halloween, October 31.

BROCCOLI MORNAY SOUP

1) Remove the flowerets from **4 bunches broccoli** and
   set aside. Use a small sharp knife to peel the stems,
   discarding the hardest bottom part. (The peeling takes
   time but the outside of the stem is too stringy and tough
   to use and the inside provides the substance and flavor
   of the soup.) Cut the peeled stems into 1 inch pieces,
   barely cover with **water** and cook until soft. When
   done, puree the stems in their liquid.

2) Meanwhile, melt ¾ **stick sweet butter.** Add
   ¾ **c. flour** and stir for several minutes. Add **2 c. heavy
   cream** and the pureed broccoli stems and liquid. Add
   ½ **c. tamari,** a **dash** of **Tabasco, 2 oz. Swiss
   cheese** and **2 oz. raclette cheese** (if available). Also
   add some **grated nutmeg,** the **juice** of ½–1 **lemon**
   and more **milk** or **cream** if soup is too thick. When
   seasoning is right, thinly slice about half of the flowerets
   lengthwise and add them to the soup. (The rest may be
   used for omelets, Raclette dinner or with salads.)
   Continue cooking until flowerets are barely done and
   still crisp. Do not overcook. Reheat leftover soup with
   care so that flowerets retain their freshness.

Serves about 8

GARLIC SOUP

1) Separate **1** whole **head** of **garlic** into cloves but do not peel them. Drop into boiling water, let cook one minute and pour into a strainer, discarding the water. Run cool water over cloves and peel with a small sharp knife.

2) Saute the peeled garlic in **2 Tb. butter** and **1 Tb. olive oil** in a soup pot. Cook over low heat for about 10 minutes, stirring, so that the cloves don't brown. Add **1½ qts. water** and simmer covered for ½ hour.

3) Dry out pieces of **French bread** in a 300° oven (or toaster oven) to make crouts. Finely chop **1 bunch straight leaf parsley.** Set crouts and parsley aside.

4) In a bowl whisk **4 egg yolks.** Add **¼ c. olive oil** slowly, beating the mixture until it thickens slightly.

5) Pour the soup through a strainer, mashing the cooked garlic cloves through as well. Return to the pot and add **2 t. salt, fresh grated nutmeg** and **pepper.** Stir about ½ c. of soup into the egg yolk and oil mix slowly so that yolks do not curdle, and then turn yolk mixture into soup pot. Heat gently, stirring, to slightly thicken the soup without letting it curdle. Serve at once, adding **2 Tb. parsley** to each bowl. Top with a crout.

Serves 6–8

CZECH MUSHROOM SOUP

This is a rich, hearty soup. From *Mushroom Cookery* by Rosetta Reitz, Gramercy Publishing Co., and used with her permission. An excellent cookbook, unfortunately now out of print.

1) In a large soup kettle bring to a boil **1 qt. water** with **1 t. caraway seed, 2 t. salt** and **½ t. pepper.**

2) Meanwhile, peel and dice **4 medium** to **large potatoes** and add to the pot. Turn down the flame to slowly cook the potatoes. Cook 15 minutes or until potatoes are soft.

3) Meanwhile, stir **4 Tb. unbleached white flour** into **2 pints sour cream** in a bowl and mix thoroughly. Stir this mixture into the soup pot and don't worry about curdling—it will smooth itself out later. Turn off flame.

4) Slice **½ lb.** of **mushrooms** (we use fresh mushrooms without preservatives—they can be found with some searching) and add them to the soup. Cover, turn the flame on low, simmer 10 minutes or until mushrooms are soft. Turn off the heat and remove from burner.

5) In a small bowl beat **2 eggs** with a whisk and spoon
   some of the hot soup over them whisking rapidly.
   Repeat until there is no danger of eggs curdling, then
   pour the egg/soup mixture into the soup pot stirring
   constantly. Add **1 Tb.** fresh chopped **dill** to the soup to
   finish the seasoning. Soup should be served
   immediately. When reheating, be very careful to stir and
   not boil.

Serves 8

*"She's a mean woman" is really a compliment,
meaning this person is serious and will not put up
with nonsense. She is not someone to trifle with or
to take lightly. It is a positive view of an
independent woman, granting her the regard she
deserves as one who will not passively accept
unjust or unkind treatment.*

Mean Mothers Independent Women's Blues
Rosetta Reitz; Rosetta Records

CREAM OF CAULIFLOWER SOUP

1) Cut out the core of **2 large heads** of **cauliflower.**
   Slice off hardest part of core and leaves and discard. Cut
   up remainder of core, barely cover with **water** in a pot.
   Peel **6 cloves garlic** and add to pot. Simmer until core
   is very tender. Puree or put through sieve.

2) Meanwhile, thinly slice flowerets of the cauliflower. You
   will be using about ½ to ¾ of them, the rest may be
   saved for salads.

3) In soup pot, melt **2 Tb. butter.** Add **2 Tb. flour** and
   cook together a minute or two. Add **⅔ c. heavy cream**
   and gently bring to a boil.

4) Add the pureed cauliflower core. Also add **1½ Tb.
   tamari, dash** of **Tabasco, freshly ground
   nutmeg,** and **fresh ground pepper.** Dice **3 oz.
   Swiss cheese** and add to simmering soup. Add **2 c.
   water, 1½ c. milk, 2 t. lemon juice.** Taste for
   seasoning. Add **salt** if necessary (despite the tamari, it
   will probably be necessary). When seasoning is right
   and a little too salty, add sliced cauliflowerets. Cook till
   barely done. Don't overcook. Serve with **chopped
   parsley.**

Serves 6

SWEET AND SOUR RICE SALAD

1) Bring to a boil **1 c. long grain white rice, ½ t. salt,**
   and **1⅔ c. water** in covered saucepan. As soon as
   water boils, turn down heat and cook slowly until water
   is absorbed and rice is fluffy. Let cool.

2) Make marinade: In a large bowl combine **⅔ c.
   vegetable oil, ⅔ c. red wine vinegar, 2½ t. honey,
   ½ t.** dry crumbled **tarragon, 2 t. salt, ½ t. pepper.**
   Mix well so that the honey is in solution.

3) Add the cooked rice to the marinade with **3 c. mung
   bean sprouts, 1 c. slivered almonds, ¾ c. raisins**
   and **½ red onion,** finely chopped. Mix well; refrigerate.

4) Arrange the salad on a bed of **lettuce.** Top with **red
   onion rings** and fresh snipped **tarragon,** if available.
   This salad will keep in the refrigerator 4–5 days.

Serves 10

*I am a woman
who understands
the necessity of an impulse whose goal or origin
still lie beyond me.*

"Artemis"
Beginning With O
Olga Broumas; Yale University Press

ROUMANIAN SALAD

From Fay Davidson.

1) Cover **½ lb. California Giant dried lima beans**
   with **water** and bring to a boil. Add **3–4 leeks,** well
   washed and finely chopped. Simmer several hours or
   until very soft. Mash with fork. Mixture should be loose
   since liquid will be absorbed.

2) Mince **1 small onion.** Chop **3 Tb. straight leaf
   parsley** and add parsley and onion to the lima bean-
   leek puree. Add **2 t. lemon juice, salt,** and **pepper** to
   taste, and **¼–⅓ c. olive oil.** Taste for lemon and salt.
   Chill.

3) Place a **whole eggplant** directly on a gas burner with
   the flame on high. (Or on a preheated electric burner.)
   Turn the eggplant every few minutes so that it steams
   inside and turns black on the outside. It will be quite
   done in 5–10 minutes. Remove from stove (which will
   be a mess), slit open and scoop out eggplant flesh into a
   bowl. Chop **½ small onion** very fine and add with **salt**
   to taste and **⅓ c. vegetable oil.** Stir together and chill.

4) Wash **2 lb. red** and **green bell peppers.** Use tongs to
   hold over gas flame or grill under broiler, turning often.
   When peppers are well blistered, remove to platter and
   use a sharp knife to skin. Slit to remove stem and drop
   into jars. Bring **1½ c. cider vinegar, 1½ c. water** and
   1½ Tb. sugar to a boil. Pour over peppers and cool;
   refrigerate.

5) Serve lima bean-leek puree, Roumanian eggplant, and strips of roasted pickled peppers on a bed of **shredded lettuce** with wedges of **tomato** and thin slices of **cucumber.** Drizzle **vinaigrette** (see recipe index) over the lettuce, tomato, and cucumber.

Serves 6–8

SUNCHOKE SALAD

1) Either grow your own **Jerusalem Artichokes** or buy them in a market. If you are harvesting your own after the first frost, scrub them thoroughly with a small brush under running water. Packaged ones need no cleaning and neither needs peeling.

2) For each diner, arrange a bed of **fresh spinach** on a dinner plate. Top with sliced **raw mushrooms** and **thinly sliced sunchokes.** Add a slice of **onion** separated into rings and finish with **vinaigrette** (see recipe index).

THREE BEAN SALAD

From Denslow Tregarthen Brown.

1) Soak in water overnight in separate pots **1 c. dried chick peas** and **1 c. dried kidney beans.** Cook the beans (separately) until soft. Allow an hour or more.

2) When the beans are done, steam or parboil **1 c. fresh green string beans** until barely soft. Do not overcook. Drain all the beans in a colander and mix them all together in a large enough bowl.

3) Make a vinaigrette while the beans are warm: Mix **⅓ c. wine vinegar, 1½ Tb. olive oil, ½ c. vegetable oil, ¾ t. celery seed, 2 cloves garlic,** crushed, **salt** and **pepper** to taste.

4) Pour the vinaigrette over the beans while they are still warm. Add **3** chopped **scallions** and mix together. Refrigerate until ready to serve.

5) Serve cold on a bed of **Boston lettuce** with **red onion slices, alfalfa sprouts** and **avocado slices.** Top with **gomahsio** (see recipe index).

Serves 6–8

ZUCCINI LATKES

From Fay Davidson.

1) Grate **2 medium zuccinis** in a food processor or by hand. Also grate **1 small onion.** Turn into a colander in a sink and let drain 5 minutes.

2) Beat **2 eggs** in a bowl large enough to hold zuccini mixture. Squeeze zuccini, handful by handful and add to the eggs. Add **2½ Tb. cornmeal, 2½ Tb. flour, ½ t. salt, fresh ground pepper,** and a **pinch** each **baking powder** and **sugar.** Stir all together and refrigerate until ready to serve.

3) Heat **2 Tb. butter** and **2 Tb. oil** in a frying pan. Use a fork to pat out small pancakes (4"–5" across) and fry until brown on one side. Turn with spatula, pressing down on the latke to flatten it.

4) Serve 3 latkes per diner with **sour cream** on the side.

Serves 6

STEAMED VEGETABLES AND ROASTED POTATOES

Having a choice of sauces makes this simple dish a treat.

1) Prepare **Mornay Sauce:** In a sauce pan melt **2 Tb. sweet butter.** Add **3 Tb. unbleached white flour** and cook the roux slowly till the butter and flour are incorporated. Add **2 c. milk, ¼ t. salt** and a grating of **pepper.** Bring to a boil, whisking constantly. Add **½ c. Swiss cheese** and whisk till the cheese has melted. Add **1 Tb. tamari.** Taste for salt and pepper. Set aside.

2) Prepare **Avgolemono Sauce** (see recipe index).

3) Prepare **Sour Cream Sauce** (see recipe index).

4) Preheat oven to 450°. Wash, peel and cut into quarters **8 medium potatoes.** Put potatoes in a roasting pan with **2 Tb. oil,** turning them on all sides to cover them. Roast for an hour or more until well browned, turning the potatoes from time to time.

5) A nice piece of kitchen equipment is a Chinese steamer with two or more tiers above the boiling water. Collapsible baskets are second choice, and of course a pan with a little water and tight fitting lid will cook vegetables without too much loss of flavor.

Peel **1 package carrots** and cut into thin sticks.
Cut **1 small head** of **broccoli** or **cauliflower** into
flowerets. Steam all the vegetables till just tender, giving
the carrots a 5 minute head start. Check with small
sharp knife and be careful not to overcook.

6) Serve vegetables together on a platter or arrange on
individual dinner plates with sauces in separate bowls.

Serves 6

in that province
we laugh without sound
the waves we send out
shake the trees
and when we love
we love in threes

"Summer, 1976 A Woman's Place"
Tribe
Martha Courtot; Pearlchild

PASTA CON FUNGHI

First find your mushrooms. **Armillaria mellea** and **Clitocybe tabescens** are exceedingly common in the northeast. They appear in the third or fourth week in September on the surface of the ground and are parasitic on tree roots. Both have decurrant gills and produce a white spore print and look remarkably alike except that Armillaria has a ring. However, before you proceed with hunting wild mushrooms, you should know that caution is *most* necessary. No matter how much you study books or mushroom field guides, they are no substitute for a course in mushroom identification or going out in the field with a knowledgable collector. Some mushrooms can kill and some can make you very sick. Be sure an expert has identified what you find!

1) Cut off stems of about **2 qt. Armillaria mellea** or **Clitocybe tabescens.** Wipe clean but do not wash. Clean and slice **8 frying peppers,** using red ones, if available. Slice **1 very large onion.**

2) Put **3 Tb. olive oil** and **2 t. hot pepper flakes** in a large frying pan and saute peppers and onions. When they are light brown, scoop them out of the pan into a large pot. Turn heat on high and fry the mushrooms, adding more **olive oil** if necessary. When mushrooms are well cooked, turn into pot and deglaze frying pan with ¼ **c. tamari** and a **#2½ can** of **tomato sauce.** Simmer, scraping up burnt bits and turn sauce into pot. Use tomato sauce can to add **1 can water** and ½ **can red wine.** Add **salt** and **pepper** to taste. Simmer 20 minutes.

3) Finish mushroom sauce with **3 Tb. pesto** (see recipe
index), if available, and ½ **bunch Italian parsley,**
chopped. Sauce should be thin and not very tomato-
tasting. Thin with equal parts water and wine, as
necessary.

4) Boil **2–3 lb. linguine** or **spinach noodles** until just
cooked. Drain and shake dry. Serve with sauce and
freshly grated **parmesan.**

Serves 6–8

*My main point is to show how so-called health
values of therapy, hormonal treatment, and surgery
have replaced ethical values of choice, freedom,
and autonomy; how these same "health" values
have diffused critical awareness about the social
context in which the problem of transsexualism arises;
how more and more moral problems have been
reclassified as technical problems; and indeed how
the very notion of health itself, as generated by this
medical model, has made genuine transcendence
of the transsexual problem almost impossible.*

The Transsexual Empire:
The Making Of The She-Male
Janice G. Raymond; Beacon Press

MOUSSAKA

1) Make filling: Melt **2 Tb. butter** in a frying pan and saute ½ **c. pignoli nuts** and **1 large spanish onion,** finely chopped. When onions are soft and light brown, add **8 oz.** canned **tomato sauce, ⅓ c. red wine** and **2 Tb. tomato paste.** Simmer together a few minutes. Add **8 oz.** (the tomato sauce can) **water, ¼ c.** chopped **straight leaf parsley,** and **1 t. salt.** Simmer another 5 minutes. Add another ¼ **c. red wine** and ¾ **t. cinnamon.** Let cool. Beat **2 small eggs** in a bowl and slowly stir cinnamon-tomato sauce into the eggs.

2) Prepare cheeses by grating ¼ **lb. kefalotiri** and ½ **lb. kasseri.** Both are available at Greek markets and are necessary to the flavor of this meatless moussaka.

3) Peel and slice lengthwise, ½ inch thick, **2 large eggplants.** Fry the slices in a very hot frying pan or on a very hot griddle in as little **olive oil** as possible to keep eggplant from sticking. Using a large, deep ovenproof casserole dish, line the bottom with half the fried eggplant slices and sprinkle with about one fourth of both cheeses. Spoon the tomato-cinnamon-pignoli sauce over and top with remaining eggplant slices. Add most of the remaining cheese.

4) Make **Bechamel Sauce:** In a pot melt **½ stick
   butter.** Add **¼ c. flour** and cook together, stirring, a
   few minutes. Add **2½ c. milk** and whisk together until
   sauce comes to a boil. Season to taste with **salt,
   pepper,** and **nutmeg.** Beat **3 egg yolks** in a medium
   sized bowl and add hot sauce gradually to yolks, stirring
   well so that they do not curdle. Spread sauce over
   eggplant casserole. Top with the last of the grated
   cheeses and bake at 350° until browned and bubbling,
   about 1 hour.

                                                    Serves 6–8

> . . . *a woman forced
> to bear witness, falsely
> against my kind, as each
> other sister was judged inadequate, bitchy, incompetent,
> jealous, too thin, too fat. I know what I know.
> What sweet bread I make
> for myself in this prosperous house
> is dirty, what good soup I boil turns
> in my mouth to mud.*

"Cinderella"
Beginning With O
Olga Broumas; Yale University Press

GREEN TOMATO PIE

A savory dish that appears to be Pennsylvania Dutch in origin. Proportions are hard to be specific about in this recipe since it depends on how big your pan is and how many green tomatoes you have. From Roberta (Sage) of *A Woman's Place*, Athol, N.Y.

1) Make pie crust (see recipe index) using **9 c. white flour, 2¼ t. salt, 1 lb.** plus **½ stick sweet butter, ⅔ c. vegetable shortening,** and **1½ c. ice water.**

2) Using a large pan, for example, one 11" x 17", roll out enough pie crust to fit and line pan.

3) Thickly slice **8–10** very hard **green tomatoes,** removing stem end.

4) Slice **2** very **large onions** and saute in fry pan in **½ stick sweet butter.**

5) Slice **1 lb. Swiss cheese** and **1 lb. muenster cheese.**

6) Sprinkle pie crust lined pan with **bread crumbs.** Layer tomato slices, cheeses and sauteed onions in pan. Sprinkle with **coarse salt** and lots of **fresh ground pepper.** Also sprinkle over about **2 Tb. brown sugar.** Repeat layers until ingredients are used up. Top with more **bread crumbs** and a sprinkle of **wine vinegar.**

7) Roll out crust to top pie. Crimp edges and slash. Bake at
   375° until brown. When it begins to brown, the top crust
   can be brushed with milk to glaze it. Leftover portions
   can be reheated in an oven or toaster oven.

Serves 10–12

*When we got married it was fairly dull. I was fairly
lonely there as Derek didn't like hanging around
with just me so he'd go off somewheres and I'd
watch the TV and eat. Actually I got pretty fat then.
In the beginning I'd just tell myself it's the baby but
of course I knew and Derek would say pig at me and
I'd try to diet say on tomatoes and coffee then just
eat about six loaves of bread and jam like crazy I'd
get so funny about it.*

The True Story of Ida Johnson
Sharon Riis; The Women's Press

MAPLE APRICOT MOUSSE

1) Soak **3 c. dried apricots** overnight in **water** to cover.

2) Puree the softened apricots in their liquid with
   2 Tb. sherry and **1 t. lemon juice.** A food processor
   does this best, but a blender or food mill are other
   possibilities. (If apricots are not soft enough to puree,
   they may be cooked in their liquid until soft before you
   puree.) Put puree in large mixing bowl and set aside.

3) Beat **⅓ c. egg whites** (approx. 3) stiff in mixer. Fold
   into apricot puree. Into mixer (no need to wash) place
   **1⅓ c. heavy cream, ¼ t. almond extract, ¼ t.
   vanilla extract,** and **3½ Tb. grade A maple syrup.**
   Beat stiff and fold into apricot-egg white mixture. Chill
   thoroughly.

4) Beat together until stiff **1 c. heavy cream, 1 Tb. syrup,**
   and **¼ t. almond extract.**

5) To serve, pile mousse in glass sherbert or dessert dishes.
   Top with maple whipped cream. **Slivered almonds,**
   lightly toasted, are nice on top.

                                        Serves 10

RICOTTA HONEY CHEESECAKE

1) Soften **1 lb. cream cheese.** Preheat oven to 325°.
   Melt ½ **stick butter** and cool to room temperature.

2) Separate **4 eggs,** whites in a mixer, yolks in a food
   processor or a bowl. Add **2 extra whites** to the ones in
   the mixer and beat until stiff.

3) If you have no food processor, turn whites into another
   bowl and add egg yolks to mixer. In either case, add
   grated rind of **1 lemon, 4 t. lemon juice, 1 lb.
   ricotta cheese,** the softened cream cheese, and
   the melted butter to the yolks. Begin to mix or turn
   processor on. Add ¾ **c. honey, 3 Tb. flour, 3 Tb.
   cornstarch, 2 t. vanilla extract,** and mix well. Fold
   2 c. sour cream into the yolk-cheese mixture gently
   but thoroughly.

4) Fold the stiff beaten egg whites into the cake carefully.
   Turn cake into an ungreased 12″ spring form pan. Bake
   cake 1 hr. and 15 min. Turn off oven and leave cake in it
   for 2 hours. Remove from oven and cool. Chill before
   serving.

LEKACH

Jewish Honey Cake.

1) In a small pot, heat ⅔ c. brewed **coffee, 1 Tb. instant coffee** (or coffee substitute), **1 Tb. unsweetened cocoa, ½ t. cinnamon, ¼ t. ground cloves, ¼ t. allspice, ¼ t. nutmeg.** When all is blended, remove from heat and let cool. Preheat oven to 350°.

2) Separate **6 eggs,** placing **whites** in a mixer and **yolks** in a bowl or food processor. Beat yolks with **½ c. oil** and **1¼ c. honey.** When yolks seem light in texture, add cooled coffee and spices.

3) In a bowl, use a whisk to stir together **2½ c. flour, 1½ t. baking powder,** and **1½ t. baking soda.**

4) Beat egg whites until stiff. Meanwhile, fold together flour mix and egg yolk mix, adding ⅔ c. chopped **walnuts** and **½ c. raisins** as you fold. Now fold in the stiff beaten egg whites gently but thoroughly.

5) Turn batter into one greased and floured tube pan or two loaf pans. Bake at 350° until cake has browned and pulled away slightly from the sides of the pan. Turn out onto a rack and cool.

6) Honey cake is traditionally served with afternoon tea or coffee or as a dessert with brandy. However, you may serve it with **honey sweetened whipped cream:** Beat until stiff **2 c. heavy cream, 1½ Tb. honey, 1½ t. vanilla extract.**

Christianity is rather naive compared with the earlier patriarchal yarns. Eve (whose name means Hava, life) doubtless the Goddess in her Mother form, eats from the apple tree! This is most absurd, since the apple or quince always belonged to her and symbolized Wisdom. The fact that the snake made her do it, is transparent as well. The Snake belongs to her; it is the death and rebirth symbol of the Goddess. At her shrines, the sacred snakes used to be consulted by the priestesses for oracles. Hecate, Mary, Medusa, and Eve—they are never without their sacred animal, the snake. Just as Life is never without Death as a necessity.

The Holy Book of Women's Mysteries Part I
Z. Budapest; Susan B. Anthony Coven No. 1

LIME TART

1) Preheat oven to 400°. Roll out **pie crust** (see recipe index) and fit crust into a pie pan. Prick at intersection of rim and bottom with a fork. Line crust with aluminum foil and weight with dried beans or lentils. Bake for 5–10 minutes, or until edges are light brown. Carefully remove foil and beans and bake until crust is nicely browned, about 10 minutes more. Remove from oven and cool.

2) In a stainless steel pot, combine **6 eggs, 5 egg yolks, ⅓ c. honey, grated rind** and **juice** of **4 limes.** Place over medium to low flame and stir with whisk. When mixture warms, add **1½ sticks sweet butter,** cut into pieces. Continue stirring until mixture starts to thicken. Cook, whisking constantly, another 30 seconds until mixture is creamy and slightly thick. Do not overcook. Remove from heat and continue whisking another minute. Let cool 10 minutes and then pour into the baked pie shell. Place in refrigerator until set up, about 2 hours.

3) Before serving, top pie with **honey whipped cream:** Beat together until stiff **1 c. heavy cream, 1½ t. honey** and **½ t. vanilla** extract. A grating of **lime rind** over the whipped cream is a finishing touch.

APPLE CUSTARD TART

1) Preheat oven to 400°. Roll out pie crust (see recipe
   index) for 1 pie pan. Prick around bottom of crust with
   fork tines. Use foil and dried beans, lentils or corn to
   weight down the crust while it bakes 5–10 minutes.

2) Meanwhile, peel, core and slice enough **crisp apples**
   like Macoun or Staymen Winesap to yield **3 c.** sliced.

3) Remove partially baked crust from oven, remove foil
   and beans and arrange apple slices in shell. Sprinkle
   lightly with **cinnamon,** lower heat to 375° and bake
   20 minutes.

4) Beat **1 large** or **2 small eggs** with ¼ **c. honey.** When
   well mixed, add ¼ **c. flour** and ½ **c. heavy cream.**
   Mix well to be sure honey is dissolved. Flavor with
   2½ Tb. cognac or ¾ **t. vanilla,** as you prefer.

5) Sprinkle **1½ Tb. currants** over apples in pie crust and
   pour custard over the apples. Bake another 25–30
   minutes. This pie is best served warm and can be
   reheated either entire or serving by serving.

APPLE COBBLER

This is a variation of Anne Raulerson's Peach Pudding.

1) Preheat oven to 400°. In mixer combine **3 c. unbleached white flour, ¾ t. baking powder, ¾ t. salt.** While mixing, add **½ lb. sweet butter** cut into small pieces. Do not worry about overbeating. Remove from mixer and press into 9" x 12" baking dish.

2) Peel and core **5 apples** and cut into slices. Press the apple slices into the dry mix. Pour **¾ c. honey** over slices and sprinkle lightly with **cinnamon.** Bake 10 minutes.

3) Meanwhile, whisk together thoroughly in large mixing bowl: **3 c. sour cream, 3 egg yolks,** and **⅓ c. honey.** If too thick for pouring, add up to **¼ c. apple juice** or **cider.** Open oven and pour sour cream mixture over apples. Spread evenly. Sprinkle lightly with **cinnamon** and continue baking for about ½ hour more. Cobbler is done when top is golden brown and there is a minimum of movement when pan is jiggled.

4) Serve warm with **heavy cream.**

APPLE MUFFINS

1) Preheat oven to 425°. Butter muffin tins or line them with papers.

2) Melt ½ **stick sweet butter.**

3) Use a whisk to stir together **2 c. unbleached white flour, 4 t. baking powder, ½ t. baking soda, ½ t. salt, scant ⅔ c. sugar, ¼ t. nutmeg,** and **½ t. cinnamon.**

4) Beat **2 eggs** well; stir in **1 c. sour cream** and the melted butter.

5) Peel, core and dice **1½ c. apples.** Do not peel, but core and slice an additional **apple** into 14 segments.

6) Combine wet and dry mixtures and the diced apples. Do not overmix. Spoon batter into prepared muffin tins. Gently press one of the apple slices (skin side up) into the center of each muffin. Bake at 425° until lightly browned, about 20 to 25 minutes. These can be frozen and then reheated in a 350° oven or toaster oven.

Yields 12–14

CHAPTER 9   BREAKFASTS
Omelets, eggs and breakfasts.

OMELETS

Having an omelet pan doesn't guarantee you will be good at making omelets; not having one requires your being especially skilled before your omelets slide out mottled brown and gold on the outside and moist and tender within. Heavy aluminum or other metal designed especially for omelet making, preferably with a wooden handle, is best. Season an omelet pan as you do a crepe pan by slowly heating a tablespoon of oil in it for 15–20 minutes and then wiping it clean with absorbent paper. Don't ever wash it. Any burnt-on material can be removed with oil and salt.

Two or **three eggs** make a nice omelet. Do try to obtain eggs from free-running chickens. You will be amazed at their superior flavor. Fork beat them in a small bowl with a **dash** of **Tabasco** and **1 Tb. beer,** which add flavor and lightness. Very little beating is necessary, just enough to mix the eggs. Have your filling ready. Heat **1 Tb. butter** in the omelet pan until it just begins to turn brown. Turn heat moderately high, add egg mixture and shake the pan vigorously until the omelet sets up. Or you can use the fork, flat side down, to stir the mixture as it sets, or a combination of stirring and shaking may please you best. In any case, the egg mixture should end up opposite the omelet pan handle. Turn heat down, **salt** the omelet and add filling. Now holding the handle in your right if you are righty, in your left if you are lefty, keep your palm under the handle, thumb on top with pan at a right angle to your arm. Hold the plate in your other hand and roll the omelet out onto the plate by gradually turning the pan upside down against the plate. It does take a little practice, but not too much!

The most popular omelet here is **Cheese and Sprout.** We use thin slices of **Doux de Montagne** ("sweet of the mountain") cut with a cheese plane, and **alfalfa sprouts.** A **dash** of **tamari** before rolling finishes it.

Leftover **Creamed Spinach** (see page 284) is also popular and so are **Mushrooms in Port Wine.** Fry sliced mushrooms and onions (**1 small onion** to **1 lb. mushrooms**) in **butter** until liquid has evaporated and mushrooms begin to brown. Turn off fire and add a **splash** of **port wine.**

Omelets are an excellent way to use up leftovers. Leftover **applesauce** in Autumn may be laced with **brandy** for an omelet filling and **Cranberry Applesauce** (see recipe index) is good as is. Leftover cooked peeled **asparagus** stalks from the asparagus platter can be cut up for a Spring omelet filling. If there is leftover cooking liquid, it can be thickened with a roux (**1 Tb. butter, 1 Tb. flour** cooked together before **1 c. asparagus liquid** is added), and a little **Swiss** or **raclette** cheese melted in this sauce. Warm the asparagus in the sauce and top the omelet with it as well. Washed shredded **sorrel leaves** cooked in their own liquid with a **splash** of **heavy cream** is another Spring omelet specialty.

Leftover **Ratatouille Nicoise** (see recipe index) makes a wonderful late Summer omelet. For a **Zuccini and Pesto** omelet, simmer ½ **c. pesto** (see recipe index) and a **#2½ can tomatoes** together for 5 minutes. Slice **1 medium zuccini** and a **small onion** and fry in **1 Tb. butter** with ½ **t. oregano** over high heat. Use the zuccini as the omelet filling, add some grated **parmesan cheese** and a little of the pesto sauce. Turn the omelet out and top with more sauce.

Whenever you have leftover cooked **broccoli** it can be cut up, warmed in a little **butter,** and used as an omelet filling with a little **Sour Cream Sauce** (see recipe index) inside the omelet and a lot more on top.

Omelet Grandmere is made up of several ingredients Grandma had on hand. Stale **homemade bread** is cut in cubes and toasted in the oven. The last **herbs** of the garden year or the first ones of Spring are chopped fine and mixed with the eggs. We prefer **burnet** and **garlic leaves,** but almost any herbs will do. You will need leftover gravy (see recipe index for **miso gravy**) and **sour cream.** Fill the herb omelet with the croutons, moisten with a little heated gravy, and turn out onto the plate. Top with more gravy and a dollop of sour cream.

As good as many foods are reheated for omelets, potatoes have to be fresh cooked to make good **homefries** or filling for a **Spanish Omelet.** Idahos are best. Cook scrubbed **potatoes** in their skins until tender. Peel or not as you like and cut up into small slices. Add chopped **onion** and chopped **green pepper, salt** and fresh ground **pepper** and moisten with **oil.** Fry potatoes in your largest well heated cast iron skillet or on a griddle, turning occasionally and sprinkling with **paprika.** When browned and crisp, turn out to serve with **fried eggs** and **Johnson's Table Sauce** (available at Health Food Stores) or use the potatoes as an omelet filling with slivers of **Swiss cheese.** Top with **Spanish Sauce:** Chop **1 small onion** fine and saute in **olive oil** with **2** crushed **cloves garlic, 2 t. oregano, 1 t. basil (dried).** After a few minutes, add **15 oz.** canned **plain tomato sauce.** Rinse out can with ¼ **c. red wine** and add **1 Tb.** finely chopped canned **hot peppers.** Taste for **salt,** and simmer 10 minutes.

Home grown **Mung Bean Sprouts** make an excellent omelet. Fry them in a little **oil** with chopped **scallions.** When they are barely cooked and still crisp, add a **dash tamari** and a little **sesame oil,** if you have it. Use as an omelet filling alone or with **cheese,** as you like.

If you can find good quality **Rose Hip Jam,** it makes a nice omelet filling. Top the omelet with **sour cream.** Finally, for an elegant orange omelet, thinly slice and cut **oranges.** Heat in orange marmalade in a small pot. Fill omelet and add a **splash** of **Grand Marnier liqueur** to remaining juices in the pot. After the omelet is rolled onto the plate, heat the sauce and tilt the pot to flame it. Pour over the omelet and serve for a fancy breakfast.

Did you ever think that you lived in a cage?
Well, they're calling you a "chick,"
And the name just seems to stick—
And you still don't think you're living in a cage?

"High Flying Woman", Helen Hooke
The Deadly Nightshade
Shanti Productions

POACHED EGGS IN SPINACH NESTS

1) Thaw **2 ten oz. packages** of **frozen chopped spinach** several hours or overnight. Drain and gently squeeze liquid from spinach. Melt **3 Tb. butter** in a pot. Add **3 Tb. flour** and stir together for a few minutes. Add **½ c. heavy cream** and bring to a simmer. Add the drained spinach and cook over low heat, stirring occasionally. Add **1 t. salt, fresh ground pepper,** and **fresh grated nutmeg.** Don't overcook; cover and set aside.

2) Prepare **Hollandaise Sauce:** Melt **1 stick unsalted butter.** Set aside. In a stainless steel pot, use a whisk to blend **2 egg yolks, 2 t. lemon juice** and **2 t. water.** Whisk over low heat until mixture foams and thickens slightly. Add melted butter very slowly, whisking and cooking over lowest heat until mixture becomes the consistency of thick cream. Remove from heat, whisking for another minute. Add **salt** to taste and **a drop** of **Tabasco.** Cover. Sauce will keep warm enough for an hour.

3) In a shallow sauce pan, bring enough **water** to a boil to adequately cover the eggs you will be poaching. Don't try to poach more than 4 eggs at a time. You may add **1 t. white vinegar** to the water to help egg whites coagulate, but the best way to get good poached eggs is to find a source for **fresh fertile eggs.** Bring water to a boil, drop in eggs, turn heat down to a simmer and cover. If you are making **toast,** the eggs and toast will usually take the same amount of time to get done. Without toast, allow three minutes to poach the eggs.

4) Make a spinach "nest" by heaping spinach in the middle of a plate and using a small spoon to make a central depression in it. Use a slotted spoon to dip eggs from simmering water, drain on absorbent paper, and slip into "nest". We serve 2 eggs in each nest. Toast goes around the sides and the hollandaise sauce over the top.

Serves 6.

POACHED EGGS
IN ARTICHOKE BOTTOMS

Artichoke bottoms may also provide a rather small receptacle for poached eggs. Allow **1 large artichoke** per diner and boil in **water** to cover until just done. Overcooked artichokes fall apart. Pull off one outer layer of leaves, cut off stem so that bottom sits flat on a plate. Pull out central leaves a few at a time (they may be scraped for artichoke mushroom soup). Scoop out choke, using a small spoon and discard. Now use a kitchen scissor to snip away the outer leaves, leaving a ½ inch rim remaining. The artichokes may be prepared in advance and stored in the refrigerator. When ready, they may be heated in an oven or toaster oven. Top with **poached eggs** and **Hollandaise** or **Maltaise Sauce** (see recipe index).

MUSHROOM QUICHE

1) Preheat oven to 400°. Prepare **pie crust** (see recipe index) and line a 10″ quiche pan with it. Prick intersection of rim and bottom with a fork and line pie crust with foil and weight with dried beans, corn or lentils. Bake 5–10 minutes, or until edges of the crust are a very light brown. Remove foil and beans and turn oven down to 375°. Remove pie crust from oven.

2) Meanwhile, wipe clean (do not wash) and slice **1 lb. mushrooms.** Finely chop **3 Tb. onions** and saute onions for about a minute in a large fry pan in **2 Tb. butter.** Add mushrooms, turn heat up high until liquid evaporates and they begin to brown. Stir occasionally. Add **1 t. salt** and ¼ **c. tawny port.** Set aside.

3) Beat **3 eggs** together in a mixer or a bowl. Add a **grating** of **nutmeg, 1½ c. heavy cream,** and some **fresh ground pepper.**

4) Add mushrooms to pie crust. Sprinkle ½ **c. grated Swiss cheese** over them and return pie to oven. Carefully add custard to the quiche. Bake until puffed and browned, ½ hour to 45 minutes. (Individual pieces of quiche may be wrapped, frozen, and later reheated in a toaster oven.)

GRANOLA

From *A Woman's Place*, Athol, N.Y.

1) Preheat oven to 375°. In a large shallow pan, combine **⅓ c. sesame seeds, ⅓ c. sunflower seeds, 3 Tb. flax seed, ⅓ c. wheat germ, ⅓ c. bran, ½ c. powdered milk, ⅓ c. dried coconut, ½ c. mixed nuts** (such as cashew pieces or chopped Brazil nuts), **2 c. oats, ⅓ c. soy powder, ½ t.** ground **cardamom** and a **dash salt.** Roast, stirring occasionally, for 30–40 minutes.

2) Meanwhile, mix together **⅓ c. honey, ⅓ c. vegetable oil, ½ t. vanilla extract.** Pour over mixture in oven; stir well and bake another 30 minutes. When done and still quite warm, add **½ c. raisins.** Other dried fruits can be added as well. Store in covered container. Serve with **milk** or **yoghurt** as breakfast food or keep as a snack.

Makes about 6 cups

*I thought women who worked together
would become naturally close
but I learned women who were close first
had to find ways
to work together later*

"Talking With Woman"
Dyke Jacket
Fran Winant; Violet Press

SOUR DOUGH PANCAKES

Sour dough starter produces pancakes, biscuits, and breads of wonderful lightness and "clean" flavor. The starter is made up of wild strains of yeast which must be fed fresh water and flour every two or three weeks, so once you have starter, you must use it with some regularity. Always turn it all out, add as much flour and water (potato, if available) as seems necessary to make a thin batter, and stir well. The batter will be lumpy. Leave overnight. Be sure to remember to return some starter to the refrigerator before adding spoilable ingredients, such as milk or eggs, to the batter. We have had some very close calls. In each instance some of our original starter had been given to a friend who was able to replenish our supply.

You can obtain starter in one of three ways. Getting some from a friend is best, since it will be oldest and therefore will have the best developed flavor. Ours is over fifteen years old. Some gourmet or health food stores sell sour dough starter as a dry powder. Or you can try to grow your own: Wash, peel and shred **2 large potatoes.** Add ⅓ **c. honey** and **flour** and **water** to make a thin mixture. Or, cook the potatoes, mash, and add honey, flour and water. Either way, leave this mixture uncovered in a warm place in the kitchen for 5–7 days, stirring every day. When it smells fermented and like alcohol, it is ready to use. If it smells rotten, however, discard it. See *Uncle John's Bread Book*, by John Rahn Braué, Exposition Banner Press, and *Breads and Coffee Cakes* by Ada Lou Roberts, Hearthside, for more on sour dough.

Once you have the starter, you will note that it has a changeable personality. Weather, humidity, and time of year affect its liveliness. Many times we thought we were preparing a batter which was either too thick or too thin only to have the yeasts grow in an opposite fashion from our expectations.

To make pancakes, turn out the **starter** into a bowl the night before and add as much **flour** and **water** as seems necessary to make as much batter as you need. Stir well. Batter will be lumpy. The next morning return some starter to the refrigerator. Beat **eggs** (about **4** to **2 qt. starter**) and melt some **butter,** about **1 stick** to the above proportions. Stir butter and eggs into the batter. Heat griddle very hot. A tiny test pancake will prove how hot the griddle is. Cut up fruit of the season to add to the batter, or have the pancakes plain, but do plan to use real **Grade A 100% maple syrup** on the pancakes. We mix in **apples, cranberries, bananas, pineapple, strawberries, blueberries, mulberries** and **peaches** at different times of the year. Dip out a ladle of fruit filled batter or use a pitcher to pour pancakes out. Turn when bubbles form and begin to burst. Serve with **butter** and syrup.

The most notable fact that culture imprints on women is the sense of our limits. The most important thing one woman can do for another is to illuminate and expand her sense of actual possibilities . . . To refuse to be a victim: and then to go on from there.

Of Woman Born
Adrienne Rich; Norton

Sunflower

~~~~~~

CHAPTER 10   BREADS

BREAD BAKING

Making your own bread differs from other cooking in that it depends less on accuracy of measured ingredients and time elapsed between steps than it does on learning the "feel" of the dough and sensing how temperature and humidity are affecting it. So bread baking is more subjective and intuitive than calculated. It is very satisfying in that it is hard to produce an inedible loaf. Once you have some practice, there's no reason you can't make excellent bread, and no excuse for oversweetened and overyeasted loaves that pass for "good" homemade.

Having a bread mixer is a necessity for us. Kneading by hand takes time and one is tempted to add more flour than necessary to make the dough stop being sticky sooner than is possible. You can knead by hand if you don't mind the mess and will give the kneading enough time before more flour goes in.

We rise bread twice: once after kneading and once in the pans. We don't make a "sponge" or proof the yeast since both procedures seem a waste of time. The first rising is long, 1½–2 hours. This requires a cool place in the kitchen and if that is not possible, then a cool place elsewhere in the house. Rising that is too rapid produces a yeasty tasting bread with underdeveloped flavor. The second rising should be brief, ½ hour to 45 minutes. The remaining yeast growth takes place in the oven.

Potato cooking water (and mashed potatoes themselves)
seem to do something wonderful to bread. Some old
fashioned sour dough starters begin with potatoes, which
purportedly attract very particular wild yeasts. We save
potato cooking water in the refrigerator for sour dough
pancakes and for bread making.

You will note that except for the whole wheat bread, all
others are made with unbleached white flour in
combination with whole grains. Producing a well risen
loaf requires high gluten, which the white flour provides.
We add gluten flour to the whole wheat to help it up,
together with potatoes and a little sour dough starter.

If you have never baked bread before, begin with an easy
one like the rye bread. After you have made bread a few
times, you can experiment with your own additions. Our
recipes here are basic and are restaurant favorites. We
always suggest bread for children who are unused to our
menu, and they love it.

Bread freezes very well. Place cooled bread in a plastic bag
and freeze. To reheat, remove from bag and heat in a 350°
oven for half an hour.

putting a positive value on hunger
not starvation but a little unfilled hunger
all the time
its something vegetarians dont talk about

"Dyke Jacket"
Dyke Jacket
Fran Winant; Violet Press

POTATO RYE BREAD

From Bud Schwartz. Note that this bread has and needs no sweetening.

1) Wash **4 medium potatoes,** cover with **water** and boil until tender. Remove and peel, reserving potato water. Mash in mixer or by hand.

2) When cool, add **2 Tb. salt, 2 Tb. caraway seed, 2 c. rye flour** (fresh ground from health food store is best), and **2 Tb. dry yeast.** Be sure potato water is no more than tepid before proceeding. Add alternately, **2½–3 c. potato water** and **6–7 c. white flour,** beating well. Flour should be added gradually to determine how much is needed. You should knead dough about ½ hour by hand or about 10 minutes in a Kitchenaid mixer. Rye bread is especially sticky. Be careful not to add too much flour, resulting in heavy bread.

3) Turn bread out into a bowl and let rise in a cool place for 2 hours, covered with a cloth. Deflate the dough and divide into 2–3 loaves, oval shaped or round. Shape the dough by tucking in ragged edges and turning it round and tucking it in again and again. It will feel silky and alive. Butter a cookie sheet and sprinkle it with cornmeal. Place loaves on cookie sheet and don't let bread rise more than 30 minutes. Meanwhile, preheat oven to 400°. Slash top of loaves the instant before bread goes into the oven.

4) Fork beat **1 egg white** with **1 Tb. water.** When loaves
   have risen and are very slightly brown, brush with egg
   white mix and sprinkle with **czerniska** (Russian
   caraway seed), if available. Continue baking until well
   browned. Cool breads on racks. Don't cut them until
   they have cooled at least ½ hour.

Yields 2–3 loaves

*The blues women had a commanding presence
and a refreshing robustness. They were nurturers,
taking the yeast of experience, kneading it into
dough, molding it and letting it grow in their minds
to bring the listener bread for sustenance, shaped
by their sensibilities.*

Mean Mothers Independent Women's Blues,
Rosetta Reitz; Rosetta Records

OATMEAL SUNFLOWER SEED BREAD

1) Pour **4 c. boiling water** over **3 c. rolled oats** and let cool for ½ hour in a large bowl. Oatmeal must be no more than warm when yeast is added.

2) In bread mixing machine or by hand, add **2 Tb. yeast** to the oatmeal and stir in **2 Tb. salt,** ¼ **c. oil,** ½ **c. molasses,** and gradually add **5–8 c. unbleached white flour.** Knead a good 20 minutes if working by hand and at least 10 minutes in a machine. Add enough flour to make dough silky, not tough and dry. When dough seems the right texture, add ½ **c. sunflower seeds** and ½ **c. sesame seeds.** Mix into bread dough thoroughly and set dough aside to rise for 1½–2 hours, covered with a dish towel. Be sure your kitchen is not too hot. A long slow rising produces best flavor.

3) Butter 3 small loaf tins (9" x 5" x 3") or 2 larger ones. Punch down bread on a floured board and shape into loaves. Place in pans and let rise ½ hour to 45 minutes.

4) Preheat oven to 350° and bake bread until done, about ¾ hour. Turn out onto racks to cool.

Yields 2–3 loaves

FOUR GRAIN WALNUT BREAD

From Nancy Pressley.

1) Combine **3 c. oatmeal** and **6 c. water** in a pot. Bring to a boil, remove from heat and let cool.

2) In a mixer or large bowl combine **3 Tb. salt, ¾ c. molasses,** and **1½ sticks sweet butter.** Add oatmeal and mix. When mixture is tepid, add **¼ c. yeast, 3¾ c. water** (potato water, if available), **3 c. rye flour, 3 c. whole wheat flour, 1½ c. wheat germ, 1 c.** plus **2 Tb. bran flakes, 1½ c. cornmeal** and beat until smooth. Add up to **11 c. unbleached white flour** and beat or knead to make dough silky smooth. Mix in **2⅔ c. chopped walnuts.** Turn out into bowl and let rise 2 hours in a cool place, covered with a dish towel.

3) Grease 4–5 large loaf pans. Punch down bread and shape into loaves. Pat each piece flat, roll up and tuck in ends. Let rise in pans about 45 minutes.

4) Preheat oven to 375°. Bake loaves until brown and hollow sounding when rapped. Turn out onto racks to cool.

Yields 4–5 loaves

SPROUTED WHOLE WHEAT BREAD

1) Three or four days before making the bread, cover **1 c. wheat berries** with water for a few hours, drain and keep in a dark cupboard. Rinse twice a day, draining well each time to produce sprouts by the third or fourth day. Sprouts stop growing quickly when refrigerated. They can be omitted from this bread, but they add protein and texture.

2) Boil **2 c. potatoes,** peeled and cut up, in **water** to cover. Cool to lukewarm. Drain, reserving potato liquid, and mash potatoes. Potatoes add delicious flavor to whole wheat bread. And if you have **sour dough starter** in your refrigerator, prepare **1 c.** of it to add additional flavor and leavening.

3) In mixer or bowl, place **3½ c. potato cooking liquid** (tepid) and add **4 Tb. yeast.** When yeast has dissolved, add potatoes, **¼ c. oil, 2 Tb. salt, ½ c. honey, 1 c. gluten flour** and sour dough starter if available, and begin beating or mixing. Gradually add up to **10 c. whole wheat flour.** Be sure to use hard wheat, not that provided as "pastry flour". The gluten flour will help the bread rise and be light. Now add **2 c. wheat berry sprouts** and **¾ c. sunflower seeds.** When bread is well beaten and silky, turn out to rise for 1½–2 hours.

4) Grease 2–3 large bread pans. Turn bread out, cut into loaf sized pieces. Flatten out each one and roll up to make neat loaves. Tuck in ends and place in pans. Let rise 45 minutes more.

5) Preheat oven to 375°. Bake bread until brown and
   hollow sounding when you tap on the loaves. Turn out
   onto racks to cool.

Yields 2–3 loaves

. . . we will begin to see lesbian history as a history of
subversion and resistance, not necessarily
consciously feminist, but representing an
underground river which has fed the open and
conscious forms of women's resistance and rebellion. . .

Adrienne Rich
"Questionnaire on Issues in Lesbian History"
Frontiers, a journal of women studies
Judith Schwarz Vol. IV, No. 3, Fall 1979

COTTAGE CHEESE DILL BREAD

From Menga Thurm.

1) Gently warm **2½ lb. cottage cheese** in a pot over low heat, stirring occasionally.

2) Dissolve **4 Tb. yeast** in **1 c. warm water** (potato water if available), in a mixer or large bowl, and add **⅓ c. honey, 2½Tb. caraway seed, 2 bunches** fresh **dill,** chopped, **1 stick sweet butter,** cut into pieces, **1 onion,** peeled and chopped fine, **1½ Tb. salt, 1 t. baking soda,** the warmed cottage cheese, and **4 large unbeaten eggs.** Turn mixer on or begin to beat, adding about **10 c. unbleached white flour.** Beat thoroughly. This dough should be made drier than other breads, so you may need up to **8** more **c. flour.** There should be no dampness or stickiness when you pinch it. When well beaten and silky smooth, turn out into bowl and let double for 2 hours, covered with a dish towel or tablecloth.

3) Punch down, grease 3–4 large bread pans and divide dough. This bread rises more than most, so shape dough into smaller loaves than you would ordinarily. Let rise in pans 30–40 minutes. Preheat oven to 350°. If you like, brush loaves with beaten **egg white** while they are baking and sprinkle with **coarse salt.** Bake until brown and hollow-sounding when rapped.

Yields 3–4 loaves

CHEESE BABKA

A coffee cake.

1) In mixer or bowl, dissolve **1 Tb. yeast** in **1 c. tepid water** with **1 Tb. sugar**. After 5 minutes, add **2 t. salt, 1½ sticks sweet butter,** cut into bits, **⅓ c. sugar, 2 eggs, 2 egg yolks** and mix well. Begin adding **3 c. unbleached white flour** and knead until dough is silky smooth. Up to **3** more **c. flour** may be added if dough is too loose, but be sure it remains soft. Turn into a bowl to rise about 1½ hours in a cool place.

2) Meanwhile prepare filling. Plump **2 Tb. yellow raisins** in **1 Tb. brandy** or **cognac**. Cream together **1 c.** dry **cottage cheese** or **pot cheese** with **¼ c. sugar, 1 Tb. flour, 1 egg yolk, ½ t. grated lemon rind, ½ t. vanilla extract** and **1 Tb. sour cream.** When well mixed, add raisins and brandy and stir.

3) Deflate dough on a floured board and shape into a rough rectangle. Brush with melted **butter** and spread filling over. Roll up like a jelly roll and fit into a large buttered loaf pan or coil into a buttered angel food or other large circular pan. Don't use a pan that is too small. Bread should come no more than ¾ up the sides of the pan. Let rise 45 minutes.

4) Preheat oven to 350°. Bake babka until well browned, about 45 minutes to one hour. Optional: after bread has risen in the oven, it may be brushed with beaten **egg white** and sprinkled with **streusel:** use your fingers to rub together **⅓ c. butter, ½ c. sugar,** and **½ c. flour.**

POPPY SEED CAKES

These are made from a yeast dough. However, other recipes for poppy seed cakes use cake batter or cookie dough and hold strong emotional connotations ranging from grandmother-lore in Eastern Europe to celebration of Jewish rebellion against oppression in the form of triangular shaped cookies called "Humantashin," made for Purim. We chose to make poppy seed cakes in memory of ancient Jewish women's celebration of the new moon, when lit candles were floated on water and round or crescent shaped cakes filled with seeds or nuts were eaten.

1) Start filling. Cover **1½ c. poppy seeds** with boiling water and soak 1–2 hours.

2) Make dough. Soften **1 stick sweet butter.** In a small pot, warm **½ c. milk** with **¼ c. honey** until honey dissolves and milk is lukewarm. Turn into mixer or bowl and add **3 Tb. yeast.** Beat in **3 c. unbleached white flour,** 1 cup at a time. Add **2** unbeaten **eggs** and the softened butter, cut into pieces. Beat or knead dough thoroughly. Add **1** more **c. flour** and beat until dough is quite dry and well mixed. Shape into a ball and place in a bowl covered with **cold water.** In 15 minutes to half an hour, the dough will have risen above the water. Pat it dry, return to mixer or place on floured board and knead again for 5–10 minutes. Place in a buttered bowl, cover and let rise in a cool place 1–2 hours.

3) Finish filling. Drain poppy seeds well in a fine mesh strainer. Place in a blender with **1 c. milk** and **2 Tb. flour** and blend for a few minutes to grind poppy seeds as fine as possible. Turn into a small pot, add ⅓ c. **honey** and cook, stirring, until smooth and thick. Add ⅓ c. chopped **almonds, 1 c. raisins,** coarsely chopped, and **2 t.** grated **lemon rind.** Fork beat **1 egg** and add to filling, mixing well.

4) Divide dough in half to shape. Melt ½ **stick sweet butter.** Roll one piece at a time on a floured board to ¼″ thickness and in as square a shape as possible. Brush each half with half the melted butter and spread thinly with half the poppy seed filling. To form "moons," roll up jelly roll fashion, slice in ½″–¾″ rounds and place on a buttered baking sheet. To form crescents, divide dough into 9–12 squares and cut each square diagonally into triangles. Roll each triangle from a wide end to the point and curve to form crescent. Place on buttered baking sheet.

5) Heat oven to 375° and wait 5 minutes for it to warm. Place rolls in oven. When they have puffed and browned a little, brush with **1 egg yolk** beaten with **2 Tb. cream.** Bake till medium brown. Rolls may be frozen and reheated in an oven or toaster oven. Serve with **butter,** if you like.

Yields 35–40

*You say to us: if this is a tribe, why do you
never stay still? Why do you meet only long
enough to exchange stones, shells, feathers,
amulets? Why can you pass through the center
only alone and in absolute darkness? You say,
if this is a tribe, what is the given language?
What is its name, who belongs? You challenge
our assumptions. You say, what kind of people
is always on the road, alone, only speaking to
each other in crisis, at connecting points, in
crowded intersections in dying cities, in drug-
stores in small towns where no one knows your
name, and then dispersal?*

*This is our answer: our language is poetry. Do
you understand? Our language is signs, symbols,
sacred objects; we are a sacred people. We have
magical properties. There are many things to
be done, people to be healed, houses to be
built. It is not a time to be together. It is
a time to be separate, to learn what it means
to be alone.*

*We tell you this: we are doing the impossible.
We are teaching ourselves to be human. When
we are finished, the strands which connect us
will be unbreakable; already we are stronger
than we have ever been . . .*

Thus we move: silently, separately; our name is buried in various sacred spots all over the land. We are waiting until it is safe to claim it. Though we move silently, separate, can you hear our joint voices singing, singing our women's songs in ever widening circles?

Listen. We are making ready. Hear our music across the dying land. . .

"Tribes"
Tribe
Martha Courtot; Pearlchild

BIBLIOGRAPHY

FAVORITE COOKING RESOURCES

Jordan, Julie, *Wings of Life*. Trumansburg, N.Y.: Crossing Press, 1976.

Dinaburg, Kathy and D'Ann Akel, *Nutrition Survival Kit*. San Francisco: Panjandrum Press, 1976.

Shurtleff, William and Akiko Aoyagi, *The Book of Tofu*, Brookline, Mass.: Autumn Press, 1975.

_____, *The Book of Miso*, Brookline Mass.: Autumn Press, 1976.

_____, *The Book of Tempeh*, New York: Harper & Row, 1979.

Bumgarner, Marlene Anne, *The Book of Whole Grains*, Brookline, Mass.: Autumn Press, 1978.

Rhoads, Sharon Ann, *Cooking With Sea Vegetables*, Brookline, Mass.: Autumn Press, 1978.

Whyte, Karen Cross, *The Complete Sprouting Cookbook*, San Francisco: Troubadoor, 1973.

Child, Julia, Louisette Bertholle, and Simone Beck, *Mastering the Art of French Cooking Vol. 1.*, New York: Alfred A. Knopf, 1961.

_____, and Simone Beck, *Mastering the Art of French Cooking Vol. II.*, New York: Alfred A. Knopf, 1970.

_____, *From Julia Child's Kitchen*, New York: Alfred A. Knopf, 1975.

Field, Michael, *Michael Field's Cooking School*, New York: Holt Rhinehart Winston, 1965.

_____, *All Manner of Food*, New York: Alfred A. Knopf, 1970.

David, Elizabeth, *French Provincial Cooking*, Harmondsworth, Middlesex, England: Penguin Books, 1960. Her other cookbooks are also excellent.

Stockli, Albert, *Splendid Fare: The Albert Stockli Cookbook*, New York: Alfred A. Knopf, 1970.

McCully, Helen and Jaque Pepin, *The Other Half of the Egg*, New York: William Morrow, 1971.

Perkins, Wilma Lord, revised the 10th edition *The Fannie Merritt Farmer Boston Cooking School Cookbook*, Boston: Little Brown & Co., 1959.

Time-Life Books, *Foods of the World,* New York: Time Inc., 1968–1971. All books in this series are excellent and in particular: *American Cooking: the Eastern Heartland, American Cooking: New England, American Cooking: Southern Style, The Cooking of Japan, Latin American Cooking, Pacific and Southeast Asian Cooking,* and *A Quintet of Cuisines.*

Lewis, Edna, *The Taste of Country Cooking,* New York: Alfred A. Knopf, 1976.

Bowser, Paula, and Joan Eckstein, *A Pinch of Soul,* New York: Avon, 1970.

Women of St. Paul's Greek Orthodox Church, Hempstead, L.I., N.Y., *The Art of Greek Cookery,* Garden City, N.Y.: Doubleday & Co., 1961.

Corey, Helen, *The Art of Syrian Cookery,* Garden City, N.Y.: Doubleday & Co., 1962.

Detroit Women's Chapter of the Armenian General Benevolent Union, Inc., *Treasured Armenian Recipes,* New York: Armenian General Benevolent Union, Inc. 1949.

Kasdan, Sara, *Love § Knishes,* New York: The Vanguard Press, 1956.

Morton, Marcia Colman, *The Art of Viennese Cooking,* New York: Bantam, 1963.

Ortiz, Elizabeth Lambert, *The Complete Book of Mexican Cooking,* New York: Bantam, 1965.

Miller, Gloria Bley, *The Thousand Recipe Chinese Cookbook,* New York: Grosset & Dunlap, 1970.

Lin, Florence, *Florence Lin's Vegetarian Cookbook,* New York: Hawthorn, 1976.

Claiborne, Craig, and Virginia Lee, *The Chinese Cookbook,* Philadelphia: Lippincott, 1972.

Romagnoli, Margaret and G. Franco, *The Romagnolis' Meatless Cookbook,* Boston: Little Brown & Co., 1976.

Peck, Paula, *The Art of Fine Baking,* New York: Simon & Schuster, 1961.

Reich, Lilly Joss, *The Viennese Pastry Cookbook,* London: Collier-MacMillan Ltd., 1970.

Tatum, Billie Jo, *Billie Jo Tatum's Wild Foods Cookbook and Field Guide,* New York: Workman, 1976.

Kavasch, Barrie, *Native Harvests,* New York: Vintage Books, Random House, 1977, 1979.

Lincoff, Gary, *Edible Wild Plants,* c/o N.Y. Botanical Gardens. A pamphlet.

Mycological Society of San Francisco, *Kitchen Magic with Mushrooms*, San Francisco: Mycological Society of San Francisco, Inc.

Reitz, Rosetta, *Mushroom Cookery*, New York: Gramercy Publishing Co., 1955. Out of print.

Hawkes, Alex, *A World of Vegetable Cookery*, New York: Simon & Schuster, 1968.

Pellegrini, Angelo M., *The Food Lovers' Garden*, New York: Alfred A. Knopf, 1970.

A FEMINIST BIBLIOGRAPHY
FOOD FOR THOUGHT: A SUBJECTIVE LIST

GENERAL

Rich Adrienne, *On Lies, Secrets, and Silences,* New York: Norton, 1979.

_____, *Of Woman Born: Motherhood as Experience and Institution,* New York: Bantam, 1976.

Daly, Mary, *Gyn/Ecology: The Metaethics of Radical Feminism,* Boston: Beacon Press, 1978.

_____, *Beyond God the Father,* Boston: Beacon Press, 1973.

Griffin, Susan. *Woman and Nature: The Roaring Inside Her,* New York: Harper & Row, 1978.

Woolf, Virginia, *A Room of One's Own,* New York: Harcourt Brace Jovanovich, 1929.

_____, *Three Guineas,* New York: Harcourt Brace Jovanovich, 1938.

Brownmiller, Susan, *Against Our Will: Men, Women and Rape,* New York: Bantam, 1975.

Johnston, Jill, *Lesbian Nation,* New York: Simon & Schuster, 1973.

Dworkin, Andrea, *Woman Hating.* New York: E.P. Dutton, 1974.

Vida, Ginny. *Our Right to Love,* Englewood Cliffs, N.J.: Prentice Hall, 1978.

Davis, Elizabeth Gould, *The First Sex,* New York: Penguin, 1971.

Stone, Merlin, *When God Was A Woman,* New York: Harcourt Brace Jovanovich, 1976.

Fisher, Elizabeth, *Woman's Creation: Sexual Evolution and the Shaping of Society,* New York: McGraw Hill, 1979.

Ehrenreich, Barbara, and Deidre English, *Witches, Midwives, and Nurses: A History of Women Healers,* Old Westbury, N.Y.: The Feminist Press, 1971.

_____, *Complaints and Disorders: The Sexual Politics of Sickness,* Old Westbury, N.Y.: The Feminist Press, 1973.

_____, *For Her Own Good: 150 Years of the Experts Advice to Women,* Garden City, N.Y., Doubleday, 1978.

Mander, Anica Vesel and Anne Kent Rush, *Feminism as Therapy,* New York: Random House, 1974.

Chesler, Phyllis, *Women and Madness,* New York: Avon Books, 1972.

Lewis, Sasha Gregory, *Sunday's Women,* Boston: Beacon Press, 1979.

Rule, Jane, *Lesbian Images,* New York: Pocket Books, 1976. Out of Print.

Hazelton, Leslie, *Israeli Women: The Reality Behind the Myths,* New York: Simon & Schuster, 1977.

Chicago, Judy, *Through the Flower: My Struggles As A Woman Artist,* New York: Garden City, N.Y.: Doubleday, 1975.

_____, *The Dinner Party: A Symbol Of Our Heritage,* Garden City, N.Y.: Doubelday, 1979.

JEB, *Eye to Eye: Portraits of Lesbians,* Washington, D.C.: Glad Hag Books, 1979.

Olsen, Tillie, *Silences,* New York: Dell, 1965.

Deming, Barbara, *On Anger,* Palo Alto, Ca: Frog in the Well (pamphlet)

Fritz, Leah, *Dreamers and Dealers: An Intimate Appraisal of the Women's Movement,* Boston: Beacon Press, 1979.

Stanley, Julia Penelope, and Wolfe, Susan, *The Coming Out Stories,* Watertown, Mass.: Persephone Press, 1980.

Cruikshank, Margaret, *The Lesbian Path,* New York: Caroline House, 1980.

Raymond, Janice, *The Transexual Empire: The Making of the She-Male,* Boston: Beacon Press, 1979.

Martin, Del, *Battered Wives,* New York: Pocket, 1976.

Corea, Gina, *The Hidden Malpractice: How American Medicine Mistreats Women,* New York: Harcourt Brace Jovanovich, 1977.

Brown, Rita Mae, *Plain Brown Rapper,* Oakland, Ca: Diana Press, 1976.

Abbott, Sidney and Love, Barbara, *Sappho Was a Right-On Woman,* Stein & Day, 1972.

Stoltenberg, John, *Disarmament and Masculinity,* Palo Alto, Ca.: Frog in the Well (pamphlet).

Wallace, Michelle, *Black Macho and the Myth of the Superwoman,* New York: Warner Books, 1978.

Smedley, Agnes, *Daughter of the Earth,* Old Westbury, N.Y.: The Feminist Press., 1973.

Smith, Lillian, *Killers of the Dream*, New York: Norton, 1949.
_____, *The Winner Names the Age*, New York: Norton, 1978.

Niethammer, Carolyn, *Daughters of the Earth*, New York: Collier Books, MacMillan, 1977.

Gyorgy, Anna, and friends, *No Nukes: everyone's guide to nuclear power*, Boston: South End Press, 1979.

Koen, Susan, and Nina Swaim, *A Handbook for Women on the Nuclear Mentality*, Norwich, Vt.: Wand, 1980.

Singer, Peter, *Animal Liberation: A New Ethics for Our Treatment of Animals*, New York: Avon, 1975.

Mason, Jim, and Peter Singer, *Animal Factories*, New York: Crown Publishers, 1980.

McFadyen, Barbara and Marilyn Gayle, *Bring Out Your Own Book*, Portland, Ore.: Godiva, 1980.

West, Celeste, and Valerie Wheat, *The Passionate Perils of Publishing*, San Francisco: Booklegger, 1978.

Van Deurs, Kay. *The Notebooks that Emma Gave Me*, Youngsville, N.Y.: Kady Van Deurs, 1978.

Molloy, Alice, *In Other Words*, Oakland, Ca: Women's Press Collective.

O'donnell, Mary, *Lesbian Health Matters!* Santa Cruz, Ca: Santa Cruz Women's Health Center, 1979.

Women's Educational Project, *High School Sexuality*, Eugene, Or.: Amazon Reality, 1977.

Gage, Suzanne, *When Birth Control Fails*, Hollywood, Ca: Speculum Press, 1979.

Reitz, Rosetta, *Menopause: A Positive Approach*, NY: Penguin Books, 1977.

POETRY

Grahn, Judy, *The Common Woman, A Woman is Talking to Death*, and *Edward the Dyke*. All from Oakland, Ca: Women's Press Collective.

_____, *She Who*, Oakland, Ca: Diana Press, 1972.

_____, *The Work of a Common Woman*, New York: St. Martin's Press, 1978. Includes all of her work to date.

Rich Adrienne, *The Dream of a Common Langauge*, NY: Norton, 1978.

McDaniel, Judith, *Reconstituting the World: the poetry and vision of Adrienne Rich*, Argyle, N.Y.: Spinsters, Inc., 1978.

Lorde, Audre, *The Black Unicorn*. New York: Norton, 1978.

_____, *Coal*, New York: Norton, 1968.

_____, *New York Head Shop and Museum*, Detroit: Broadside Press, 1974.

Broumas, Olga, *Beginning With O*, New Haven, Ct: Yale University Press, 1977.

Winant, Fran, *Dyke Jacket,* New York: Violet Press, 1976.

Courtot, Martha, *Tribe,* San Francisco: PearlChild, 1977.
————, *Journey,* San Francisco: PearlChild, 1977.

Shange, Ntozake, *For Colored Girls Who Have Considered Suicide When the Rainbow is Enuf,* New York: Bantam, 1975.

Morgan, Robin, *Lady of the Beasts,* New York: Random House, 1962.

Piercy, Marge, *To Be of Use,* Garden City, N.Y.: Doubleday, 1969.

Parker, Pat, *Movement in Black,* Oakland, Ca: Diana Press, 1978.

WOMANSPIRIT

Starrett, Barbara, *I Dream in Female,* Cassandra Publication, 1976.

Wittig, Monique, *Les Guerillères,* New York: Avon Books, 1969.

Hall, Nor, *Mothers and Daughters,* Minneapolis: Rusoff Books, 1976. (Apparently out of print)

Rush, Anne Kent, *Moon, Moon,* Berkeley, Ca. and N.Y.: Moon Books and Random House, 1976.

Budapest, Z., *The Holy Book of Women's Mysteries,* Los Angeles, Ca: Susan B. Anthony Coven No. 1, 1979.

Starhawk, *The Spiral Dance,* San Francisco: Harper & Row, 1979.

Potts, Billie, *A New Women's Tarot,* Woodstock, N.Y.: Elf and Dragons Press, 1978.

Stone, Merlin, *Ancient Mirrors of Womanhood,* New York: New Sibylline Books, 1979.

Goldenberg, Naomi, *The Changing of the Gods,* Boston: Beacon Press, 1979.

Thorsten, Geraldine, *God Herself,* Garden City, N.Y.: Doubleday, 1980.

CHILDREN

Allison, Rosemary, *The Green Harpy at the Corner Store,* Toronto: Kids Can Press, 1976.

George, Jean, *Julie of the Wolves,* New York: Harper & Row, 1972.

Maury, Inez, *My Mother and I are Growing Strong—Mi Mamá y yo nos hacemos fuertes,* Stanford, Ca: New Seed Press, 1978.

————, *My Mother the Mail Carrier—Mi Mamá la cartera,* Old Westbury, N.Y.: The Feminist Press, 1976.

Lichtman, Wendy, *Blew and the Death of the Mag,* Albion, Ca: Freestone, 1975.

Farrell, Sherrie, *Gabriel's Very First Birthday,* Seattle, Wa: Pipeline Books, 1976.

Waxman, Stephanie, *What is a Girl, What is a Boy?* Culver City, Ca: Peace Press, 1976.

Widerberg, Siv, *I'm Like Me,* Old Westbury, N.Y.: The Feminist Press, 1973.

Russ, Joanna, *Kittatinny,* Houston, Tx: Daughters, Inc., 1978.

FICTION

Riis, Sharon, *The True Story of Ida Johnson,* Toronto: The Women's Press, 1976.

Halegua, Lillian, *The Pearl Bastard,* London: The Women's Press,1959.

Brady, Maureen, *Give Me Your Good Ear,* Argyle, N.Y.: Spinster's Ink, 1979.

Geller, Ruth, *Seed of a Woman,* Buffalo, N.Y.: Imp Press, 1979.

Olsen, Tillie, *Tell Me A Riddle,* New York: Dell Publishing, 1956. (Short stories.)

Bryant, Dorothy, *Miss Giardino,* Berkeley, Cal.: Ata Books, 1978.

Warner, Silvia Townsend, *Lolly Willowes,* London: The Women's Press, 1926.

Atwood, Margaret, *Surfacing,* New York: Popular Library, 1972.

Gould, Lois, *A Sea Change,* New York: Avon, 1976.

Morrison, Toni, *The Bluest Eye,* New York: Pocket Books, 1970.

————, *Sula,* New York: Bantam, 1973.

Piercy, Marge, *Small Changes,* New York: Fawcett, 1972, '73.

Woolf, Virginia, *Orlando,* New York: Harvest/Harcourt Brace, Jovanovich, 1928.

Gilman, Charlotte Perkins, *The Yellow Wallpaper,* Old Westbury, N.Y.: The Feminist Press, 1973.

Chopin, Kate, *The Awakening,* London: The Women's Press, 1979.

————, *Portraits,* London: The Women's Press, 1979.

Arnold, June, *The Cook and the Carpenter,* Houston, Tx: Daughters, Inc., 1973.

————, *Sister Gin,* Houston, Tx: Daughters, Inc., 1975.

Rule, Jane, *Theme for Diverse Instruments,* Vancouver B.C., Canada: Talon Books, 1975.

————, *Desert of the Heart,* Vancouver B.C., Canada: Talon Books, 1977.

Miller, Isabel, *Patience and Sarah,* New York: Fawcett, 1969.

Isabell, Sharon, *Yesterday's Lessons,* Oakland Ca: The Women's Press Collective, 1974.

Clausen, Jan, *Mother, Sister, Daughter, Lover,* Trumansburg, N.Y.: Crossing Press, 1980.

SCIENCE FICTION

Charnas, Suzy McKee, *Motherlines,* New York: Berkley Publishing, 1978.

_____, *Walk to the End of the World,* New York: Berkley Publishing, 1974.

Russ, Joanna, *the Female Man,* New York: Bantam Books, 1975.

_____, *The Two of Them,* New York: Berkley Publishing, 1978.

Piercy, Marge, *Woman on the Edge of Time,* New York: Fawcett Crest, 1976.

Tiptree, James, "The Women Men Don't See" and "The Last Flight of Dr. Ain" in *Warm Worlds and Otherwise,* New York: Ballantine, 1975. And "Houston, Houston, Do You Read?" from *Star Songs of an Old Primate,* New York: Ballantine, 1978.

_____, *Up the Walls of the World,* New York: Berkley, 1978.

Carrington, Leonora, *The Hearing Trumpet,* New York: Pocket, 1974.

Gearhart, Sally Miller, *Wanderground,* Watertown, Mass: Persephone Press, 1979.

MUSIC

Adam, Margie, *Margie Adam Songwriter,* Pleiades Records, Berkeley, Ca: 1976.

_____, *Naked Keys,* Pleides Records, Berkeley, Ca. 1980.

Berkeley Women's Music Collective, *Berkeley Women's Music Collective,* Windbag Records, Box 23894, Oakland, Ca 94623.

_____, *Trying to Survive,* Olivia Records, 4400 Market St., San Francisco, Ca: 1975, 1978.

Christian, Meg, *I Know You Know,* Olivia Records, San Francisco, Ca: 1977.

Culver, Casse, *Three Gypsies,* Urana, Wise Women Enterprises, N.Y.C. Distributed by Olivia Records, San Francisco, Ca.

Dobkin, Alix, *Lavender Jane Loves Women,* Alix Dobkin Project #1, Preston Hollow, N.Y.

_____, *Living with Lesbians,* Project #1, Preston Hollow, N.Y.

Edell, Therese, *From Women's Faces,* Sea Friends, P.O. Box 20015, Cincinatti, Ohio, 1977.

Etzler, Carol. *Sometimes I Wish,* Sisters Unlimited, 1492-F Willow Lake Dr., Atlanta, Ga 30329.

_____, *Woman River,* Sisters Unlimited, Atlanta, Ga.

Ferron, *Ferron,* Lucy Records, Ltd., Box 67, Saturna Island, B.C. VON240.

_____, *Testimony,* Lucy Records, B.C.

Flying Lesbians, *Flying Lesbians, fbv frauenbuchvertrieb, gmbh, mehring damm 32"34, 1000 Berlin 61,* Available from Ladyslipper, Durham, N.C.

Gardner, Kay, *Emerging,* Wise Women Enterprises, N.Y.C.

————, *Mooncircles,* Wise Women Enterprises, N.Y.C.

Izquierda, *Quiet Thunder,* Riverbear Music, Portland, Or.

Jaeckel, Monika, and Barbara Bauermeister, *Witch is Witch,* Vertrieb durch Troubadisc, Frauenplatten vertrieb, Erhaltich in allen Frauenbuchladen. Available in Europe.

Kosse, Roberta, *The Return of the Great Mother,* Ars Pro Femina, Brooklyn, N.Y., 1978.

Kvindeballade, *Kvindeballade,* Kvindeballade Ind spillet, Knabrostr 3, DK1210 KOBH.K. Available inEurope.

Near, Holly, *Hang in There,* Redwood Records, P.O. Box 996, Ukiah, Ca.

————, *Imagine My Surprise,* Redwood Records, Ukiah, Ca.

————, *A Live Album,* Redwood Records, Ukiah, Ca.

————, *You Can Know All I Am,* Redwood Records, Ukiah, Ca.

New Harmony Sisterhood, *". . . And Ain't I a Woman?"* Paredon, Box 889, Brooklyn, N.Y. 11202: 1977.

Nugent, Trish, *Foxglove Woman,* Olivia Records, San Francisco, Ca:1977.

Reynolds, Malvina *Held Over,* Cassandra Records, 2027 Parker St., Berkeley, Ca.

————, *Malvina,* Cassandra Records, Berkeley, Ca.

————, *Mama Lion,* Cassandra Records, Berkeley, Ca.

Rosetta Records, *Mean Mothers Independent Women's Blues Vol. I,* and *Sorry But I Can't Take You Women's Railroad Blues,* Rosetta Records,   115 W. 16th St., N.Y.C.

Shear,Linda, *A Lesbian Portrait,* Old Lady Blue Jeans, Northampton, Mass.

Simmons, Woody, *Oregon Mountains,* Olivia Records, San Francisco, Ca.

Sweet Honey in the Rock, *B'lieve I'll Run On . . . See What the End's Gonna Be,* Redwood Records, P.O. Box 996, Ukiah, Ca.

Tillery, Linda, *Linda Tillery,* Olivia Records, San Francisco, Ca.

Tyson, Willie, *Full Count,* Lima Bean Records, P.O. Box 447, Madison, Tn.

————, *Debutante,* Lima Bean, Madison, Tn.

————, *Willie Tyson,* Lima Bean, Madison, Tn.

Watkins, Mary, *Something Moving,* Olivia Records,San Francisco, Ca.

Winter, Cathy, and Betsy Rose, *Sweet Sorcery,* Origami Records, P.O. Box 8012, Albany, N.Y.

Williamson, Cris, *The Changer and the Changed,* Olivia Records, San Francisco, Ca.

PERIODICALS

Conditions, P.O. Box 56 VanBrunt Station, Brooklyn, N.Y. See especially V, the Black Women's Issue.

Sinister Wisdom, Box 30541, Lincoln, Nebraska.

Chrysalis, P.O. Box 28761, San Diego, Ca.

Heresies, 225 Lafayette St., New York, N.Y. The Great Goddess issue, currently out of print, is superb. See also Issue 8 on Third World Women.

Womanspirit, P.O. Box 263, Wolf Creek, Oregon.

Frontiers, Vol. IV #3, Fall 1979. Lesbian History issue. University of Colorado, Boulder.

SpareRib, 114 George St., Berkhamsted, Herts, Great Britain.

Off Our Backs, 1724 20th Street NW, Washington, D.C. 20009.

Sojourner, 143 Albany Street, Cambridge, Ma. 02139.

Big Mama Rag, 1724 Gaylord, Denver, Co. 80206.

WomaNews, P.O. Box 220, Village Station, N.Y.C. 10014.

New Directions for Women, 223 Old Hook Road, Westwood, N.J. 07675.

Plexus, 545 Athol Ave., Oakland, Ca. 94606.

The women say that they could not eat hare veal or fowl, they say that they could not eat animals, but man, yes, they may. He says to them throwing his head back with pride, poor wretches of women, if you eat him who will go to work in the fields, who will produce food consumer goods, who will make the aeroplanes, who will pilot them, who will provide the spermatozoa, who will write the books, who in fact will govern? Then the women laugh, baring their teeth to the fullest extent.

Les Guérillères
Monique Wittig; Avon

INDEX

320

3